THE
HISTORY OF
INDONESIA

ADVISORY BOARD

THE
HISTORY OF
INDONESIA

Steven Drakeley

The Greenwood Histories of the Modern Nations
Frank W. Thackeray and John E. Findling, Series Editors

Greenwood Press
Westport, Connecticut • London

Library of Congress Cataloging-in-Publication Data

Drakeley, Steven.
    The history of Indonesia / Steven Drakeley.
        p. cm. — (The Greenwood histories of the modern nations, ISSN 1096–2905)
    Includes bibliographical references and index.
    ISBN 0–313–33114–6 (alk. paper)
      1. Indonesia—History.   I. Title.   II. Series.
DS634.D73 2005
959.8—dc22   2005018298

British Library Cataloguing in Publication Data is available.

Library of Congress Catalog Card Number: 2005018298
ISBN: 0–313–33114–6
ISSN: 1096–2905

First published in 2005

Greenwood Press, 88 Post Road West, Westport, CT 06881
An imprint of Greenwood Publishing Group, Inc.
www.greenwood.com

Printed in the United States of America

The paper used in this book complies with the
Permanent Paper Standard issued by the National
Information Standards Organization (Z39.48–1984).

10 9 8 7 6 5 4 3 2 1

Contents

Series Foreword

The *Greenwood Histories of the Modern Nations* series is intended to provide students and interested laypeople with up-to-date, concise, and analytical histories of many of the nations of the contemporary world. Not since the 1960s has there been a systematic attempt to publish a series of national histories, and, as editors, we believe that this series will prove to be a valuable contribution to our understanding of other countries in our increasingly interdependent world.

Over 30 years ago, at the end of the 1960s, the Cold War was an accepted reality of global politics, the process of decolonization was still in progress, the idea of a unified Europe with a single currency was unheard of, the United States was mired in a war in Vietnam, and the economic boom in Asia was still years in the future. Richard Nixon was president of the United States, Mao Tse-tung (not yet Mao Zedong) ruled China, Leonid Brezhnev guided the Soviet Union, and Harold Wilson was prime minister of the United Kingdom. Authoritarian dictators still ruled most of Latin America, the Middle East was reeling in the wake of the Six-Day War, and Shah Reza Pahlavi was at the height of his power in Iran. Clearly, the past 30 years have been witness to a great deal of historical change, and it is to this change that this series is primarily addressed.

With the help of a distinguished advisory board, we have selected nations whose political, economic, and social affairs mark them as among the most important in the waning years of the twentieth century, and for each nation we have found an author who is recognized as a specialist in the history of that nation. These authors have worked most cooperatively with us and with Greenwood Press to produce volumes that reflect current research on their nations and that are interesting and informative to their prospective readers.

The importance of a series such as this cannot be underestimated. As a superpower whose influence is felt all over the world, the United States can claim a "special" relationship with almost every other nation. Yet many Americans know very little about the histories of the nations with which the United States relates. How did they get to be the way they are? What kind of political systems have evolved there? What kind of influence do they have in their own region? What are the dominant political, religious, and cultural forces that move their leaders? These and many other questions are answered in the volumes of this series.

The authors who have contributed to this series have written comprehensive histories of their nations, dating back to prehistoric times in some cases. Each of them, however, has devoted a significant portion of the book to events of the last 30 years because the modern era has contributed the most to contemporary issues that have an impact on U.S. policy. Authors have made an effort to be as up-to-date as possible so that readers can benefit from the most recent scholarship and a narrative that includes very recent events.

In addition to the historical narrative, each volume in this series contains an introductory overview of the country's geography, political institutions, economic structure, and cultural attributes. This is designed to give readers a picture of the nation as it exists in the contemporary world. Each volume also contains additional chapters that add interesting and useful detail to the historical narrative. One chapter is a thorough chronology of important historical events, making it easy for readers to follow the flow of a particular nation's history. Another chapter features biographical sketches of the nation's most important figures in order to humanize some of the individuals who have contributed to the historical development of their nation. Each volume also contains a comprehensive bibliography, so that those readers whose interest has been sparked may find out more about the nation and its history. Finally, there is a carefully prepared topic and person index.

Readers of these volumes will find them fascinating to read and useful in understanding the contemporary world and the nations that compose it. As series editors, it is our hope that this series will contribute to a heightened sense of global understanding as we embark on a new century.

Frank W. Thackeray and John E. Findling
Indiana University Southeast

A Note on Spelling

Over time there have been significant variations in the spelling of Indonesian words, a problem made more complex by regional variations and diverse spellings of loan words from languages such as Arabic. Here the standard modern Indonesian spelling introduced in 1972 is utilized, but with certain exceptions. Personal names have not been converted to the new spelling unless it seems that this was the preference of the individual concerned. Thus Soekarno is here rendered as Sukarno, but Soeharto is not changed. The names of organizations, however, have been converted to the new spelling. Thus Masjumi is spelled Masyumi. Place names are generally spelled in accordance with modern Indonesian spelling except where another form exists that is more likely to be familiar to the English-speaking reader. Thus I use Malacca rather than Melaka and Java rather than Jawa. Personal names present another complication when shortening for the reader's convenience. Here the choice most commonly made in English-language publications is used, although Indonesians often would make a different choice. Thus Abdurrahman Wahid is shortened to Wahid rather than to Abdurrahman. All of these spelling decisions are somewhat arbitrary, but they have been made with accessibility to the reader uppermost in mind.

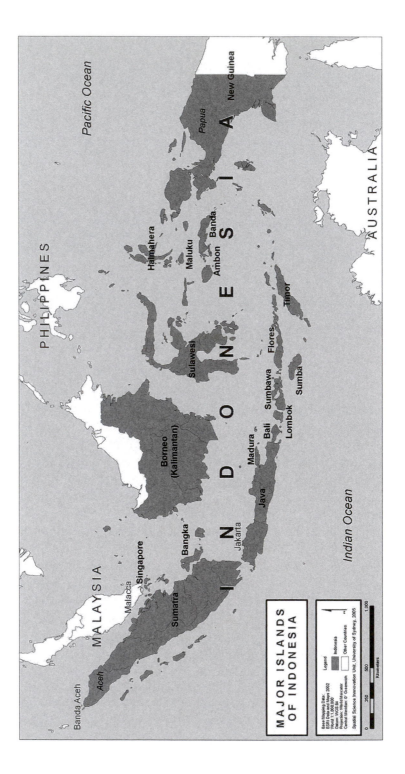

MAJOR ISLANDS
OF INDONESIA

Legend

Indonesia

Other Countries

Base Mapping Data:
ESRI Data and Maps 2002
World 1:10,000,000
Datum: WGS 84
Projection: World Mercator
Central Meridian: 0° Greenwich

Spatial Science Innovation Unit, University of Sydney, 2005

0   250   500   1,000
Kilometers

PHILIPPINES

Pacific Ocean

MALAYSIA

Malacca

Singapore

Banda Aceh

Aceh

Sumatra

Bangka

Jakarta

Borneo
(Kalimantan)

INDONESIA

Madura

Java

Bali

Lombok

Sumbawa

Sumba

Sulawesi

Flores

Timor

Halmahera

Maluku

Ambon

Banda

Papua

New Guinea

Indian Ocean

AUSTRALIA

Introduction

PEOPLE AND PLACE

Indonesia, an archipelago nation consisting of no fewer than 17,508 islands strung over 5,200 kilometers, is situated astride the equator between Australia and mainland Asia. With the Pacific Ocean to the east and the Indian Ocean to the west, Indonesia's location could hardly be more strategically significant, an importance underlined by being easily the largest country in Southeast Asia in terms of both landmass and population. With a population of 220 million people (in 2005), Indonesia is the world's fourth-most populous country (after China, India, and the United States).[1] Culturally and politically it is also one of the more complex countries in the world, with over a thousand ethnic and subethnic groups speaking many hundreds of languages and dialects.[2] It is only in comparatively recent times that these peoples have been contained within one political framework, brought together through the construction of the Dutch colonial empire, the Netherlands Indies. Throughout most of history, Indonesia's inhabitants were divided politically in many different ways as over the centuries a bewildering array of kingdoms and empires rose and fell within the region. Indeed, parts of Indonesia were previously united with territories and peoples now included in the neighboring countries of Malaysia and Singapore. Thus one of the many challenges confronting Indonesia since independence in 1945 has been the construction of a unified national identity, given the lack of shared historical experience.

Many of Indonesia's islands are small and uninhabited. Others, such as Sumatra and the Indonesian portions of the islands of New Guinea (Papua) and Borneo (Kalimantan), are very large, the size of Spain, California, and France, respectively. Paradoxically, Sumatra, Papua, and Kalimantan have relatively small populations, while some smaller islands are densely populated, including Java, home to 135 million people (including the city of Jakarta) and tiny Bali with 3.3 million people.[3] At one extreme the population density for Papua is only 6 people per square kilometer compared with 951 people per square kilometer for Java at the other extreme.[4] The reasons for these wide discrepancies have much to do with terrain and soil quality. Java and Bali have rich, volcanic soils and abundant rain, making them suitable for growing many crops, including large quantities of rice, the staple of most Indonesians. Large parts of Sumatra are suitable for plantation crops, but much of the island is mountainous or swampy and the soil is not as rich. The same can be said for Kalimantan and Papua, while much of eastern Indonesia is dry with relatively poor soils.

Each of Indonesia's many ethnic groups expresses its own cultural identity through dance, dress, music, carving, and other artistic forms, as well as through laws, customs, and etiquette. And despite the many languages, most of the population also speaks the national language, Bahasa Indonesia (Indonesian), the language of the school and the office and increasingly of the street. Moreover, even in the most isolated corners of the country (anywhere that television, if not schools and government services, can reach), Indonesians participate in the national culture. The largest single ethnic group is the Javanese, a little under 42 percent of the population.[5] The Javanese are concentrated in East and Central Java, though there are also significant Javanese populations in parts of Sumatra and elsewhere. In addition to the Javanese, other ethnic groups indigenous to Java include the Sundanese of West Java, the Bantenese of Banten, and the Betawi of Jakarta. And for many years Java, especially East Java, has been home to large numbers of Madurese, who have spread from the neighboring island of Madura.

Other prominent ethnic groups include the Bataks, Minangkabau, Acehnese, and Malays of Sumatra; the Buginese, Makassarese, Torajans, and Minahasans of Sulawesi; as well as the Dayaks, Balinese, Banjarese, Ambonese, and Papuans from other places in the archipelago. There are also small but significant numbers of nonindigenous ethnic groups, including Chinese, Arabs, and Eurasians. As a modern nation with 43 percent[6] of the population living in urban centers, Indonesians of all ethnic groups can be found almost everywhere, particularly in the large cities such as the capital Jakarta, home to 9.5 million people according to conservative official estimates.[7] Many Indonesians are no longer easily classifiable as belonging to specific ethnic groups. For example, the former president, Megawati Sukarnoputri, is generally regarded as Javanese. She was born in Yogyakarta, Central Java. But her mother was a Minangkabau, and her famous father, Sukarno, Indonesia's first president, had a Javanese father and a Balinese mother. Moreover, many people in the larger, more cosmopolitan cities no longer speak any language other than Indonesian, except where they also speak Prokem, the notoriously swiftly evolving slang dialect primarily used by Jakarta's youth.

Indonesians are almost universally religious. The majority of the population, around 88 percent, is Muslim,[8] making Indonesia the country with the largest Muslim population in the world. Islam is one of the five officially sanctioned religions; the others are Catholicism, Protestantism, Hinduism, and Buddhism. Christians, Hindus, and Buddhists make up just less than 9 percent, 2 percent, and 1 percent of the population, respectively.[9] In addition to their official religion, many Indonesians subscribe to older beliefs that vary according to place but usually contain elements of mysticism and involve local spirits and deities, including ancestral spirits. For convenience these beliefs can be categorized as animism, but this anthropological term barely begins to capture the complexity, variety, and sophistication of these older beliefs, not least because they are often integrated with one or another of the world religions. An Indonesian term that is often employed in this context is *kebatinan*. For the most part, Indonesia's religious communities are tolerant of one another, and the state, officially at least, does not discriminate among them. The state, however, does not tolerate atheism. "Belief in the One God" is the first of five principles known as the Pancasila that appear in the preamble to the constitution and compose the nation's philosophical basis. The other four principles are nationalism, humanitarianism, social justice, and democracy.

POLITICS AND ECONOMY

Indonesia is a republic with an executive president and, following a series of four constitutional reforms between 1999 and 2002, three representative levels of government. These are a national parliament, the People's Representative Council (DPR), a Regional Representative Council (DPD), and regional assemblies at the provincial and *kabupaten* (regency) levels (DPRD–I and DPR–II, respectively). The people directly elect all of these bodies, including the presidency since 2004. There is also a People's Consultative Assembly (MPR), which consists of the combined members of the DPR and DPD. The MPR inaugurates the president and vice president and upholds the constitution. It also has the power to amend the constitution and impeach the president or vice president under certain conditions. Elections take place every five years, and the political process is now vigorous and relatively open with many parties and candidates, a relatively free and lively media, and a considerable degree of freedom of speech. In formal terms, therefore, Indonesia is a modern democracy with built-in checks and balances as power is shared between different arms of government. But Indonesia's democracy is very much a work in progress with many serious imperfections. The present political system is the product of recent reforms, and it is unclear how they will work in practice, including key features such as the power sharing between the presidency and parliament and between the central government and other tiers of government.

Few would have described Indonesia as a democracy until recently (and many still would not). For 40 years (roughly between 1959 and 1999), Indonesia had authoritarian governments that allowed only an extremely limited degree of political plurality. During these four decades, the presidency was the primary political institution and the army had a powerful formal role in the political process, while the parliament and other institutions were weak, all common features of an authoritarian system of government. But the formal political structure in these years was in many respects much less important than the informal features, which combined to make the system far more authoritarian and personalized than its formal features suggested. Indonesia's current political process bears the legacy of these decades of authoritarian and highly personalized rule. Thus, although the formal political process is quite democratic, much of the actual political practice continues to closely resemble that of the past, in particular the tendency for informal and personalized channels of authority to bypass and undermine the formal structure. There are also serious problems of corruption and intimidation and an absence of the rule of law that impede or distort democratic functioning. Concerns are also expressed about the continued influence of the army. While it no longer has a formal political role, the army still retains a regional command structure that parallels the civilian bureaucracy, facilitating interference by both local and central military authorities.

Indonesia has a mixed economy of private and state enterprise, including large sections in the hands of companies controlled by the Indonesian army. In recent decades a more liberal economic environment has been created for the private sector, but Indonesia retains a strong inclination toward economic nationalism. Oil, gas, and mineral products have been Indonesia's principal sources of export earnings for several decades. Indonesia also exports a range of agricultural products, including palm oil and rubber. Light manufacturing, such as textiles and electronics, are also important but were much more so during the boom years of the early 1990s. Tourism is also a significant export-earning industry, but it too has suffered in recent years from political instability and terrorism. Indonesia's economy is currently estimated to be growing at 5 percent per year, a modest improvement over recent levels.[10] But around half the population subsists on less than US $3.00 a day, and life expectancy is a comparatively low 64.9 for males and 67.9 for females.[11] Indonesia's rate of annual population increase is declining. It fell to 1.37 percent during the 1990s from its peak of 2.37 percent during the 1960s, and the proportion of people below the age of 15 has dropped from 44 percent in 1971 to 30.4 percent in 2000.[12] Nevertheless, the population will continue to rise for several decades, posing an enormous difficulty for policymakers seeking to tackle unemployment and poverty.

Thus Indonesia, a most complex and intriguing country, faces serious challenges ahead. This book will have served its purpose if it contributes to an understanding of the history that has contrived to pose those challenges. There are so many people to thank—not least my wife, Melissa, whose love and laughter light up a thousand lives, mine especially. I also wish to thank my colleagues in the School of Humanities at the University of Western Sydney and the students I have taught there and elsewhere for their stimulation and forbearance. All the Indonesians I have ever met have contributed immeasurably to this work (and to my life) and thus earn my humble thanks. A special thanks also to Jim Angel, teacher and friend.

NOTES

1. 220 million is the official figure projected for 2005 based on the 2000 census. It is widely regarded as an underestimation, and figures of up to 240 million are often given. Badan Pusat Statistik Republik Indonesia (Central Bureau of Statistics of the Republic of Indonesia). http://www.bps.go.id.

2. Leo Suryadinata et al., *Indonesia's Population: Ethnicity and Religion in a Changing Political Landscape* (Singapore: ISEAS, 2003), p. 6.

3. My calculation is based on figures projected from the 2000 census by Badan Pusat Statistik.

4. World Bank Organization. http://www.worldbank.org.id.

5. Suryadinata, *Indonesia's Population*, p. 32.

6. World Bank.

7. Badan Pusat Statistik.

8. Suryadinata, *Indonesia's Population*, p. 105.

9. Suryadinata, *Indonesia's Population*, p. 105.

10. Deutsche Bank Research. http://www.dbresearch.com.

11. World Health Organization 2005. http://www.who.int/countries/idn/en/.

12. Suryadinata, *Indonesia's Population*, pp. 1–5.

Timeline of Historical Events

2500 B.C.E.	Austronesian people begin arriving in Indonesia via Taiwan and the Philippines
500 B.C.E.	North Java ports begin trading with southern China, mainland Southeast Asia, and India
600 C.E.	Srivijaya emerges near Palembang-Jambi in Sumatra
820	Construction of Borobudur begun by Hindu-Buddhist Mataram state in Central Java
1200s	First Muslim kingdoms established in Indonesia (northern Sumatra)
1300	Majapahit becomes biggest state in Indonesia
1512	Portuguese establish base on Ambon
1527	Hindu-Buddhist Majapahit defeated by Muslim Demak, most of Java now Muslim
1596	First Dutch expedition to the Indies arrives in Banten

1611	VOC establishes trading post in Jayakerta (Jakarta)
1613–46	Sultan Agung is ruler of Mataram, conquers most of Java
1620–23	Dutch massacre or expel population of Banda to monopolize nutmeg
1799	VOC becomes bankrupt, administration taken over by Dutch government
1816	British hand back Indies to Dutch after conclusion of Napoleonic Wars
1821–38	Padri War
1824	Treaty of London between Dutch and British
1825–30	Java War
1830	Cultivation System established
1873	Dutch invasion of Aceh
1901	Ethical Policy begins
1908	Budi Utomo, first nationalist organization, formed
1911/1912	Sarekat Islam founded
1912	Muhammadiyah founded
1920	Indonesian Communist Party (PKI) formed
1926	Nahdlatul Ulama founded
1926–27	PKI revolt
1927	Indonesian Nationalist Association (PNI) founded
1928	PNI becomes Indonesian Nationalist Party
1928	Second All Indonesia Youth Congress adopts Youth Pledge
1934	Sukarno sent into internal exile without trial
1942	Japan occupies Indonesia
1943	Peta established, later forms nucleus of Indonesian army
1945	Japanese create an investigating committee to prepare for Indonesian independence

1945	Declaration of Independence by Sukarno and Hatta
1948	S. M. Kartosuwirjo launches Darul Islam Rebellion
1948	PKI's Madiun Rebellion
1948	Second Dutch "Police Action," Republican government and capital captured
1949	Dutch transfer sovereignty to Republic of the United States of Indonesia
1950	Unitary Republic of Indonesia formed
1950	Indonesia admitted to UN, sponsored by India and Australia
1953	Daud Beureueh launches rebellion in Aceh in alliance with Darul Islam
1955	Bandung Asian-African Conference
1955	National parliamentary elections and elections for constituent assembly held
1958	PRRI-Permesta rebellion begins
1959	Sukarno abolishes constituent assembly and returns to 1945 constitution by decree
1960	Sukarno dissolves parliament by decree
1961	All political parties dissolved except for 10
1962	Kartosuwirjo captured and executed
1962	Settlement of Irian Jaya/Papua issue
1963	Sukarno begins Confrontation campaign against Malaysia
1965	September 30 Movement failed coup attempt, hundreds of thousands massacred
1965	Soeharto appointed army commander
1966	Sukarno pressured to sign March 11 Order giving Soeharto extraordinary powers
1967	Special MPRS session replaces Sukarno with Soeharto as acting president

1967	ASEAN established, with Indonesia as a founding member
1969	Act of "free choice" in Papua
1971	General elections deliver stunning Golkar victory
1973	Muslim parties forced to merge to form PPP, the remainder merge to form PDI
1975	Indonesia invades East Timor
1976	Hasan de Tiro proclaims independence of Aceh
1980	Petition of Fifty group founded
1985	All organizations obliged to adopt Pancasila as sole foundation
1997	Attack on Megawati's supporters occupying PDI headquarters in Jakarta
1997	Asian economic crisis
1998	Four students shot dead at Trisakti University during anti-Soeharto demonstration
1998	Soeharto resigns and Habibie sworn in as president
1999	First free general election since 1955
1999	Referendum result in East Timor delivers independence amid much bloodshed
1999	Wahid elected president with Megawati as vice president
2001	Wahid dismissed from presidency, Megawati becomes president
2002	Bali bombing by Islamist terrorists, JI blamed
2004	General elections and first direct presidential election, Susilo Bambang Yudhoyono becomes president

1

Early History to the Coming of Islam (5000 B.C.E.–1600 C.E.)

A note of caution needs to be expressed when discussing Indonesia's early history. Much research remains to be done, and the evidence historians have to work with is fragmentary at best. Rising sea levels after the last ice age, some seventeen thousand years ago, have rendered inaccessible archeological evidence that might exist of early coastal-dwelling societies, and the humid climate is unkind to archeological evidence that might survive in colder and dryer locations. Ethnographic evidence and studies of comparative linguistics can help, but this material is often open to quite different interpretations and generally offers only history of the very "broad brush strokes" variety. Written records do not exist until comparatively late for Indonesia, and we are overly reliant on the writings of the Chinese and the observations of occasional visitors until Dutch and other European records began in the sixteenth century. These written sources are very valuable but inevitably contain errors and bias. There are some indigenous written records such as court chronicles and literary works, but opinion is divided as to their value. Certainly it takes considerable skill to make use of them, as they were not composed with the intention of providing a literal record of events.

SETTLEMENT AND SOCIAL DEVELOPMENT

Thanks in part to the famous fossil discoveries of "Java Man," made in 1891 in Central Java, we know that the early species *Homo erectus* inhabited parts of Indonesia well over a million years ago. For the presence of our species, *Homo sapiens*, there is evidence from around forty thousand years ago. Whether or not the latter were partially descended from the *Homo erectus* inhabitants remains unknown; indeed, this question remains one of the great scholarly mysteries of human prehistory in general. According to the current view, Indonesians are predominantly the descendants of Austronesians (formerly referred to as Southern Mongoloids), who began arriving around five thousand years ago, having spread slowly from southern China through Taiwan and the Philippines. The term *Austronesians* comes from the name given to the language family associated with them (a group of languages spoken from Indonesia to Polynesia). To a lesser extent, Indonesians are also descended from earlier occupants of the archipelago, the Australo-Melanesians, whose descendants survive on the island of New Guinea and in some isolated areas as distinct ethnic groups such as the Semang of the Malay Peninsula. Throughout most of Indonesia, these earlier inhabitants probably blended gradually over many centuries with the eventually far more numerous Austronesians to produce contemporary Indonesians. Due to more recent historical developments, many Indonesians now have Indian, Arab, Chinese, or European ancestry. Throughout the wider region embracing southern Thailand, Malaysia, the Philippines, Singapore, and Brunei, as well as Indonesia, the descendants of the predominantly Austronesian people are often referred to as Malays. Somewhat confusingly, the term *Malay* is also generally applied to a particular ethnic group within the region who inhabit many (mainly coastal) areas throughout the archipelago.

The considerable cultural and linguistic diversity that is now evident in Indonesia is sometimes attributed to successive waves of migration. The most likely explanation is that it developed over a long time frame as groups of settlers interacted with the particular environments they inhabited. This phenomenon would have been greatly facilitated by the nature of the physical environment that early inhabitants encountered. The prevalence of thick forest, mountainous terrain, and extensive swamps meant that communities naturally tended to establish themselves in the more hospitable and more accessible areas along coastal plains and rivers. Having done so, their settlements would usually have been relatively isolated from those of other communities due to the prevalence of these natural barriers. It has to be remembered that until the last few centuries Indonesia's population was small, inhabiting only pockets of an extensive land area with large areas probably completely uninhabited. Larger areas still probably contained fewer people than they did elephants, orangutans, and tigers. It requires a considerable stretch of the imagination to envisage Indonesia like this, as conditions have altered dramatically. As their population has exploded, Indonesians have encroached relentlessly on the natural habitats of these animals over the last few hundred years. Once plentiful, these animals now hover on or close to the brink of extinction, mostly confined to reserves that are too small and too poorly policed to provide adequate sanctuary.

Thus although considerable distances are involved in Indonesia, the cultural diversity is less attributable to a tyranny of distance than to a tyranny of terrain. In this earlier period, distance was much less of a physical barrier than was forest, mountain, and swamp because the archipelagic setting meant that nearly all great distances could be traveled by boat and usually with relative ease and speed. Unlike the natural land barriers, the seas that separate the islands of Indonesia contributed little to the tendency described above for separate cultural developments. For the most part, the sea was a highway that connected settlements and societies throughout the archipelago, especially those situated on the coasts. Thus we have the phenomenon in which coastal societies, though separated by hundreds of kilometers of sea, often exhibit considerable cultural similarity with each other while simultaneously exhibiting significant cultural differences from other societies located only short distances inland from them. The Bataks and the Malays of northern Sumatra provide a good example. The latter inhabit the eastern coastal plain and are broadly similar to other coastal Malay communities scattered throughout the region. The Bataks inhabit the highland areas of northern Sumatra, where in relative isolation they evolved a culture quite dissimilar to that of the Malays.

Facilitating the ease of sea travel throughout the Indonesian archipelago (and importantly between it and other parts of Asia) are the monsoon winds, which blow roughly from the northwest during winter in the northern hemisphere and from the southeast in the northern summer. Relatively predictable, the pattern of these winds meant that people could travel large distances quite quickly by sea. Because the monsoon wind roughly reverses its direction season-ally, people could return to their homes as readily as they left them merely by timing their travel to the pattern of the winds and thus were much more likely to travel than if their departure were to be permanent. Naturally the capacity to come and go had a significant impact on the process and pace of cultural exchange. Apart from the monsoon winds, the archipelago's physical geography further con-tributed to the relative ease and safety of sea travel. There are few large distances between landfalls because there are so many islands scattered throughout the archipelago, and large areas of water are quite well sheltered. Crucial in this latter respect are the waters of the Malacca Strait between the Malay Peninsula and Sumatra that pro-vide a natural sea gateway into the region from the Indian Ocean.

Rivers were also major highways that connected scattered settle-ments throughout the archipelago. Few rivers in Indonesia are nav-igable for any great length; nevertheless, their importance should not be discounted in a context in which terrain often made land travel difficult. Rivers not only connected communities of people living along their banks, they also connected all communities, even those living in the upper reaches of the smallest tributaries, to people living on other islands via the sea.

Thus while we should acknowledge the separate cultural devel-opments throughout the archipelago produced over centuries by the influence of terrain, we should not exaggerate the degree to which settlements were isolated and unconnected. Only those who inhabited the most inaccessible forests and mountains, who also usually lived the most nomadic of lifestyles and in the small-est community units, could truly be placed in such a category. At the other end of the spectrum are those communities that actively exploited the waterway links to other communities. Most pertinent in this context is the seminomadic Malay sea people (sometimes referred to as "sea gypsies") that have wandered the archipelago's seas for many centuries. Most communities in the archipelago lived lives somewhere between these extremes. They had contact with the world beyond their immediate cultural and physical horizons, but these contacts were usually infrequent and were often mediated through neighboring communities or else through seafaring peo-ples. In this way plenty of room existed for separate cultural devel-opments while technologies, terminologies, art forms, and ideas could be shared throughout the region and adopted and adapted in particular settings. Thus despite the striking cultural and linguistic diversity, there is a considerable degree of commonality. For example, the music and musical instruments of the gong-chime musical form (such as the gamelan orchestra of Java, Bali, and Madura) are remarkably widespread throughout the archipelago.

AGRICULTURE AND THE EMERGENCE OF EARLY STATES

Indonesia's early inhabitants lived by hunting and gathering. Many areas at this time were able to provide more than adequate nutrition for communities of moderate size living by these methods. Water was rarely scarce as Indonesia has many rivers and receives ample rainfall, except in some of the eastern islands. With rare exceptions, vegetation was abundant, providing edible plants and fruit and sustaining wild game. The plentiful rivers and coastlines abutting nutrient-rich waters made fishing and the collection of other edible sea products a rich source of food. Yet however benevolent the environment, communities living by hunting and gathering techniques are inherently limited in size and can rarely settle in one location for long before local food supplies become depleted. Perhaps at some coastal and wetland locations where the fishing was especially good, slightly larger and more settled communities could have developed, but still only those of moderate size. Other environments, such as the inland equatorial rainforest areas (which once covered much of the islands of Sumatra and Borneo) could only have supported very small and widely scattered hunting and gathering communities.

In Indonesia, as it did elsewhere, the development of agriculture brought dramatic change. Even primitive agricultural techniques could sustain much higher population densities in most areas than could hunting and gathering. Higher population density is in itself a dramatic development, but its greatest significance lies in its allowing for many other profound social developments such as enhanced specialization of labor and the emergence of cities and urban life. The earliest practice of agriculture in Indonesia occurred in the highland areas of New Guinea around nine thousand years ago, where Melanesian people cultivated plants such as taro (a root crop) and sugar cane to supplement their hunting and gathering.[1] But these agricultural developments remained localized. Perhaps there were some other localized intrinsic developments of agricultural techniques that we do not yet know of, but certainly the widespread introduction of highly successful agricultural practices in Indonesia can be attributed to the later Austronesian immigrants.

The agricultural technology that the Austronesians introduced was truly revolutionary, providing those who brought it (and those who adopted it) with a massive advantage in terms of both being better able to reproduce themselves as well as their capacity for greater social sophistication. The principal technologies introduced initially were dry-rice farming and pig rearing. Both produced high protein levels in relatively small areas and were very well suited to large parts of Indonesia. Agricultural practices now made it possible for a far greater proportion of Indonesia's inhabitants to settle in one place. They could also settle in greater numbers and in closer proximity to other settlements since the amount of territory needed to sustain a settlement was much less than when people depended on hunting and gathering. This was true even though the new agricultural technology, known as shifting cultivation, was relatively primitive. Shifting cultivation involves clearing virgin land for the planting and harvesting of crops. When the land becomes unproductive the site is abandoned and the process is repeated elsewhere. Naturally the size of settlements and their degree of proximity to others still varied enormously, depending upon the fertility of the soil and other features of the local environment that affected agricultural productivity. The same geographical features remained important but now with some significant variations. Mountains and jungles still constituted barriers, but they were now environments from which a living could more readily be extracted for modest communities, with the application of shifting cultivation to supplement hunting and gathering, or vice versa in more favorable areas. Coastal areas where fishing provided a valuable source of protein remained important, but where the coastal plain was fertile, agriculture then provided an additional, perhaps more important, food source. The same applied to rivers, where deltas and river valleys sometimes offered an environment vastly more productive with the application of agriculture. This latter development represented a significant change, making sizable inland settlements possible for the first time.

The introduction of agriculture accentuated the settlement pattern already evident during the era of hunting and gathering. Since equatorial forest areas were significantly less conducive to human settlement than intertropical forests, the inland areas of Sumatra, Borneo, central Sulawesi, and Papua were already much less densely populated than the inland areas of Java, Bali, and to a lesser extent the southern areas of Sulawesi and Sumatra. While agriculture allowed for some increased population in equatorial forest areas, it allowed for even greater population increases in the intertropical areas. Agriculture benefited greatly from the rainfall pattern associated with the latter areas, where there are distinct and regular dry and wet seasons of an appropriate length, rather than the almost year-round rain in the equatorial regions. These conditions were particularly favorable to cereal crops such as rice that need an extended, dry, sunny period for them to ripen. Farther east, in the intertropical zone past Bali, the opposite problem begins to take effect, with extended dry seasons of six months or longer for the islands of Nusa Tenggara (or Lesser Sundas) such as Lombok, Sumbawa, Sumba, Flores, and Timor. The rainfall pattern was not the only natural feature that interacted with agriculture to enhance the already established settlement trend. The islands of Java and Bali were also favored by the fertile soils produced by the activity of their volcanoes, part of the active volcanic belt that stretches from the northern tip of Sumatra to the islands east of Bali. The emissions of the Sumatran volcanoes produce more acidic and thus less fertile soils. Borneo lies in a volcanically inactive area.

The introduction of wet-rice cultivation in Indonesia saw further dramatic changes. Dry-rice cultivation (a form of shifting cultivation), as the term suggests, involves planting rice seeds in dry ground, often after the existing vegetation has been cut down and burned to provide nutrients (so-called slash-and-burn agriculture). Wet-rice cultivation typically involves germinating seeds of rice before planting them closely packed in watery mud in a corner of a field that serves as a nursery. When the seedlings reach a certain point of maturity, usually after about two months, they are pulled out and individually pruned and washed before being transplanted. They are pressed gently into the mud, covered by a few centimeters of water in regular, dense rows. The water level is carefully maintained so that the roots and bottoms of the stalks remain covered by water. After a few months when the grain has appeared, the water is gradually drained away and the rice plants are allowed to ripen before harvesting. The origins of wet-rice cultivation are unclear, but it appears to have been practiced in Indonesia quite early in the Common Era. It is also not clear exactly how or when it was introduced. India has been suggested as the source, but there is no evidence to support this contention except that contact between India and Indonesia had clearly become frequent by this point. The same, however, could be said for southern China and mainland Southeast Asia, and by this point, all of these areas knew and practiced the technology where the conditions were suitable.

Wherever its origins, wet-rice cultivation further accentuated the already established settlement patterns favoring Java and Bali. If Java and Bali provided an excellent combination of soil, rain, and climate for dry rice, then these conditions could hardly have been more ideal for wet rice. Of even greater significance, wet-rice techniques also massively increased the capacity for large concentrations of population. Rice and therefore calorie yields from land brought under wet-rice cultivation were much higher per unit of land than where dry-rice techniques were employed. Moreover, in the good rice-growing areas of Java and Bali, two crops of wet rice could be grown per year without degrading the soil. Dry rice could only produce one crop per year, and even the best fields needed to be rotated in and out of production, as yields would otherwise decline sharply. These extraordinary levels of productivity are significant because now, for the first time, the areas best suited for population concentrations were river valleys and riverine plains because they were the best suited for wet-rice production. The combination of these developments would have profound consequences for social and historical development in Indonesia.

Larger settlements allow for the development of more sophisticated societies with specialization of labor and other social functions but typically also see the development of social stratification and the emergence of a state. It is not surprising therefore that these social phenomena began to occur in Indonesia in tandem with the establishment of large and densely settled communities based on the stable food source provided by wet-rice cultivation. Small (for the most part) states based on a system of government best termed *kingship* gradually emerged. With this development came courts and thus courtiers, and the needs of the state saw the emergence of specialist administrators and soldiers. Courts also brought together the best musicians, dancers, artisans, and others highly skilled in crafts and arts, a concentration that raised the level and sophistication of all these skills. Intellectual and spiritual developments were also stimulated by these greater concentrations of people, especially around the courts. Full-time religious officials or priests, and other trappings of a religious bureaucracy, tended to emerge, together with more detailed and rigorous religious ideas and more stylized rituals, compared with the part-time and highly localized religious practices and practitioners that persisted at village level.

Exactly when these developments began is unknown; however, by around 400 C.E. the kingdoms of Tarumanegara in West Java and Kutai in East Kalimantan had appeared. It is likely, however, that other states, albeit probably less sophisticated, had existed on Sumatra, Java, and Borneo for some time prior to this point. Unfortunately their history remains elusive. An early state, known only by its Chinese name of Ho-Ling, was located on the northern Java coast, from where it came to dominate much of Java. Ho-Ling was sophisticated and powerful enough to send a delegation to China in 640. Some time early in the eighth century, Ho-Ling merged with Mataram, then centered on the fertile Kedu plain in southern Central Java. It is this Hindu-Buddhist state that in the early ninth century constructed the famous Borobudur, the largest Buddhist monument in the world, situated some 50 kilometers north of the present-day city of Yogyakarta. This massive stone and beautifully carved stupa was an enormous project that took decades to build and serves as eloquent testimony to the resources that this state could command as well as to its lofty ambition and pride.

It has been suggested that one of the reasons why wet-rice agriculture on a large scale tends to lead to the emergence of a state is the need for construction and regulation of complex irrigation works . It is certainly true that in Java and Bali the irrigation works involving terracing and channels are incredibly sophisticated. Water is brought to fields at just the right time and in the right quantity and then allowed to flow on to other fields with the same exquisite timing and measurement. But at least until recently, these irrigation works at least were not the product of large-scale construction such that a state might be required to organize. The farmers built them themselves out of earth and bamboo pipes. Indeed, part of their genius is precisely the primitive nature of the materials that allow for constant and immediate adjustment at the micro level. A few minutes' work with a hoe, and a new channel is opened or a channel closed off or the rate and direction of flow adjusted. Moreover, in Indonesia the regulation of the complex irrigation systems was achieved not through the coercive power of the state, but through cooperation mediated by *adat* (customary law or traditional law).

Kings and states were remote from what can only be described as a remarkable process of grassroots cooperation and organization; nevertheless, their coincidence in time and place suggests some relationship. It is easy to see why states needed the agricultural surplus and the population that such wet-rice irrigation systems made possible, but why the state was needed is less obvious. States provided a framework of peace and common belonging within which the complex grassroots cooperation and regulation could take place. They also provided protection from other states and brigands. In addition to these sociological functions, the state also provided a similar protective function in the spiritual dimension. The prevalent religious view at the time saw rulers as having a spiritual function inseparable from their temporal role. As the linchpin between an intimately interconnected heaven and earth, a crucial part of the ruler's role was to preserve harmony between these spheres to maintain good fortune for the realm. According to this worldview, threats posed by brigands and invasion were perceived to be identical in source to those posed by volcanic eruptions and poor weather. The source ultimately was spiritual, and thus averting these threats was ultimately dependent on the spiritual health of the state, usually personified by the ruler. Ostentatious displays of ritual and glory by the state demonstrated diligent performance of its designated functions, thereby legitimizing its existence and attendant claims to material support in the form of rice and labor from the people. It is likely that this combination of spiritual and practical motives provided sufficient reason for peasant populations to accept their lot. To leave and find an isolated region where a community could live and farm without putting up with the onerous extractions of a state also would have meant abandoning many years of labor investment in irrigation works and other tasks associated with preparing fields. Conditions were sometimes such that people did take this drastic option, one that existed for many centuries due to the small population relative to the amount of fertile land suitable for agriculture. This population-to-land ratio was why the object of war between states in this period was often the seizure of a rival's population rather than its territory.

TRADE AND THE EMERGENCE OF EARLY STATES

Trade was another important factor facilitating the emergence of states in Indonesia. By around 2000 B.C.E. (perhaps earlier), most of the world was linked in a market network. (The American continent was the major exception.) Most trade remained local or regional, but some products were so valued that their transportation over many thousands of kilometers was evidently worthwhile. Within this semiglobal network, the Indian Ocean, together with the Arabian Sea, the South China Sea, and the other seas in and around Indonesia came to perform a role similar to that of the Mediterranean, only on a much larger scale, larger in terms of both distance and trading volumes. Goods were conveyed among India, China, and Southeast Asia in enormous quantities for the time, and then from the western coast of India the products of these areas were then traded in West Asia, the Mediterranean, and northern Europe. From the very beginning, Indonesia was part of this trading network, but by the fifth century, circumstance and geography had combined to place Indonesia at the crossroads of the large-scale seaborne trade between China and India. Indonesian traders became prominent participants in the regional trading networks, along with their products, as did Indonesian sailors and boat builders and their boats. The preeminence of the latter is manifested in the type of vessel that became dominant on the region's seas until the arrival of the Europeans. Originally built by Indonesians of the northern Java and southern Borneo coasts, we know it by the name *junk*, a Portuguese corruption of the Malay word *jong*. These vessels were neither primitive nor small for their day, often being more than three times the size of the first European boats to arrive in Southeast Asian waters.

Prior to the fifth century, products of Indonesia had already been carried far afield. Cloves from Maluku (the Moluccas) and sandalwood from Timor had been reaching Rome since at least the beginning of the Common Era. But it seems that a surge in trade in Indonesian products was stimulated when the established trade route shifted sometime in the middle of the fourth century. Hitherto, traders operating the seaborne trade between China and India unloaded at the narrow Kra Isthmus (in present-day southern Thailand), where their goods were portered to the other side to be loaded onto other boats to continue the journey. By the beginning of the fifth century, the sea route through the Malacca Strait was preferred. No doubt it was more economical, but the change of route also reflected the growing number of Indonesian sailors and traders in the regional trade who knew the waters and winds. It also reflected the growing demand for Indonesian products, which made the diversion attractive. In China, cloves, nutmeg, and mace (all from Maluku), pepper (from Sumatra and West Java), as well as rhinoceros horn (from Java and Sumatra) and tortoiseshell (from Bali and elsewhere) were in high demand. Certain rainforest products, especially aromatic woods and resins such as camphor and benzoin (mainly from Sumatra) were also highly prized as substitutes for the extremely expensive frankincense and myrrh. The blocking of the land route between northern and southern China in 439 due to a phase of hostilities provided further stimulation of the sea-route trade between southern China and Indonesia.

Once Indonesian involvement in trade reached significant proportions, then port city-states began to emerge in particular locations around the archipelago. Trade on a large scale, just like wet-rice cultivation, could now sustain a relatively large population in a small area, a development likely, as noted previously, to result in a more sophisticated and stratified society and some form of state. Arguably the requirements of running a port and marketplace lent even more impetus to state development. The need to establish and maintain port facilities, to maintain order between residents and assorted communities of transient merchants and sailors, and the need for a navy to ensure the safety of vessels coming and going from port were all needs best met by a state. These port city-states tended to develop where a number of fortuitous circumstances converged to provide an advantage. The mouth of a navigable river could provide a safe harbor for shipping, and the river itself could provide access to the interior where forest products could be collected for trade and brought to market. Proximity and ease of access to a source of sought-after products was necessary, as was proximity or ready access to a substantial food and water supply. The latter was necessary because trading ports needed to feed not only their own populations, but also the transient traders who would usually have to wait several months for the wind to shift before they could leave with their cargoes. Proximity to established trade and sailing routes was highly desirable, as was the capacity to control the surrounding waters. "Choke points," such as the Malacca Strait and the Sunda Strait, through which shipping had to pass, were geographical features that facilitated the latter two desirable elements. Many significant trading states emerged on or near the coasts of these straits over the centuries: for example, Aceh and Srivijaya on the east coast of Sumatra, Johor and Malacca on the west coast of the Malay Peninsula, and Banten on the north-west coast of Java. Singapore at the mouth of the Malacca Strait is a contemporary example. Access to timber suitable for shipbuilding was also advantageous. Again, it is striking how many trading states emerged on the northern coast of Java, where such timber was abundant, including Jayakerta, Demak, Tuban, and Jepara. These Java coast states also benefited from the rice surplus produced by the wet-rice-based states located inland. But probably of most importance to their commercial success was their acquisition of Maluku spices, which they procured from the source and traded to the world.

The best known of the trading states to emerge in Indonesia was Srivijaya, which came to prominence in the seventh century. Srivijaya was located in southern Sumatra, somewhere near the present site of the city of Palembang, some distance up the large, navigable Musi River, which flows into the Malacca Strait. The river provided access to large quantities of forest products and a safe harbor for Malacca Strait shipping. Initially it seems that Srivijaya could produce sufficient food locally to meet the needs of its sizable population. As it expanded to become the preeminent port in the region, it was able to secure rice from Java through a symbiotic relationship it established with the state of Mataram. Leaving aside sundry episodes of warfare, such as that of 1016, which resulted in a temporary defeat for Mataram, these two states coexisted in a mutually beneficial, if competitive, fashion, a relationship they cemented with intermarriage. The latter was by no means the only example of astute diplomacy on the part of Srivijaya. Regular diplomatic missions to China established an excellent relationship with Chinese emperors, one that the Chinese liked to see as tributary in nature though was probably more ambiguous from the Srivijayan perspective. Whatever its precise character, the arrangement paid off handsomely for Srivijaya as thereby, traders operating with the imprimatur of Srivijaya and its allies and clients gained privileged access to the lucrative China trade. By such means Srivijaya expanded its power until it acquired the size and status of a major maritime empire extending its sway over the Malacca and Sunda Straits and for a considerable distance along the north coast of Java. Srivijaya's dominance eventually proved unsustainable, however. Although victorious in its battle with Mataram, the victory evidently proved draining. Less than a decade later, in 1025, another blow came when an expeditionary force dispatched by the Indian kingdom of Chola briefly captured Srivijaya's capital. Rivals to the north as well as to the south now confronted Srivijaya. But

Srivijaya's biggest problem was probably its inability to sustain the monopoly on trade with China because during the twelfth century Chinese merchants began to engage directly in regional trade.

INDIC INFLUENCES ON STATE AND SOCIETY

Until recently, Southeast Asia's pre-Islamic civilizations were usually perceived to be the product of "Indianization."[2] Although there was clearly much borrowing from India, most scholars now regard the Indianization theory as having exaggerated the degree of Indic influence to the point of rendering virtually invisible the indigenous cultural elements. Moreover, it is now considered important to grasp the way Indic influences were absorbed but simultaneously transformed in an interactive process of adoption and adaptation. It is also now considered likely that the initiative for the Indic borrowing came largely from Southeast Asians rather than from Indians deliberately exporting ideas or emigrating.

Some past Indic influences on Indonesia are quite obvious. Clearly, religious beliefs that emanated from the Indian subcontinent, essentially Hinduism and Buddhism, were widely and well received in Indonesia from early in the Common Era. At the time it sent delegations to China, Ho-Ling was a Buddhist state. The Buddhist monument of Borobudur (a major site for international Buddhist pilgrimage for many centuries) has already been mentioned. Hindu temples were erected on the Dieng Plateau in the eighth century, and during the late ninth century the magnificent Hindu temple complex of Prambanan, also located close to Yogyakarta, was constructed. Majapahit, to be discussed below, was also a Hindu state. Srivijaya, although not leaving us any impressive stone evidence, was nevertheless a Buddhist state of some religious repute, known as an international center of Mahayana Buddhist learning. Clearly, Indonesia was not a backwater that had merely absorbed a pale reflection of Buddhism, but a major center of Buddhism in its own right. Indic influences were not confined to religion alone, although religion was the primary vehicle through which they arrived. These Indic religious beliefs were not confined to the realm of theology. They were imbued with a worldview that included politics, social organization, ethics, and philosophy and were also embodied in arts, crafts, and technologies. Thus apart from matters we might categorize as spiritual, Indic-influenced courts of this era in Indonesia also adopted conceptions of kingship and statecraft, as well as things like the Hindu epic poems, the Ramayana and the Mahabarata, and techniques of stonemasonry and writing.

That so much of the evidence of Indic influence is associated with the Indonesian courts is an important clue to understanding the phenomenon. The Indonesians who had by far the most direct contact with India were the traders and sailors who traveled to India and who also encountered Indian merchants in Southeast Asian ports. But there is no evidence that these Indonesians were sufficiently impressed with things Indian to adopt Indian customs and religions, certainly not in significant numbers or to any great extent. This is unsurprising. Except where it is sometimes successfully imposed by conquest, cultural transmission usually occurs due to a perceived utilitarian value on the part of those accepting the new ways of living and of seeing the world. Those Indonesians who could perceive such a benefit and who were also well placed to know something of the world beyond their immediate vicinity were the new rulers and elites that rose with the states. They could also access it, most probably by inviting Brahman priests to their courts.

To the Indonesian rulers and elites, Indian rulers must have embodied the apotheosis of power, state majesty, wealth, and cultural sophistication. But their impulse to emulate Indian rulers was not merely a matter of self-aggrandizement. It was also driven by pragmatic motives that were as much spiritual as they were secular. The Indic conception of kingship as the embodiment of an essential link between heaven and earth provided powerful religious legitimation and greatly enhanced authority for a ruler. Sometimes rulers took this as far as representing themselves as the embodiment of a god, as did Airlangga, the ruler of Mataram from 1016 to 1049, who claimed to be the incarnation of Vishnu. No doubt the concept was convenient. But embracement of the concept and its proper implementation can also be regarded as merely responsible behavior on a ruler's part. At a time when belief in the supernatural dimension and its intimate relationship with the material world was unquestioned, it was regarded as incumbent upon rulers to do their utmost to maintain harmony and to negotiate between the two worlds on behalf of their people. After all, according to both indigenous and Indic beliefs, it was they who were uniquely placed to do so. Furthermore, according to the circular logic intrinsic to these ideas, the evident power and wealth of Indian rulers proved the efficacy of their religious beliefs and intertwined practice of statecraft. It was merely practical therefore for

Indonesian rulers to embrace these beliefs and practices. Among other things, this entailed a responsibility for rulers to behave and to present themselves as a king should, but also an obligation for the people to respect the ruler's authority. The state itself was a religious ritual and, like all religious rituals, had to be conducted properly for its propitiation objectives to be met, not merely for the sake of the ruler but also for the sake of the realm.

It is difficult without a lot more evidence to judge how deeply Indic influences penetrated into Indonesian society. Part of the problem is that many Indic ideas, such as those underlying king-ship, overlapped with ideas about the world already prevalent in Indonesia. Indeed, this is precisely why many Indic ideas were so readily accepted. Another part of the problem is that Indic ideas (the same can be said for Indic technologies and art forms) were not simply accepted, they were also assimilated. The earli-est examples of Indonesian writing we know of, dating from the fourth century, is in South Indian Pallawa script. Usage of the script became widespread, but within a few centuries it evolved into a localized script known as Kawi.[3] The two thousand bas-relief sculptures of the Borobudur are evidently influenced by similar great works of art produced in India during the Gupta Empire (320-540 C.E.). Likewise, the stonemasonry skills involved are considered to be Indic in origin, as is the story (the life of the Buddha) that the panels depict. But the faces that look back at us from these exquisite carvings are Indonesian faces, and the details of everyday life and dress depicted are clearly indigenous. Similarly, literary forms of Indian origin such as the Mahabarata and the Ramayana were not merely reproduced, but were modi-fied or became material for indigenous literature. For example, the famous Javanese epic poem the Arjunawiwaha (The Marriage of Arjuna), composed in the Mataram court during the first half of the eleventh century, although based on the Mahabarata, is quint-essentially Javanese.

Key Indic religious ideas were also modified for domestic con-sumption or were applied on a selective basis. A prime example is the Hindu caste system, which in Indonesian contexts was never practiced with anywhere near the rigor and complexity that gen-erally pertains in India. Hindu and Buddhist ideas were often blended with each other and with indigenous beliefs to construct what was arguably a new belief system. For example, Kertanegara, the ruler of Singasari from 1268 to 1292, established a syncretic cult of Shiva-Buddha attached to local religious beliefs associated with ancestral spirits.[4] These syncretic tendencies were facilitated by the prevailing attitude of this era, which rarely saw the adoption of Hinduism or Buddhism as necessitating the abandonment of existing religious beliefs, but merely as adding more strands into an ever-richer woven fabric of connections to the supernatural world. Even where Indic forms became dominant, they rarely totally eclipsed local elements. Moreover, the apparent domination of Indic elements was not always what it seemed. In the famous Javanese *wayang* performance art form (usually involving puppets), which utilizes episodes loosely drawn from the Mahabarata, new clown characters were introduced into the story, the best known of whom is Semar. In the Javanese version the joke is that while he appears common, coarse, and foolish he is really a local god in disguise (Ismaya, protector of the island of Java). Semar, despite his appearance, is more powerful (as well as kinder and wiser) than the Hindu gods who are otherwise central characters in the story. A closer look at the *wayang* reveals that the Indic elements that appear so central are actually relatively unimportant: the *wayang* is a rich embodiment of Javanese values and culture.

Our brief survey of the rise and fall of the Indic-influenced states of Indonesia in this period would be incomplete without some further mention of Majapahit: as the greatest state to exist in Indonesia before the late colonial period, it is often heralded as a precursor of the Republic of Indonesia.

After Airlangga's death, Mataram divided into two states, Kediri and Janggala. Kediri went on to become a powerful state in the late twelfth and thirteenth centuries, controlling the key ports in southwestern Borneo, Bali, and southern Sulawesi for a time. The mysterious adventurer, Ken Angrok, seized power in the smaller kingdom of Janggala and conquered Kediri in 1222. Having done so, he established a new capital at Kutaraja and renamed it Singasari, which also became the name of the state. Majapahit emerged from Singasari in 1292, a product of complex political conflicts involving rival princes within the Singasari dynasty and a punitive Mongol invasion force from China. The successful rider of these waves of domestic and international conflict and intrigue, Vijaya (also known as Kertarajasa), established his new capital at Majapahit. Majapahit, situated on the Brantas River plain, was better located than was its principal predecessor, Mataram. Like Mataram, Majapahit had access to a significant rice surplus. But unlike Mataram, Majapahit had much better access to the coast and thus was much better able to control and thereby to extract wealth from trade. Moreover, located at the eastern end of Java, it was better placed to control access to the spices emanating from Maluku. This was important, as international demand for spices had risen dramatically. Majapahit made itself the supplier of Maluku spices to the world, acquiring them in exchange for rice. Majapahit also used its power to prevent rivals from accessing the spices. On the back of its strategic advantages Majapahit, also blessed by the astute statecraft of "Minister" Gadjah Mada from roughly 1330 to 1364, sought to control the entire archipelago, including the remnants of Srivijaya. The extent and degree of its power almost certainly never matched this ambition, but there seems little doubt that for a time Majapahit exerted power and influence throughout the archipelago as no power had before it. As such it established a model of greatness to which many have aspired since and is an evocative "legend" of indigenous prowess and power, especially for the Javanese. The greatness resided not only in the realm of politics and power, but also in arts and culture. For instance, during the Majapahit era, the great epic poem Nagarakertagama was composed (probably in 1365), and the Semar character was introduced into the *wayang*.

THE COMING OF ISLAM

The dramatic territorial expansion of Islam from the environs of Medina and Mecca in present-day Saudi Arabia occurred for the most part within decades of the prophet Muhammad's death around 632. The major exception to this phenomenon is Indonesia, which ironically today is home to the world's largest Muslim population. As far as we know, Islam made few if any Indonesian converts until around 1200 and was probably not the majority religion in Indonesia before around 1700. The first indigenous Muslim community in the region that we are fairly certain about was in the port of Pasai in northern Sumatra in 1290.[5] In the same area, however, it seems likely that there was a Muslim state in existence perhaps as early as a century earlier. Trengganu, on the northeastern coast of the Malay Peninsula, seems to have been an indigenous Muslim state around 1300. Prominent (perhaps royal) indigenous Muslims were present at the Hindu-Buddhist Majapahit court from the 1360s.[6] The state of Malacca became Muslim around 1410, and at approximately the same time there seem to have been Muslims at Gresik on the northeastern coast of Java, but whether they were indigenous remains unclear. Demak (northern coast of Central Java), Sulu (the Philippines), and Ternate (Maluku) apparently adopted Islam during the second half of the fifteenth century. Early in the sixteenth century, Brunei (northeastern Borneo), Banten, and Cirebon (northwestern Java) were Muslim, and by the end of the century other key points such as Buton (southeastern Sulawesi) had followed suit.

Roughly up until the sixteenth century, Islam's presence in the region had been largely confined to coastal areas prominent in the trading network, but it seems to have begun spreading inland in some areas. More key centers converted to Islam in the early seventeenth century, during which Islam also penetrated farther inland. By around 1650, Islam was dominant in most coastal areas of Indonesia except those toward the eastern end of the archipelago and had spread inland to most of Java and Sumatra. Since that time, Islam has continued to spread throughout Indonesia; indeed, it is still spreading today in remote parts of Kalimantan and Papua. Some parts of Indonesia and some ethnic groups have largely rejected Islam, usually where they adopted Christianity, which arrived in Indonesia with Europeans in the sixteenth century. An important exception is the island of Bali, which has largely clung resolutely to its Balinese version of Hindu-Buddhist beliefs. There is another dimension of the Islamization of Indonesia process that warrants mentioning. Alongside the geographical spread of the religion, there is a process whereby Indonesian Muslims, particularly over the last century, have deepened their overt commitment to the faith. The pace of the geographical spread may have slowed in recent decades, but at the same time the pace and intensity of the movement toward a deeper or more manifest commitment to the faith has increased markedly.

Indonesians may have begun adopting Islam much earlier than the thirteenth century, but this is unlikely. Assuming that the process did only begin around 1200, then this raises two questions: why then and why not before? Arab traders, already a presence in the region long before the Prophet's time, increased markedly in number after most of the Arab world embraced Islam. Moreover, it was not long before that these Muslim Arab traders were joined in the region by Persian, Indian, and Chinese Muslims. Thus despite ample contact it appears that Islam initially held little appeal to Indonesians.

As A. H. Johns has pointed out, the period in which Indonesians began to adopt Islam coincides with the period when Sufi forms of Islam became popular throughout the Islamic world.[7] Sufism's significance in this context is that, as a mystical form of Islam, it likely found ready echoes in beliefs and practices, both Indic and indigenous, already well established in Indonesia. It is reasonable to assume that these and other characteristics of Sufism, such as an accepted place for magic and a generally tolerant approach to other religious beliefs, would have appealed to Indonesian religious tastes that were for the most part openly syncretic at the time. It is worth noting that Islam in Indonesia still has a distinct Sufi tinge, although it is a characteristic in decline. Perhaps nowhere was Sufism likely to have had more appeal than in the courts, where sophisticated and eclectic religious practices were avidly pursued. Another reason why rulers and courtiers may have begun to find Islam attractive around this time is the spread throughout the Islamic world of Persian ideas about kingship and associated forms of pomp and ceremony surrounding royal ritual, including elaborate royal titles.[8] It is unlikely, however, that the changes in the nature of Islamic practice from the thirteenth century were sufficient in themselves to persuade many rulers to adopt Islam. More likely, their importance lies in smoothing the way for rulers to adopt Islam for more practical reasons to do with trade and politics.

As the number of Muslim traders in the region began to rise significantly in tandem with rising volumes of trade with West Asia and the Mediterranean, their presence began to have profound commercial and political consequences. These consequences were first felt in the Malacca Strait, in the ports where Muslim traders were to be found in the greatest numbers, having come there to trade for the region's sought-after spices. Their common religious membership facilitated business transactions among themselves because Islam includes rules for commercial behavior and encourages assistance to fellow Muslims. Commercially astute local traders seeking access to these growing commercial networks would have found it conducive to adopt Islam, and once a point of critical mass had been reached, the same would have applied to the local port cities and their rulers. Indeed, it appears that rulers (who were often involved in trade) were usually at the forefront of such shifts. The significantly increased presence of Muslim traders in the region also facilitated a related development—the founding of Muslim states or settlements in Indonesia by foreign Muslims who intermarried with Indonesians and adopted many aspects of local culture.

Adopting Islam is likely to have provided the port states on the northern coast of Sumatra with a commercial advantage in their competition with Srivijaya, since thereby Muslim traders were encouraged to utilize North Sumatran ports rather than those of Srivijaya or of any other rivals. The religious change also probably signaled their independence from lingering Srivijayan claims to authority over them. It is probably for reasons such as these that, approximately a decade after founding the new state of Malacca around 1400, Malacca's ruler Parameswara converted to Islam and took the name Iskandar Syah. Having obtained Chinese trading preference and protection, Malacca, strategically situated at the narrowest point in the strait that now bears its name, quickly became the dominant power in that vicinity. During the fifteenth century, its trading empire came to surpass that of Majapahit, extending beyond the Malacca Strait to embrace ports along the northern Java coast and the southern coast of Borneo, across the South China Sea to Brunei, and beyond to Sulu and Maluku. Some of the states that came within its sway were already Muslim, but most adopted Islam due to Malacca's influence, which embodied all the advantages that accrued to rulers who became Muslims.

Two other key aspects of the regional political context were conducive for these developments. The decline of Buddhist Srivijaya, which had for so long dominated the Malacca Strait, provided the political space in which new political forces and social forms could arise. The state policies of the Ming dynasty (founded in 1368) placed trade in the hands of the state and forbade Chinese from traveling overseas, thus reducing competition for Muslim traders. The renewed interest in the region by the Chinese Empire proved particularly fortuitous for Malacca because its establishment coincided almost exactly with the period in which Chinese Admiral Zheng He's fleets visited the region in awesome force, thus underlining Malacca's protected vassal status in a highly visible manner.

The rise of Muslim Malacca's great trading empire was the major turning point in Islam's fortunes throughout the region. Under the auspices of this maritime empire's political and commercial power, Islam spread to almost all the significant trading ports and political centers, thereby gaining the initial momentum that carried it to its subsequent dominant position in Indonesia. In passing, one should also note another important historical phenomenon facilitated by Malacca. Malacca's power and influence were largely responsible for turning Malay into the region's lingua franca, the language upon which the national languages of Indonesia and Malaysia are based.

NOTES

1. Robert Cribb, *Historical Atlas of Indonesia* (Richmond: Curzon, 2000), p. 22.

2. The classic expression of this view is G. Coedes, *The Indianized States of Southeast Asia* (Canberra: Australian National University Press, 1968).

3. Cribb, *Historical Atlas*, p. 38.

4. Coedes, *Indianized States*, p. 199.

5. The dates in this paragraph are taken from Cribb, *Historical Atlas*, pp. 44–45. Although these dates are generally accepted, there is some dispute among scholars regarding the dating and locations of Islam's spread through the archipelago.

6. M.C. Ricklefs, *A History of Modern Indonesia Since c. 1200* (Basingstoke: Palgrave, 2001), p. 4.

7. A.H. Johns, "Muslim Mystics and Historical Writing," in *Historians of South East Asia*, D.G.E. Hall (London: Oxford University Press, 1961), pp. 39–41.

8. A.C. Milner, "Islam and Malay Kingship," in *Readings on Islam in Southeast Asia*, comp. Ahmad Ibrahim et al. (Singapore: ISEAS, 1985), pp. 27–28.

2

Indonesia during the Colonial Era (1600–1940)

The colonial impact on Indonesia's historical development was certainly of great significance and therefore provides a convenient overarching theme for this chapter. But colonialism was not so central a historical phenomenon that it subsumed everything else for three or four hundred years. The great significance of the European impact needs to be recognized but without neglecting the considerable degree of continuity with long-established historical patterns. Indonesians were not the passive recipients of a colonial history that was imposed upon them. The vital parts played by Indonesian historical actors should not be overlooked: Indonesians and Europeans both acted and also reacted to each other and to the new circumstances with which they were confronted. It is precisely in the interplay between European and indigenous elements that we can locate the shaping of modern Indonesia, largely in ways that were unintended.

SPICE WARS

Europe's fifteenth-century elite was well aware that another world existed beyond the Mediterranean, one they believed to be enormously wealthy. But Europeans knew little else about this world, and even that little was riddled with error and distortion. For example, a lost Christian kingdom was believed to exist somewhere in the "Indies." Between Europe and the half-glimpsed other world stood a feared and formidable enemy, the Muslim Ottoman Empire, the dominant power in the Mediterranean between Morocco and Constantinople (Istanbul). Apart from the serious military threat the Ottomans posed to Christian Europe, Europeans were aggrieved by the effect Ottoman taxation policies had on the already high prices of products, especially spices, originating in the Indies. Thus driven by a mix of religious, political, and above all economic motives, European powers led by rivals Spain and Portugal began to seek another route to the Indies. Within a century the English and the Dutch followed.

The Portuguese were the first to arrive in the region. Vasco de Gama reached the West Coast of India in 1497, his representative informing the bemused traders of Gujerat that they came "in search of Christians and of spices."[1] Within a few years, under the leadership of Alfonso de Albuquerque, the Portuguese sought to monopolize the spice trade through absolute domination of the Indian Ocean trading region. This was ambition of breathtaking proportions, given that Portugal was a modest European power with a population of approximately a million at the time. Nevertheless, in pursuit of their audacious objective, the Portuguese captured Goa in 1510, Malacca in 1511, and Hormuz in 1515; acquired Macau in 1557; and blockaded the Arab port of Aden for decades. They also made several attempts to capture Johor and built a string of forts around the region, including on the Indonesian islands of Ambon, Banda, and Java.

For a time, the Portuguese strategy brought considerable commercial success as they supplanted Muslim traders as spice suppliers to Europe. For example, in the last decade of the fifteenth century, Muslim traders, lacking any competition, supplied Europe with 50 tons of cloves, but during the sixteenth century, 573 tons were shipped to Europe by the Portuguese compared with only 170 tons by Muslim traders.[2] Nevertheless despite their initial successes, the Portuguese lacked the ships and men to fulfill their grandiose ambitions, but this is not to say that their efforts were without significant effects. The Portuguese capture of Malacca left the region without a dominant indigenous power, ending a historical pattern (Srivijaya, Majapahit, and Malacca) that has not been replicated since. Because the Portuguese proved unable to fill Malacca's shoes, power in the region was effectively splintered among numerous smaller units, a condition that continued until the colonial state of the Netherlands Indies attained regional hegemony in the late nineteenth century. Trade was seriously disrupted by Portuguese actions for decades, and its patterns shifted as traders bypassed Portuguese-held ports. Some of the alternative port-states, such as Johor (the new location of the dynasty expelled from Malacca) and the emerging Aceh seized the opportunity to become significant powers.

The Portuguese impact was certainly of considerable significance, especially in the long term, but it should not be overrated. Periods without a dominant power were not unknown in the region's history, and the dominant powers of the past had never completely smothered the region's fractious political patterns. These patterns now simply continued to operate largely as they always had, only without the moderation that an overarching regional power would have provided. The Portuguese, having tried and failed to establish themselves as the region's dominant power, effectively became merely another powerful participant in regional affairs, operating largely by the long-established local rules. Thus the Portuguese tried to coerce shipping into the ports they controlled as local states had always done. Also, like local states, they negotiated alliances, such as with Hindu-Buddhist Banten in 1522 (against Muslim Demak) and in the same year with Muslim Ternate (against Muslim Tidore, which was allied to the newly arrived Spanish). The Portuguese also seized cargoes as regional pirates had always done when opportunities arose, and, as local states in alliance with pirates often did, they generally targeted shipping that bypassed their ports. Like local and other visiting merchants, they also traded freely, usually behind the back of the Portuguese Crown.

A third important effect attributed to the Portuguese is their introduction of Christianity into the region, and with it the Christian-Muslim friction central at the time to the politics of the Mediterranean and southern Europe. The first part of this proposition is correct, although spreading Christianity was not the Portuguese's primary objective except for a zealous few. Nevertheless, by the end of the sixteenth century, there were probably around a hundred thousand indigenous Christians in eastern Indonesia,[3] a considerable number given the total population of Indonesia at this time, estimated to be less than ten million.[4] The second part of the proposition is also true but should not be exaggerated. Whatever religious animosity there was between Christians and Muslims that arrived with the Portuguese was insufficient to prevent occasional political alliances between the Portuguese and Muslim kingdoms of the region, even against other Muslim kingdoms, when it seemed mutually beneficial. Apart from the Ternate-Tidore example mentioned above, Johor and the Portuguese were sometimes allied against Aceh. At other times, Aceh and Johor, together with Jepara, were allied against the Portuguese.

Other historical developments continued in the Indies, usually with little if any Portuguese involvement. On Java, for instance, declining Majapahit shifted its capital farther inland to Kediri around the turn of the century. Muslim Demak became a major power on Java about the same time, expanding its power eastward at Majapahit's expense, incorporating Tuban around 1527, Madiun around 1530, Pasaruan and Surabaya in the 1530s, and Malang in 1545. Simultaneously, Demak swept into its orbit hitherto independent port-states strung to its west along the northern coast of Java in the 1520s, including Banten and Sunda Kelapa (renamed Jayakerta afterward). In 1546 the death of Sultan Trenggana stalled Demak's ascent, leaving a power vacuum on Java that was not filled until a new Mataram state emerged in that part of Central Java, which centuries earlier had produced the Borobudur and Prambanan. Mystery and legend surround the origins of the new Mataram, but clearly by the time it conquered Demak and Madiun in the late 1580s, it had embarked on a path that would see it emerge as the most powerful state on Java early in the seventeenth century.

THE COMPANY ERA

The beginning of the seventeenth century also brought another important historical development. Having been the only Europeans in the region for almost a century, apart from minor Spanish and English incursions, the Portuguese were confronted by a formidable new European rival—the Dutch, whose first Indies expedition arrived in 1596. More Dutch ships quickly followed, and in 1602, prominent Dutch merchant-financiers agreed to maximize their resources by forming the Vereenigde Oost-Indische Compagnie (United East Indies Company) usually known as the VOC. About this time, the Spanish and English presence increased, and thus a four-cornered contest between European rivals for the lucrative spice trade became another factor in already tangled regional affairs. In their efforts to form exclusive trading agreements with local rulers, the Europeans often became embroiled in local conflicts as well as clashed with each other.

A few examples must suffice to convey the flavor of these "spice wars." During 1605 and 1606, the Dutch, in alliance with the Hituese, seized Ambon and Ternate from the Portuguese, only for a Spanish fleet to immediately seize Ternate and Tidore. In 1641, the VOC, in alliance with Johor, captured Malacca from the Portuguese. In 1620, the English, having already established several trading posts throughout Indonesia, secured reluctant agreement from the VOC to establish a post on Ambon. This unhappy arrangement ended in 1623 with the notorious "Ambon massacre." All but 2 of the 18 English traders and all 30 Japanese mercenaries in Ambon were executed after being tortured to confess to conspiracy against the Dutch. Apt indeed was the comment of one contemporary Portuguese who described the clove as "an apple of discord. And one could curse it more than gold itself."[5]

Competition and conflict between the Europeans in the Indies continued throughout the seventeenth and eighteenth centuries; but gradually, the Dutch emerged as the strongest European power. Their supremacy was partly due to a fortuitous waning of interest in the region from the other Europeans. The Spanish, always somewhat distracted by their substantial lucrative interests on the American continent, withdrew from Maluku in 1663 and shortly thereafter contented themselves with the Philippines. The Portuguese, once the other European powers had arrived in force, simply did not have the resources to compete effectively. Their efforts were also hamstrung by the unification of the Spanish and Portuguese Crowns from 1580 to 1668.

The English competed fiercely with the Dutch for much longer. Although generally bested in the Indies during the seventeenth century, the English remained a persistent thorn in the Dutch side. For example, when the VOC finally secured the expulsion of the English from Banten in 1683, the English merely responded by establishing a base at nearby Bengkulu on Sumatra's southwestern coast. By the time Britannia ruled the waves in the late eighteenth century, the English (British after 1707) were largely preoccupied with greater prizes including India and North America. Eventually, British interests in the region coalesced on the territory that now comprises Malaysia, Brunei, and Singapore. Thus the British and the Dutch divided Borneo between them and turned the Malacca

Strait from a water doorway into a border for the first time. The other great potential competitors, the French, were also generally busy elsewhere. Later, paradoxically, fears of French involvement bolstered the Dutch position in the Indies by providing the British with incentive to favor the Dutch presence, if only to obstruct their French enemies.

VOC actions should not be discounted, however, as factors vital in establishing Dutch dominance in the Indies vis-à-vis their European rivals. The substantially greater amount of capital at the VOC's disposal in the vital early years, roughly nine times the amount invested in the VOC's English counterpart, the East India Company, was crucial. Of at least equal importance, the VOC did not disburse its capital after each expedition returned. Instead, investors were paid a periodic dividend while the capital remained intact, and most profits were ploughed back into VOC operations. Thus the VOC could hire more men, obtain more and better ships and other equipment and, crucially, could take a longer-term view of its activities. Consequently, the VOC could maintain a stronger and more persistent regional presence, vital for protecting positions of influence won as well as for defending forts and maintaining continuity of supply. A good example of what greater capital and the capacity for a longer-term perspective could achieve is provided by the construction in 1611 of Fort Belgica, on Neira, one of the Banda islands. This massive, thick-walled, star-shaped fortress that still commands Neira's natural harbor was built from stone shipped to the island. This was a massive investment, but one that ensured that VOC control of Banda could not be supplanted. Fort Belgica also illustrates another element vital to VOC success, the sheer determination to succeed whatever the cost. No rival sailing into Banda's harbor at the absolute mercy of the fort's guns could fail to miss the emphatic statement in stone of VOC intent.

VOC determination was displayed, equally emphatically, by its ruthlessness when dealing with Indonesians who obstructed its efforts to secure a monopoly over the most valuable spices: nutmeg, mace, cloves, and pepper. The Portuguese had sought to attain a monopoly position through controlling the key trading ports. The Dutch pursued a similar objective largely by attempting to control spice production at the source, an objective lent some feasibility by the limited area in which three of these four spices could be found. Indeed, nutmeg and mace both come from the fruit of the nutmeg tree that at this time only grew, by a fluke of nature, on the group of six tiny islands that is Banda, the protruding remnants of a volcano, situated more than a hundred kilometers from the nearest landfall. The clove tree grew a little more widely but was still confined to Maluku. Pepper in this period was produced mainly in Sumatra and West Java but also on the Malay Peninsula and southwestern India, where it originated.

Fort Belgica deterred foreign and local military rivals, but the local inhabitants still presented a problem. Evidently, they were loath to abandon a livelihood that had been theirs for over a thousand years. The pragmatic Dutch solution implemented during 1620–23 was to expel Banda's entire population, massacring those who resisted, and replacing the locals with slaves. Securing a monopoly over clove production was more difficult, given the clove tree's wider habitat. The VOC issued "regulations," but local rulers and traders continued to "smuggle" cloves. Vigorous efforts were made to implement the monopoly, including treaties involving annual cash payments, such as those signed with the rulers of Ternate and Tidore in 1652 and 1657, respectively. Additional conquests and military actions were also employed, for example, a war conducted during 1652–58 against Ternatean rebels based on the small island of Hoamoal. Here, as elsewhere throughout Maluku, before success was achieved, the VOC resorted to burning clove trees and expelling populations to restrict production to areas under its control or that of its allies. Less drastic methods were employed in pursuit of a pepper monopoly, such as a treaty with Palembang in 1642 and the Painan Treaty with the pepper ports of northwestern Sumatra in 1663. But there was simply too much pepper-producing territory for the VOC to police it effectively, much of it relatively inaccessible in the Sumatran interior. There were also too many states engaged in the pepper trade, including Banten, Jambi, Palembang, and Aceh, as well as numerous other interested parties including Chinese and English traders.

As we have seen, the VOC was willing to commit massive resources to secure dominance over the "spice islands" of eastern Indonesia, the prerequisite for guaranteeing cheap supplies of spices. To this end, numerous engagements had to be fought, and then fortifications had to be constructed, maintained, and garrisoned. A well-equipped navy was also needed to fight battles, police the waters, and protect Dutch shipping. Moreover, the VOC quickly realized that to protect its position in Maluku, it needed a strong presence in other parts of the archipelago. It is largely in this light that the attainment of a base at Jayakerta in 1611 through an arrangement with the local ruler, and the conquest of Malacca 30 years later, should be seen. All of these requirements involved incurring significant initial costs, for which the VOC was prepared, as it was prepared for the substantial costs of maintaining its position, although it expected that costs would decline sharply once its position had been secured. Of course, the VOC also expected that the profits would soon dwarf both the initial and the ongoing costs.

To the VOC's considerable chagrin, however, high costs continued. To protect the VOC's position, it seemed that further battles had to be fought, more local states conquered, and additional defensive positions established. Worse, the decisive (and often costly) measures implemented to maximize profits generally failed to return the hoped-for level of profit. To defray the costs associated with security, the VOC quickly adopted the strategy of acquiring local allies, but this strategy also proved disappointing. All too often, VOC allies required costly military assistance as they became threatened by rival local powers, by rebellion from vassals, or by usurpation from rival claimants to their thrones. Frequently too, negotiated treaties proved worthless as rulers failed to meet the terms, either because they preferred not to or because they were simply unable to. A persistent error the Dutch made in this regard was to overestimate the capacity of Indonesian rulers to control their subjects and vassals. The frequency of regime change also caught the VOC off guard, as new rulers rarely saw any obligation to fulfill the terms of a treaty agreed by a predecessor. Both of these miscalculations derived from a failure on the part of the Dutch to understand the fragile and contingent nature of traditional kingship in the region.

Wherever the VOC was confronted by a situation that contributed to either of the twin problems of high costs and "low" profits, a remedy always seemed apparent to its representatives on the spot. Almost invariably, the solution involved another military or diplomatic intervention, and almost invariably, the immediate problem seemed solved, but only at the cost of incurring additional expenses. This would not have mattered in the long run if only new problems had not immediately arisen, very often as a consequence of the measures just implemented. Thus in the pursuit of elusive profitability, there was always one more costly war to fight, one more deal to make with one more local ruler, one more ally to bolster, one more royal succession to manipulate, or one more piece of territory to take and then defend. The real problem for the VOC was neither these individual problems nor their individual solutions, but the pattern of ever-increasing and ever-costlier entanglement in the affairs of the region in futile pursuit of the chimera of stability and profitability.

By far the most significant of the many costly entanglements resulting from VOC efforts to protect or extend its interests were on Java. Here, the VOC was confronted by the most powerful indigenous state in the region at that time—Mataram—and also by an extremely complex political context. When the VOC had its first meaningful dealings with Mataram in 1613, the latter was already the most powerful state on Java but was still struggling to subdue other states. In this year, Mataram permitted the VOC to establish a trading post at Jepara to add to its toehold at Jayakerta. In 1618 the VOC became embroiled in hostilities at both points. The ruler of Jepara, a Mataram vassal, attacked the VOC trading post there in August. In December the Dutch were besieged in their fort at Jayakerta, first by the local ruler and then by the Bantenese, until relieved in 1619 by forces led by Jan Pieterszoon Coen, the VOC's new Governor General of the Indies. Coen annexed the port, having already decided to make Batavia (as the Dutch now called it) the VOC's Indies headquarters. On route to relieve Batavia, he paused to burn Jepara, an act that did not bode well for good relations with Mataram.

Mataram, under the leadership of its greatest ruler, Sultan Agung, finally achieved hegemony over Java with the defeat of Surabaya in 1625. Almost all of Java was brought under Mataram's sway over the next 20 years, including the island of Madura in 1634. But Agung was unable to achieve his ultimate objective of ruling the entire island of Java, due ultimately to his failure to expel the VOC from Batavia, which also effectively protected Banten to its west. Agung's failure was not from want of trying. In 1628 and again in 1629 he dispatched massive armies against Batavia, but both efforts ended in ignominious and costly failure. By the time of Agung's death, Banten was the only indigenous state on Java independent of Mataram. Banten retained its independence until 1682 when the VOC intervened in a succession crisis, effectively turning Banten into a VOC vassal. But by this point, much else had also changed on Java.

While Agung had been unable to drive the Dutch from Java, the VOC remained severely constrained by Mataram's power except at sea. At this juncture (before the industrial revolution), it was only in naval engagements that the Europeans held a decisive military advantage over Indonesians. But the real Achilles' heel of the indigenous states, on Java as elsewhere, was a lack of unity. Not until the twentieth century were the Dutch widely perceived as a special enemy that warranted setting aside indigenous enmities. On the contrary, Indonesian rulers repeatedly prioritized their conflicts with each other over those with the VOC; indeed, frequently they sought to enlist VOC aid. Thus the VOC's deepening involvement in Javanese affairs was as much a product of manipulation on the part of local rulers as it was of deliberate VOC policy. Even where VOC actions were deliberate, they were ad hoc and piecemeal rather than representing the implementation of a grand strategy. Nevertheless, with the leverage provided by the lack of indigenous-state unity, the VOC was able to transform its position of weakness on the edge of Java and Java's affairs in the 1620s to one in which, by the 1750s, it stood at the center of events on Java, if not as king, then as a literal king-maker.

Agung's successors generally lacked his statecraft skills with the result that the decades of fighting to construct Mataram's empire were replaced after his death with another century of almost incessant warfare involving rebellions and succession crises. The fighting and chaos disrupted trade and other economic activities, which adversely affected the VOC's growing interests on Java. But the troubled times also provided the VOC with opportunities to extend its power and territory and also to acquire more of Java's wealth. In 1677 Amangkurat II was driven from his court by rebels and in desperation turned to the VOC for military assistance. The VOC obliged but extracted a heavy price in the form of economic and territorial concessions. When Amangkurat II died in 1703, the VOC placed its weight behind the king's uncle, Pakubuwana I, against the claims of Amangkurat III. The former's ascent to the throne under these circumstances was accompanied by more substantial concessions to the VOC. Similarly, when Amangkurat IV, the son of Pakubuwana I, succeeded his father to the throne in 1719, a long and bloody war ensued in which, again, VOC intervention tipped the balance. This time, in addition to further concessions, the VOC's campaign expenses were added to the ruler's debt.

Barely had this turmoil settled down when the massacre of Batavia's Chinese population (whom the Dutch suspected of plotting a revolt) led to a sequence of events known as the China War of 1740–41. This developed into a complicated struggle with shifting alliances involving the Madurese, the Chinese, the VOC, and rival

Javanese royal factions. Pakubuwana II, who had initially sided with the Chinese against the VOC, ended up back on his throne thanks to the VOC, but only at the cost of further major territorial concessions, including ceding a narrow strip along the entire northern coast of Java. Within a few years, another decade of fighting ensued for the blood-splattered throne of Mataram. This time, the VOC imposed a quite different settlement. The 1755 Treaty of Giyanti essentially divided what remained of Mataram into two sultanates: one capital situated at Surakarta under Pakubuwana III, another at Yogyakarta under Hamengkubuwono I. Each claimed (and their descendants still claim) to be the legitimate Mataram kingdom, but neither was ever again in a position to settle the argument through recourse to war. (Another rebel, Mas Said, settled for a smaller fiefdom as a vassal of Surakarta, and later a fourth subordinate principality was added to Yogyakarta.)

This permanent divide-and-rule strategy worked well for the VOC, bringing peace and leaving it virtually unchallenged on Java for several decades, although such rule as it was exercised remained quite indirect except in a few areas. The Giyanti settlement had only proved possible because of the gradual bleeding of Mataram, largely self-inflicted, over the preceding century of incessant warfare. The gradual depletion of sources of wealth as successive rulers paid the VOC piper's price after each temporary settlement, combined with the wealth and resources consumed during the fighting, had weakened Mataram considerably. The parallel draining of legitimacy also rendered Mataram increasingly incapable of resisting VOC demands. It became progressively more difficult for Mataram's rulers to inspire confidence in their followers and to exert their will over their people as successive rulers failed to establish peace and prosperity and appeared increasingly beholden to the VOC. The same effect flowed from the loss or dispersal of the kingdom's *pustaka* (regalia and other court-associated objects believed to be imbued with magical power).

FROM COMPANY TO COLONIALISM

An important historical by-product of the VOC's desperate efforts to overcome its problems was the emergence of a rather strange Dutch colony in the Indies. Effectively, the VOC had become a colonial power by default, drawn in a colonialist direction simply by seeking to make its investment pay. In this pursuit, the VOC had acquired a network of territorial pockets throughout the Indies, together with an array of allies and vassals. As it did so, it had developed a peculiar hybrid form: part private company, part colony, and part local state. In Europe it behaved like any other large private company of the time. But in the Indies, although driven by the imperatives of its private-company nature, the VOC behaved much like any of the powerful maritime states of the archipelago that had preceded it, such as Malacca and Srivijaya.

A little over 150 years after the VOC's arrival, the hybrid company-colony had established a powerful political and economic position in the Indies. The ruthlessness and determination for which it is famous had certainly brought the VOC enormous successes, including fending off European rivals and defeating formidable local powers. Most major and strategically located ports (and the associated incomes) were in VOC hands, including Batavia, Banten, Surabaya, Makasar, Menado, and Malacca. Some smaller islands, such as Ambon and Banda, were totally under VOC control, as was the militarily and economically significant strip of territory along the northern Java coast and a large area around Batavia, including the Priangan highlands of West Java. In addition to its semieffective export monopoly on spices, the VOC also had acquired lucrative semieffective monopolies on the importation of items such as textiles and opium. It also enforced several treaties that obliged local rulers to supply large quantities of products such as rice, indigo, and coffee. But beneath all this success lay a problem. The VOC was secretly bankrupt.

When bankruptcy was declared in 1799, the Dutch government assumed control of the VOC's affairs and assets. But almost immediately there followed an interlude induced by the Napoleonic Wars during which the VOC's Indies possessions were administered for several years by a French governor general, Marshall Herman Willem Daendels, and then by the British lieutenant governor, Thomas Stamford Raffles, from 1811. Thus what the transfer from private company colony to state colony would mean had to await the establishment of a functioning Dutch colonial administration after the British returned the Indies to the Dutch in 1816.

How had the VOC become bankrupt? Although it overcame every individual obstacle, overall success in terms of what really matters to a business, an adequate and dependable level of profitability, had always eluded the VOC. A number of factors contributed to its eventual business failure. In the preceding paragraphs, considerable attention has already been paid to the problem of persistent high costs. At every instance where additional costs were incurred, VOC officials justified their decision by citing the compulsion of circumstance but also by the promise that the costs would be more than recouped by the higher profits that would follow. Unfortunately, the promised profits proved elusive and the costs were always much greater than expected. Corruption on the part of VOC officials was another significant factor that affected the company's profitability. It is quite likely that a great proportion of the wealth extracted from the Indies by the VOC flowed into private hands other than those of the company's investors. A year's sailing away from Amsterdam's oversight, it was extremely tempting for VOC officials in the Indies to pursue their personal fortunes by colluding with local rulers and traders at the company's expense. Probably their very high mortality rates added considerable inducement to succumb to such temptation. Those who accepted a VOC career in the Indies were gambling with their lives. They did not only have to survive the dangers of a hazardous sea journey to the Indies and those associated with possible engagement in military conflict on their employer's behalf. The greatest threat to their survival came from tropical diseases, such as malaria, against which they had no resistance and for which there was no effective remedy.

Before proceeding to examine Indonesia's colonial experience proper, it is useful to consider the historical impact of two centuries of VOC involvement, from which important social, economic, and political consequences flowed. Some consequences of considerable historical significance are not usually the first that spring to mind—the fate of Javanese shipping for example. Treaty terms imposed on Mataram and other Javanese states effectively ended a Javanese shipping industry whose sailors had been plying the seas between India and China for more than a millennium. This, together with the removal from Javanese hands of all but the smallest trading activities, accentuated an existing Javanese tendency, one especially associated with the inland courts, toward a somewhat Java-centric, less outward-looking worldview. Elsewhere in the archipelago, VOC actions had exactly the opposite effect. VOC domination of the Bugis homeland of southern Sulawesi had the unforeseen consequence of driving many of these irrepressible Indonesian "Vikings" to seek opportunities further afield. For several decades, well into the eighteenth century, these adventurers were aggressive migrants, pirates, and mercenaries throughout the archipelago. They were already outward looking and assertive, and it seems the VOC had inadvertently accentuated these renowned Buginese characteristics.

More commonly considered in this context is the general impact of the VOC on Indonesia's economy and people. Clearly, the Dutch had appropriated a significant proportion of the region's wealth, together with industries that created it. Nevertheless, indigenous traders and producers remained important, as did visiting traders including Arabs, Indians, and Chinese, as well as other Europeans. The VOC was an important economic participant, but the Indies economy was far from being in its hands. Nor was the VOC's undoubtedly rapacious behavior entirely economically negative for the region's inhabitants. VOC involvement brought with it significant additional demand for Indonesia's products, thereby providing additional economic opportunities for many indigenous traders, producers, and rulers. For example, in the Minangkabau region of Sumatra, local farmers and traders took considerable advantage of new cash crops opportunities such as coffee. The VOC impact on other Indonesian communities was much more direct and sometimes devastating, such as the dispossession of the people of Banda. But for most Indonesian communities, any impact directly attributable to the VOC was negligible. This is not surprising, given that the proportion of Indonesian territory under either direct or indirect Dutch rule by the end of the eighteenth century was still small. No doubt for many Indonesians, especially those inhabiting the hinterlands and islands that were as yet of little interest to the Dutch, there was little if any economic impact. But this was not always the case. They may never have seen a Dutchman, but for the subjects of rulers burdened with debts to the VOC, life often became much harder since it was their lot to supply the products required to service the ruler's debt. Indirect effects could be profound indeed.

Similar judgments can be made with respect to the VOC's political impact. Initially slight, VOC influence over political developments grew in tandem with its power. Despite the relatively small area under its sway at the end of the eighteenth century, the VOC had long been a power in the region that few could afford to ignore. Yet only in a few areas (such as Java and Maluku) had the VOC mustered the will and resources to shape the actual course of political developments. Elsewhere, such as in the pivotal Malacca Strait, the VOC, along with several other powers—Palembang, Jambi, Johor, Riau, Aceh, and the British—continued to vie with each other.

And in some areas, where it had no stake, political developments continued with little if any direct VOC involvement. In Bali for instance, without VOC involvement, the overall dominance of the ruler of Gelgel gave way in the middle of the seventeenth century to a long period of war and political conflict. Several smaller kingdoms emerged, at least two becoming involved in conquests beyond Bali. Mengwi of South Bali wielded a fragile suzerainty over Balambangan in East Java in the early eighteenth century, as had Buleleng of North Bali in the late seventeenth century, while Karangasem of East Bali acquired a firm grip over the island of Lombok in 1740.

EXPANSION OF THE DUTCH COLONIAL STATE

During 1780–84 the Netherlands fought a disastrous war with Britain. A decade later, France invaded the Netherlands, which remained under effective French control until the end of the Napoleonic Wars in 1815. The Netherlands emerged weak and impoverished from these events only to be struck another blow when Belgium waged a successful war for independence during 1831–32. Against this desperate background, the Indies colony inherited by the Netherlands state was viewed as an enterprise that had to be made to pay. Johannes van den Bosch, appointed governor general of the Indies in 1830, was the man for the job. It was he who proposed and first implemented the infamous mechanism known as the Cultivation System, whereby the Indies, especially Java, was to be successfully exploited. But, in continuation of the familiar pattern, the Dutch first had to fight two more major wars in Indonesia. The Padri War began in 1821 and lasted until 1838, although there was a gap in the fighting from 1825 until 1832. The Java War was waged between 1825 and 1830, not coincidentally during the hiatus in the Padri War since the Dutch lacked the resources to prosecute both wars simultaneously. Together these wars, especially the Java War, constituted a major crisis for the Dutch that threatened their position in the Indies at a time of weakness and during the early uncertain phases of transition from company to state colonial rule.

The Padri War began when the Dutch signed a treaty with the Minangkabau traditional rulers. Essentially, the deal involved Dutch annexation of the territory in exchange for their restoration of the traditional rulers' position that the "Padri" had all but supplanted. A conflict had been raging for some years between the Padri and the traditional Minangkabau elite. The Padri were a rising commercial elite who, influenced by Wahhabism, a strict fundamentalist practice of Islam that originated in Saudi Arabia in the eighteenth century, were striving to reform aspects of traditional Minangkabau society. The traditional elite had much to lose if the Padri were successful. This was not the first occasion in which resistance against the Dutch was conducted in the name of Islam, and it was not to be the last. It was, however, probably the starkest instance of this phenomenon up to this point and was certainly among the most protracted and bloody.

The Java War was a revolt against the Dutch led by Diponegoro, one of the princes of the Yogyakarta branch of the Mataram dynasty. Simultaneously, it was also a Mataram civil war, as the princes and *priyayi* (traditional aristocratic-administrative elite) of all the rival royal houses took sides with either the Dutch or Diponegoro. Evidently, Diponegoro was a charismatic and capable leader, and his campaign to gain the Mataram throne, which he believed with some justification to be rightfully his, and to reconquer what he considered to be his kingdom of Java, met with considerable initial success. Diponegoro attracted a substantial following as a traditional ruler unsullied by sordid dealings with the Dutch and who also enjoyed a considerable reputation as a mystic. As a devout Muslim, he also appealed to an emerging social tendency of more self-conscious Muslims and so was able to forge a broad and committed anti-Dutch coalition. There was also no shortage of grievances against the Dutch and the *priyayi* and Chinese with whom they were associated, including recent expropriations of land for plantations and the imposition of onerous taxes and tolls. A cholera epidemic in 1821 and an eruption of the Merapi volcano (located just north of Yogyakarta) in 1822 contributed to a sense among the Javanese of the need for a regime change to put things right.

At considerable cost of money and men, the fledgling Dutch colonial state won these wars and was not to encounter a challenge to its power of this scale again until 1942. There were many more conflicts to fight, however. Revolts against the colonial regime and its agent rulers continued sporadically into the late 1920s. There were also more wars of conquest carried out against local states, especially in the latter decades of the nineteenth century and the first decade of the twentieth century, including that of Banjarmasin between 1859 and 1863, with resistance until 1906, Lombok in 1894 and 1907, and Bone in 1905. Two wars of conquest stand out in this period. The conquest of Aceh begun in 1873 was nominally completed only in 1903 with heavy casualties for the Dutch forces and especially for the Acehnese. Resistance continued for at least another decade, fueled by a powerful mix of Islamic religious sentiment and Acehnese cultural pride. The conquest of Bali gained an even more infamous reputation. Dutch attacks on the various Balinese kingdoms began in 1846, resulting in effective Dutch rule over North and West Bali by the 1850s. But despite considerable pressure and ambiguous treaties implying some limitations on their sovereignty, the kingdoms of Badung and Klungkung remained independent until 1906 and 1908, respectively. In each case, the Dutch invasions provoked furious resistance, culminating in a practice known as *puputan,* in which, rather than surrender, the entire courts (hundreds of people) ritually purified themselves before walking into Dutch gunfire, killing their own wounded as they advanced.

With the conclusion of this last wave of conquest, the colony of the Netherlands Indies reached its final territorial extent around 1910. The process was partly driven by particular motives of commercial opportunity (coal in Kalimantan, pepper and oil in Aceh, tin in Bangka) and partly by the desire to end various annoyances that the remaining local independent states posed to Dutch interests, such as providing havens for pirates and "smugglers." In the case of Bali, for instance, the Dutch were irritated by Balinese undercutting of the colonial state's opium-monopoly prices and their habit of looting the occasional Dutch ship that wrecked on the Balinese coast. Renewed fears of rival colonial interlopers also provided a strong motivation to clearly establish the boundaries of Dutch interests. This was the period of a renewed competitive scramble among the European colonial powers, recently joined by the United States, to expand their colonial boundaries, if only to prevent potential rivals from stealing a march.

THE CULTIVATION SYSTEM

The Cultivation System was based on a simple piece of self-serving colonialist reasoning. Each Javanese village was held to owe the state a land tax (a Raffles innovation), payable in cash, but hitherto never collected in a consistent fashion. Each village was compelled to set aside a proportion of its land and provide the necessary labor to grow suitable export crops, a proportion sufficient upon sale to cover its tax bill. In theory, the village could keep any extra cash if it overproduced but had to make up the difference if it underproduced. The colonial government paid a fixed price for the export products, such as coffee and sugar, ensuring a healthy margin of profit when they were sold to the world. The beauty of this mechanism for wealth extraction can be fully appreciated when it is recalled that the money paid out to the villages for the products came back to the government as taxes. In effect, the products, and all the inputs such as labor and land that went into producing them, were free to the Dutch colonial state and thus enormously profitable. Just how profitable is indicated by the fact that sugar-production costs in Java during the Cultivation System were lower than those utilizing slave labor in the West Indies.[6]

The land tax was justified by portraying it as replacing traditional "tribute," payable in kind and labor by the Javanese people to their rulers and lords. Since under the Cultivation System the land tax was effectively paid in kind, the system closely resembled these traditional obligations, especially as the traditional local authorities were usually still in place and now responsible for overseeing the process. Unfortunately for the villagers, traditional obligations to their local lords were usually still demanded, even after 1867, when most such obligations were officially abolished. Thus a double burden was often imposed. Furthermore, enterprising traditional authorities now commonly insisted that tribute payments made to them also take the form of export crops or as labor performed on their lands now devoted to such crops. In addition, large tracts of the most fertile land were sometimes leased and utilized for export crop production, often for amounts so meager as to verge on expropriation and with little concern for those who previously had grown their food on it. These additional burdens on the peasantry were made heavier by the corruption that riddled the system's implementation, especially in its early years. It was much too easy (and too tempting since they were paid a percentage) for corrupt officials, European and indigenous, and their collection agents (usually Chinese), to squeeze additional amounts out of the villagers. Unscrupulous village heads also frequently profited from their positions at the expense of their fellow villagers, for instance, by pocketing the payments due to villagers whose land had been assigned to the production of the village's export crop quota.

Increased monetization of the economy arising from the Cultivation System also added to the peasants' problems. They now needed cash to make up shortfalls in their delivery quotas or to purchase rice if they had been unable to produce enough for their needs. Increasingly, they were forced into the hands of moneylenders (usually village authorities and Chinese middlemen), whose extortionate rates pushed much of the rural population into permanent indebtedness, always owing a large proportion of their next harvest to their creditors. Almost certainly, the Cultivation System contributed to the famines that beset parts of Java in the mid-nineteenth century. It has often been assumed that the problem was caused by too much land and labor being taken out of rice production in favor of export crops, a problem accentuated by heavy overlapping of labor-time demands during crucial phases of export-crop and rice-crop production cycles. But recent research using colonial-era statistics suggests that the greatest contributing factor to the famines and suffering of the peasants was the corruption and extortion perpetrated by the authorities.[7]

The colonial state also squeezed wealth out of Indonesia through "revenue farming." This involved "farming" out to individual entrepreneurs (again, usually Chinese) for a hefty fee the right to collect taxes and to control tollgates and the like, as well as licenses to market particular goods such as opium. This provided a lucrative revenue stream for the colonial administration and left the "dirty" work of extracting the cash to the "farm" holders. During the period 1816–1905 (when the practice was largely ended), the revenue derived by the colonial state from revenue farms averaged more than 20 percent of revenue collected in the Indies, of which more than 70 percent was from opium farms and profit from opium sales.[8] Naturally, revenue farmers were highly motivated to extract as much profit as possible, given the high cost of acquiring their "farm," usually via a public auction. Colonial officials in charge of distributing licenses and policing revenue-farming operations were also well placed to extort bribes on top of the official fees and in exchange for turning blind eyes to abuses. Their corruption added to the costs associated with the farm and thus encouraged even more extortionate behavior on the part of the revenue farmer.

The Cultivation System also held major political advantages for the colonial state. The resemblance to tradition provided a fig leaf of legitimacy, which reduced the level of animosity that might otherwise have been generated. Moreover, most of the discontent that the system did cause was directed not at the Dutch, who benefited the most, but at the traditional authorities and their agents. The traditional authorities, however, were also significant beneficiaries.

Not only could they enrich themselves from the system, but also by becoming effectively a component of the colonial state, their position of power was enhanced. Preserving their position and passing it on to whom they chose was now dependent largely upon pleasing the Dutch rather than upon skillful handling of a complex array of domestic ambitions and circumstances. The colonial authorities for their part (until the late nineteenth century) took great care to preserve the dignity of the traditional rulers, allowing them to make great displays of the trappings of power. In this way, the outer shell of traditional authority was preserved, but the content was shifted radically in favor of incumbent rulers vis-à-vis their subjects and subordinate lords. Thus, the Cultivation System created a symbiotic relationship between traditional elites and the colonial state that had hitherto been characterized more by diametrically opposed interests.

THE EMERGENCE OF MODERN PRIVATE CAPITALISM

The Cultivation System was enormously profitable for the Dutch. During almost half a century, it not only paid for the colonial administration, but also paid off the Netherlands' debts, including those left by the VOC, and deferred any need to introduce income tax in the Netherlands. The surplus was also sufficient to pay for massive public works in the Netherlands, such as the construction of the national railway system. Yet despite the system's evident success, a coalition of interests pressed for its abolition in the middle of the nineteenth century. Dutch consciences were pricked by the publication in 1860 of the novel *Max Havelaar*, written under the pseudonym Multatuli by Eduard Douwes Dekker. A former colonial official, Dekker exposed very effectively the exploitation and corruption associated with the Cultivation System. To the voices urging reform on moral grounds were added those of entrepreneurs who sought government retreat from direct economic involvement in Indonesia to make way for private enterprise. The reformers had their way, ushering in what is generally termed the Liberal Era and bringing modern capitalism to Indonesia. From the 1860s, the Cultivation System was progressively abolished, its last vestiges disappearing in 1919. That these reforms were enacted in response primarily to the wishes of commercial interests is clear from the fact that while the compulsory deliveries of export crops was phased out, the land tax was not, so villagers still needed to find a cash income. To do so, they were forced to turn to wage labor in the emerging modern sector or to grow cash crops for the open market. Levels of rural indebtedness and with it such evils as sharecropping continued to rise in this period, especially on Java.

The Agrarian Law of 1870 and the Coolie Ordinance of 1880 further facilitated the interests of private enterprise in the Netherlands Indies. The former, while preventing the purchase of land from the indigenous population, allowed for it to be leased for extensive periods, thereby providing the security of tenure required by large-scale commercial plantations. The latter, with its infamous penal sanctions, provided the mechanism whereby the plantations could secure very cheap and highly disciplined labor. The "contract coolies" were usually signed up for periods of 10 years or more and kept as virtual prisoners, unable to leave until their contracts expired. Tens of thousands of them were shipped from their villages in Java, most never to return, to the large plantations of Sumatra, where they worked in conditions that were often appalling, even by the standards of the day. Many of their descendants still inhabit the plantation areas of Sumatra. In the wake of these reforms, much private capital entered Indonesia, transforming the export-crop industry in terms of scale as well as by introducing new crops. New industries were also created. The rapid expansion of steam shipping in this period, together with the opening of the Suez Canal in 1869, further contributed to these dramatic changes, allowing for tropical products to be transported to markets in Europe and elsewhere in much larger quantities and much more quickly and cheaply. Under these circumstances, growth in the volume of exports from the Indies rose substantially toward the end of the nineteenth century, then accelerated sharply in the early twentieth century before slumping due to the Great Depression.[9]

Throughout the nineteenth century, up until around 1870, coffee was the Netherlands Indies' principal export earner until it was replaced by sugar.[10] Between a sixth and a quarter of world coffee exports came from Indonesia up until 1885, before dropping as a proportion of world exports, due largely to greatly increased levels of production elsewhere.[11] Sugar production in Java in 1850 already represented more than an eighth of world production, rising to just less than a fifth in the first three decades of the twentieth century.[12] In the latter decades of the nineteenth century, massive plantations were carved out of the Sumatran forests, where tobacco and later rubber from the 1890s proved immensely profitable. Indeed, rubber became Indonesia's main export earning commodity in the 1920s, a position it retained until the early 1950s.[13] The oil industry, which later followed rubber as Indonesia's principal export product, began in Aceh in the 1880s, expanding dramatically in the early twentieth century in Aceh and also to other parts of Sumatra and eastern Kalimantan.

The dramatic economic changes of the nineteenth and early twentieth centuries brought equally far-reaching social and political changes. As the plantation industries expanded to the scale of the industrial era, other modern industries and infrastructural development had to keep pace. Railways, roads, ports, and shipping were needed to transport the export products to market. Processing and storage facilities were also needed, as were repair yards and associated machine shops to service the transport and processing systems. Other light manufacturing industry also developed, mostly import-substitution industries producing simple consumer products, a side effect of which was the further displacement of traditional artisans and the further reduction of opportunities for indigenous entrepreneurs. In addition to the coolie labor required to tap the rubber, cut the cane, and pick the tobacco, a more skilled workforce was also required. Workers were needed to operate the crushing machinery in the sugar mills, operate the trains, carry out repairs, and manufacture replacement parts and consumer products. Armies of clerks to process the paperwork were also required. Despite a significant influx of Dutch and other European civilians, tripling in number between 1852 and 1900, they were sufficient only to fill the specialist and supervisory positions for both the private and public sectors.[14] The large Eurasian population supplemented the Europeans at the upper levels of the racially stratified workforce, but the unskilled and the semiskilled positions nevertheless came to be occupied by indigenous Indonesians in their tens of thousands.

There were similar dramatic changes in the colonial bureaucracy. Its size expanded significantly, not only in proportion to the colony's territorial expansion, but also in response to the changes in the nature and intensity of its operations as the colonial mission shifted. Part of the price for relative peace paid by the Dutch was the system of indirect rule that provided a stake in the colonial status quo for the traditional ruling elite. But the modernizing world of the Netherlands Indies began to need a modern bureaucratic form of governmental machinery. The transition was slow, as the separate Dutch and indigenous administrations (an arrangement in which the former was placed above the latter, naturally) were gradually integrated. During the reform process, much of the higher-level traditional elite was bypassed and left in largely ceremonial and symbolic rather than functional roles. Increasingly, the functional posts in the colonial bureaucracy assigned to Indonesians came to be occupied by those with a Western education, mostly drawn from lower-level *priyayi* backgrounds but including some from commoner backgrounds. The integration of the indigenous and Dutch levels of governance allowed for what had become a much more directly interventionist approach on the part of the colonial government into village-level society. Just how far the government was prepared to meddle with the basic institutions of indigenous society is indicated by the policy of forced village amalgamations begun in 1897. The number of villages on Java was reduced by 40 percent within a few decades in the name of administrative efficiency.

Thus in many ways, Indonesians were drawn further and in ever-larger numbers into the emerging modern capitalist world, coming into greater contact with it through government if not through industry. Some indication of the scale of the phenomenon can be gleaned by reflecting that by 1930 over 30 percent of those gainfully employed were working in the nonagricultural sector.[15] This represented a dramatic social shift, involving great changes within the space of one or two generations. With it came rapid urbanization, much greater geographical and social mobility, greater interethnic contacts (including marriages) and a host of attitudinal changes, particularly among those most directly affected.

THE ETHICAL ERA

The Ethical Policy was partly a response to the dramatic socioeconomic changes under way in the Netherlands Indies. It also further propelled them. The new policy effected a significant shift in the approach and outlook of the colonial government. It also reflected a historical shift, one that affected all of the European colonial powers, and one that everywhere had historical consequences as profound as they were unintended. Nowhere was this more so than in Indonesia, as we will see in the following chapter.

The Agrarian Law of 1870 had been presented as a measure implemented largely out of paternalistic concern for the welfare of the indigenous population. While it opened the way for another round of private exploitation of Indonesia, often as grasping as that perpetrated by the VOC, there was nevertheless some truth to the claims of a benevolent motivation. Other policy measures implemented during the last decades of the nineteenth century were also directed at improving indigenous welfare, albeit often from the "tough love" perspectives of Victorian-era parenting. The analogy is deliberate. At some point during the nineteenth century, the native inhabitants of the European colonies had moved from being regarded as beasts of burden to being seen as wayward children for whom Europeans had a responsibility. This "civilizing mission" or "white man's burden" as it was variously referred to involved at least an obligation to care for the native's basic welfare. For some Europeans, it also involved providing an education and other preparation for when their charges could graduate to "adulthood" (some form of self-government), usually at a remote future point. In the Netherlands, this newly popular perspective was bound up with the idea of "a debt of honor" owed to Indonesia for the wealth extracted earlier in the century after an article was published under that title in a journal in 1899 by the lawyer C. Th. van Deventer.

The shift in approach and attitude had reached such proportions in 1901 that it was explicitly acknowledged in a speech by Queen Wilhelmina. The Ethical Policy involved a significant injection of public funds and a raft of policies directed explicitly at achieving improvements in native health and education. There was also much greater infrastructural expenditure on roads, bridges, ports, storehouses, irrigation works, and the like. All of these measures no doubt benefited Indonesians, but they also dovetailed neatly with the changing needs of the Dutch capitalists and of the modernizing colonial administration, such as by providing the better-educated workforce required by the new industries and the new bureaucracy. As it turned out, the Ethical Policy, despite significant expenditure and many good intentions, produced disappointing results in the spheres of welfare and education. The scale of the task was just too large to easily make more than a dent. For instance, at the height of the educational effort in 1931, still only 8 percent of Indonesian children were at school, and a grand total of only 178 Indonesians was attending university.[16]

THE COLONIAL IMPACT

Dutch colonial rule did not bring modernity to Indonesia, as is sometimes claimed. Neighboring Thailand, which retained its independence throughout the colonial era, modernized without colonization. Moreover, it is clear that most of the formerly independent states incorporated late into the Netherlands Indies were already modernizing long beforehand. Indeed, it can be argued that it was precisely because they were modernizing effectively, and thereby becoming potential commercial and military threats, that the decision was made to forcibly bring them under colonial rule. For example, one of the reasons offered by the Dutch for their invasion of Aceh, which had become one of the world's major pepper suppliers in the early nineteenth century, was the sultan's efforts to purchase a steamer to augment his navy.

Nevertheless, Dutch colonial rule did much to shape the ways in which modernity was experienced in Indonesia and thus had a major influence on Indonesia's social, economic, and political developments. The Dutch left behind a legacy that included modern laws and regulations and a legal system, a centralized modern bureaucracy and other associated machinery of governance. The legacy also included an education system as well as health facilities and hygiene measures. Other infrastructural developments during the colonial era included railways, roads, ports, and irrigation systems. Numerous economic developments also occurred under colonial aegis, including the emergence of many new industries, industrial infrastructure such as oil-drilling rigs and storage facilities, as well as financial institutions and other commercial services.

On the other hand, it has been suggested that many of these legacies had negative aspects. The Dutch colonial legal system was highly complex, and many of its laws contradicted Islamic laws and local *adat* (customary law or traditional law). Similarly, the bureaucracy was cumbersome, and the institutions of governance were unrepresentative and alien. The education and health systems were inadequate overall, although they contained pockets of excellence. Infrastructure for the modern industrial sector was better, but economic development was lopsided, leading to claims that Indonesia was left prone to underdevelopment. In this context, a concept known as economic dualism has been employed. According to arguments along these lines, two separate economies were created in the Netherlands Indies: a modern, export-oriented sector and a subsistence sector. Most of the indigenous population remained trapped in the latter, producing their own food requirements and little else. Their only involvement in the former was as cheap and largely unskilled labor. Moreover, according to this critique, most small-scale industry and commerce not in European hands was in the hands of the Chinese, Indian, and Arab minorities, leaving the indigenes largely impoverished and locked out from modernity. This is a grossly exaggerated picture, but it contained considerable grains of truth.

By far the most significant effect of the colonial experience was the bringing into one umbrella state all the islands and their populations that make up contemporary Indonesia. It is almost inconceivable that this would have occurred without Dutch colonialist intervention in the region's historical trajectory. Without it, almost certainly the area contained within Indonesia today would consist of a dozen or more independent states. This is certainly an effect of massive proportions. But in other important respects, the colonial influence on Indonesian society and overall historical direction was negligible. The most important example of this is in the religious realm. Dutch Christian missionaries made significant numbers of converts, especially among some ethnic groups and in some parts of Indonesia. But the colonial regime never more than half-heartedly encouraged this process, and had it even done so energetically, it is doubtful that it would have made much difference. Christianity's progress compared with that of Islam in Indonesia during the colonial era was relatively slight. As we have seen, the Islamization process had already gotten under way prior to the colonial era, but it is precisely during this colonial period that Islam spread from its early footholds to become the overwhelmingly majority religion. Clearly, this important historical process was largely unimpeded by the colonial experience.

In many other respects too it is important not to overstate the colonial impact. It must be borne in mind that most of Indonesia was not brought under Dutch rule until the late nineteenth century, some of it even later. Furthermore, in much of Indonesia, traditional rulers still held much sway so that in many parts of the country, direct contact with the Dutch colonial state remained slight. Undoubtedly, the colonial experience left behind important legacies and influenced Indonesia profoundly, but Indonesian societies had encountered and then absorbed and modified many other influences throughout a long history. It should not be surprising that many of the much more deeply embedded aspects of Indonesian society reemerged in modified forms with independence. As the colonial period slips further back in time, it becomes apparent that its historical influences on Indonesia were probably less than those exerted by Indic civilizations and by Islam.

NOTES

1. John Bastin, "Early Western Penetration into Southeast Asia," in *The Emergence of Modern Southeast Asia: 1511–1597,* ed. John Bastin (Englewood Cliffs: Prentice Hall, 1967), p. 7.

2. Calculation from the table in David Bulbeck et al., *Southeast Asian Exports Since the 14th Century* (Singapore: ISEAS, 1998), p. 32.

3. M.C. Ricklefs, *A History of Modern Indonesia since c. 1200* (Basingstoke: Palgrave, 2001), p. 29.

4. Anthony Reid, *Southeast Asia in the Age of Commerce 1450–1680,* vol. 1, *The Lands below the Winds* (New Haven: Yale University Press, 1988), p. 14.

5. Cited in O.H.K. Spate, *The Spanish Lake* (Minneapolis: University of Minnesota Press, 1979), p. 87; cited in Bulbeck, *Southeast Asian Exports,* p. 19.

6. Bulbeck, *Southeast Asian Exports,* p. 110.

7. R.E. Elson, *Village Java under the Cultivation System, 1830–1870* (Sydney: Allen and Unwin, 1994), pp. 99–127.

8. F.W. Diehl, "Revenue Farming and Colonial Finances in the Netherlands East Indies, 1816–1925," in *The Rise and Fall of Revenue Farming,* ed. John Butcher and Howard Dick (New York: St. Martin's Press, 1993), p. 199.

9. Anne Booth, *The Indonesian Economy in the Nineteenth and Twentieth Centuries* (Basingstoke: Macmillan Press, 1998), pp. 30, 34.

10. Booth, *The Indonesian Economy,* p. 208.

11. Bulbeck, *Southeast Asian Exports,* p. 155.

12. Bulbeck, *Southeast Asian Exports,* pp. 110, 138.

13. Booth, *The Indonesian Economy,* p. 208.

14. Ricklefs, *A History of Modern Indonesia,* p. 161.

15. Walter Mertens, "Population Census Data on Agricultural Activities in Indonesia," *Majalah Demografi Indonesia* (June 1978), p. 50, cited in Booth, *The Indonesian Economy,* p. 46.

16. Ricklefs, *A History of Modern Indonesia,* p. 203.

3

The Struggle for Independence (1900–1949)

The dramatic economic and social changes in Indonesia of the late colonial period, explored in the preceding chapter, gave rise to equally dramatic social and political developments, which culminated in the birth of the Republic of Indonesia in 1945. In this chapter, we will focus on the various forces and events that produced independent Indonesia, many of which continue to shape Indonesia's historical direction, as we shall see in subsequent chapters.

NEW IDEAS FOR A NEW WORLD

In some important respects, the greatly accelerated pace and the sheer scale of change toward the end of the nineteenth century unhinged key aspects of traditional Indonesian society, many of which had become dysfunctional to the point at which major changes were necessary to meet the demands of the times. Colonial rule obstructed more than it facilitated this process of change, largely because it had become interwoven with many of the now dysfunctional aspects. To the limited extent that Dutch rule now offered Indonesia a way forward toward modernity, it was set to a timetable that was far too slow to be either effective or acceptable under the circumstances. In retrospect, we can see that the death knell had sounded for Dutch rule over Indonesia even as the power of the colonial state reached its zenith. But the Dutch remained oblivious until the end.

The modern world, in particular the development of a modern colonial bureaucracy, both undermined and transformed traditional authority structures. With few exceptions, traditional rulers, although often still shown deference by their people, had lost political power. They had been relegated to mere figureheads by the modern colonial state or incorporated into it. In stark contrast, traditional authorities at the village level were now generally far more powerful in their little worlds than before, but at the price of incorporation into the colonial regime and accompanying estrangement from their fellow villagers. Intermediate-level traditional authorities such as the *priyayi* had also been incorporated into the middle levels of the colonial bureaucracy, levels generally somewhat lower than those they had occupied in traditional society. Their traditional titles and family backgrounds still afforded them a degree of social status, but their social positions came increasingly to depend upon their place within colonial society, either as bureaucrats or professionals or (more rarely) in business. An effect of these combined changes was to ensure that indigenous society increasingly could no longer look to traditional rulers for political leadership and so cast about for alternatives.

Local notables excluded from Dutch power structures sometimes provided alternative political leadership at the village level. Commonly these were the local Muslim religious authorities: mosque leaders and those who ran Muslim boarding schools known as *pesantren* in Java. Since they were traditional authorities anyway in a broad sense, it was natural for villagers to turn to them for leadership under certain circumstances. That the Dutch kept them at arm's length automatically enhanced their leadership credibility when villagers had grievances against the colonial regime. It is not surprising therefore that most of the numerous peasant rebellions of the late colonial decades were led by Muslim figures. Prominent examples of this phenomenon include rebellions in Banten in 1888 and West Sumatra in 1908. Although they sometimes aroused considerable fears, these "disturbances" posed little real threat to colonial rule because they were always highly localized and so doomed to failure. The real threat to Dutch rule, ultimately, lay in the cities where new politics began to develop.

The Indonesian inhabitants of the cities, which expanded rapidly around the turn of the century, were mostly recent arrivals drawn from various social and ethnic backgrounds now suddenly thrown together. This represented a significant change in their circumstances as they were now removed from the traditions and traditional authorities that had previously governed their lives. They were also confronted by a radically different context in which the trappings and institutions of modernity were far more obvious and in which traditional templates seemed inapplicable. By necessity, therefore, Indonesian urban dwellers were much more open to innovation and so were ready to try new solutions to their problems. Urban settings were also the places where potential new solutions and the ideas behind them were on display or could be more readily encountered. Thus, in the cities, individuals with leadership ability, irrespective of their background, were much more likely to be thrust into positions of leadership. Even more important, urban Indonesians began to find new leadership through modern organizational forms, such as unions, associations, and political movements. These were organizations that they followed (through joining) due to a sense of shared interest rather than out of traditional obligation. To a lesser extent, this phenomenon also occurred in rural settings, usually among those who worked in or were adversely affected by plantation industries.

Not only could urban-dwelling Indonesians more easily come into contact with new ideas, but they were also more likely to be aware of what was happening in the wider world. This period truly was "an age in motion."[1] There was not a corner of the planet where the industrial revolution of the nineteenth century was not driving major transformations, not least in the realm of politics. Comparatively new political ideas such as democracy, socialism, and nationalism had captured the popular imagination and were powering political movements for reform or revolution in all corners of the globe. Those ideas with particular resonance in Indonesia were the rise of socialist and radical movements in the Netherlands and the Bolshevik revolution of October 1917 in Russia. Closer to home, the 1911 revolution in China, which ended imperial rule there, the rise of Japan, and the independence struggles in India and the Philippines drove home the point that the global surge toward radical political change did not exclude Asia.

Those Indonesians best placed to appreciate the flow of global events and to measure them against circumstances in the colony were the small but growing numbers of Western-educated Indonesians. Typically, they occupied lower levels of the colonial civil service, were in the professions, or had junior clerical positions in private enterprise. This new and youthful elite, created to meet the needs of the colonial state and industry, was also imagined by Dutch supporters of the Ethical Policy to be the first "brown Dutchmen," who over several generations were to be groomed to govern the country. The Dutch liberal fantasy was that these young men (only the most progressive envisioned a similar role for women) would be grateful for the Dutch civilization and knowledge bestowed upon them. Accordingly, they would share with the Dutch the desire that Indonesia remain in some form of association with the Netherlands in perpetuity and would recognize that the process toward self-governance must be slow. Some members of this new elite accepted the Dutch vision up to a point, but almost none were satisfied with the rate of progress toward its fruition. Many were much more impatient, and there soon emerged radical "noncooperators" for whom any cooperation with the Dutch colonial regime was unacceptable.

The problem for the Dutch was twofold. With few exceptions, they simply could not see that, just as they valued their own independence, so Indonesians would desire theirs. This contradiction was exposed with an exquisite blend of irony and sarcasm in an article written by the Indonesian nationalist Soewardi Soerjaningrat in 1913 entitled, "If Only I Were a Netherlander," which exposed the absurdity of Dutch commemorations of the Netherlands' independence taking place in Indonesia.

> If I were a Netherlander I would not celebrate the commemoration of independence in a country where we refuse to give the people their freedom ... it would be a tactical mistake to show this people how it should eventually celebrate its independence.... But ... I am not a Netherlander. I am only a brown-coloured son of this tropical land.[2]

Second, while the Dutch provided a Western education to train a handful of Indonesians as doctors, lawyers, and engineers, they could not prevent extracurricular studies. Thus, a young man born in 1901 in Blitar, East Java, who graduated as an engineer from the Bandung Institute of Technology in 1926, also emerged with a thorough knowledge of radical Western political philosophy. Another young man, born in Minangkabau in 1902, trained at Leiden in the

Netherlands as a lawyer and economist, where he became equally well versed in radical Western philosophy and engaged actively in politics. He became a principal leader of an Indonesian students' association in the Netherlands, which under his influence became the Perhimpunan Indonesia (Indonesian Association, or PI). Another of this organization's young leaders, also from Minangkabau, experienced the liberal atmosphere of the Netherlands to the point at which he could befriend a Dutch woman and later marry her. This was unthinkable in the racially stratified colony; indeed, she was deported within weeks of her arrival in Indonesia by the authorities who conspired to have the Muslim marriage declared void because of the furor the relationship generated.[3] These three people were Sukarno, Mohammad Hatta, and Sutan Sjahrir, who went on to be the first president, vice president, and prime minister, respectively, of Indonesia.

Feminist ideas also made their appearance among the Western-educated elite. Raden Ajeng Kartini was their most famous indigenous adherent. A daughter of a particularly progressive *bupati* (a high-level Javanese aristocrat incorporated into the senior levels of colonial administration), Kartini was one of the very few Indonesian women to receive a Western education in the late nineteenth century. Before her early death from childbirth in 1904, she was an important advocate of education for Indonesian women and an opponent of child marriage and polygamy, ideas that were very radical for the day. After her death, her supporters established "Kartini schools," and her name and ideas became internationally famous when her letters were published, originally with the title, "Through Darkness into Light." Kartini came to be an important nationalist and feminist symbol, facilitating the inclusion (albeit limited) of women and their aspirations in the Indonesian nationalist movement.

New and radical ideas did not only emanate from the West. The Islamic world was also swirling with new ideas and new movements, and these too naturally had great influence in Indonesia. During the nineteenth century, many Islamic countries had been colonized or subjugated by Western nations, which, reversing a trend of many centuries, now led the Islamic world in areas such as technology, wealth, and political power. Among a range of Muslim responses, two stand out as particularly important here. A number of Muslim thinkers expounded a set of ideas known as Modernist Islam, which combined a welcoming approach toward new technical knowledge, irrespective of its source, with significant theological reforms. In essence, the latter involved loosening the grip on Muslim thinking and Muslim communities of the established Islamic scriptural interpretations and the traditional authorities who enforced them. These reforms were justified as a return to the primacy of the original Islamic scriptures, the Qur'an and the Hadith. Another response was known as Pan Islam, which aimed to unite the Muslim world. Both of these movements were deeply anticolonialist and so struck resonant chords with Indonesian Muslims, especially among the growing number who performed the *haj* pilgrimage to Mecca. There, and in other centers of the Muslim heartlands, their sense of religious and social community with Muslims around the world was heightened. There too they gained a keen awareness of their common political subjugation and came into contact with the various theological and political ideas and movements that purported to overcome the problems confronting the Muslim world.

EARLY NATIONALIST ORGANIZATIONS

Using the concept of nationalism broadly, the first organizational expression of nationalist aspirations was Budi Utomo (Beautiful Endeavor), founded in May 1908 by Indonesian medical students in Batavia. Heavily influenced by Javanese cultural values, Budi Utomo's primary aim was to uplift the Javanese, mainly through increased access to Western education combined with cultural activities. More particularly, Budi Utomo represented the interests of its founders, the progressive-minded, lower *priyayi*. For the most part, it did not engage in explicit political activity and generally remained confined to the *priyayi* elite. Budi Utomo nevertheless constituted a vital transitional organization in which many Indonesian nationalists and reformers developed their ideas.

A much more explicitly nationalist organization was the Indische Partij (Indies Party) founded in 1911, which called for independence and promoted the radical nonracial idea of equal citizenship for all whose home was the Indies. This was a novel idea indeed in a colony where a strict racial hierarchy had been imposed and where ethnic identities divided the indigenous inhabitants deeply. The Indies Party attracted support from radical Indonesians such as Soewardi Soerjaningrat (the author of "If Only I Were a Netherlander"). Formerly a Budi Utomo leader, he changed his name to Ki Hadjar Dewantoro and in 1922 founded Taman Siswa

(Garden of Students), an important nationalist educational movement that mixed a Western education with Javanese elements. The main support base of the Indies Party remained disaffected Eurasians and thus could not survive its banning in 1913 and the exile to the Netherlands of its leaders. In 1914 another set of radical political ideas found organizational expression with the founding of the Indies Social Democratic Association (ISDV) by newly arrived Dutch Marxist H.J.F.M. Sneevlit (whom the colonial authorities exiled in 1919). The ISDV began with a Dutch membership but soon recruited Indonesians, such as Semaun, a young Javanese railway worker who quickly became a leading labor leader and communist.

Also founded in 1911 in Surakarta (Central Java) was Sarekat Dagang Islam. Originally it was founded to defend indigenous traders in the traditional Batik industry from Chinese competition. But its broader possibilities as an organization to promote indigenous interests in general soon became apparent. Accordingly, the name was changed in 1912 to Sarekat Islam (Islamic Union). Within a few years, Sarekat Islam (SI) expanded to become a mass movement with branches throughout Indonesia and became involved in a host of activities with political overtones, such as founding trade unions and peasant associations. SI's spectacular success, short lived as it turned out, is attributable to a combination of factors. The volume and breadth of pent-up grievances among the indigenous population provided the vital basic ingredient, to which was added widespread naive hopes that SI could actually redress those grievances, hopes to which inadvertently the colonial authorities contributed through their initial tolerance of the organization. The name itself played a vital role, allowing it to be seen as an organization for all indigenous Muslim inhabitants of Indonesia, regardless of ethnicity, while simultaneously distinguishing it clearly from the Christian colonial authorities and the Chinese. Rather paradoxically, the vagueness of SI's objectives, combined with its disorganization, was also crucial. The absence of a clear political agenda meant that SI provided the broadest possible umbrella for all indigenous (Muslim) aspirations, while asking nothing specific of its members. Thus, SI accidentally hit upon a magic formula that, for a time, linked urban-based politics with the disparate, semitraditional, Muslim-led, rebellious tendencies in rural areas.

Almost simultaneously, in the neighboring city of Yogyakarta in 1912, Ahmad Dahlan (another former Budi Utomo member) founded Muhammadiyah (the Way of Muhammad). Ostensibly apolitical,

Muhammadiyah worked to promote the ideas of modernist Islam in Indonesia, confining itself largely to religious and social welfare activities. Muhammadiyah devoted considerable attention to education, founding schools with a curriculum that combined Islamic teachings with the latest "secular" knowledge including science, mathematics, and history. Nevertheless there were political dimensions to Muhammadiyah. Many of its members were simultaneously members of political organizations, especially of Sarekat Islam, within which it often exercised considerable influence. Although careful to avoid provoking the authorities, Muhammadiyah was clearly anticolonialist in sentiment and contributed in many subtle but significant ways to the independence movement.

A closely related later development was the founding of Nahdlatul Ulama (the Rise of the Religious Scholars, or NU) in 1926. Alarmed by Muhammadiyah's rapid progress, traditionalist Muslims founded NU to defend their more conservative practice of Islam. Theirs was an Islam in which traditional religious authorities or scholars (*kyai* in Java) and traditional scriptural interpretations (in Indonesia the Shafi'i school) were to be followed by the Muslim community largely without question. NU was really a loose federation of the principal traditionalist Muslim leaders and their families, each with a substantial base of support in mainly rural Java and each with a network of subordinate *kyai* and their followings. Less efficient and less modern organizationally as well as philosophically than Muhammadiyah, and less dynamic, at least in this period, NU was nevertheless a significant social force. Although like Muhammadiyah not formally political, its social weight and anticolonialism also made NU an important component of the broad nationalist movement.

DIVISIONS WITHIN THE NATIONALIST MOVEMENT

Many other organizations with a role in the nationalist movement were formed in the first decades of the twentieth century, most of them short lived. As is already clear from the organizations mentioned above, significant differences existed, both in terms of ideas and social bases. It is therefore unsurprising that sharp political differences soon emerged.

In these early years the nationalist movement was quite fluid. A smorgasbord of new ideas was available, and the boundaries between them were unformed and shifting as individuals wrestled with how to fit them to contemporary needs and how to blend them comfortably with indigenous culture. The lack of clear distinction in these circumstances between ideas now usually regarded as mutually exclusive, such as between Islam and Marxism, was enhanced by the deep-seated Indonesian inclination toward syncretism. Just as it was natural for Indonesians to blend Hinduism, Buddhism, and indigenous beliefs together in a previous era, so it was for Indonesians of the early twentieth century to do the same with Marxism, Islam, nationalism, and indigenous beliefs. An extreme example of this phenomenon is the strenuous efforts by H. Mohammad Misbach (whom the Dutch referred to as a "red *haji*"), to reconcile Marxism and Islam in a new philosophical "system."[4]

The three important nationalist figures mentioned above— Sukarno, Hatta, and Sjahrir—are more typical of the range of efforts made to incorporate Western ideas and adapt them to the Indonesian environment. Of the three, Sjahrir was clearly the most Westernized. A committed social democrat and rational thinker, his approach was to jettison the traditional ideas and cultural features that he regarded as backward. Hatta, also a rational thinker of considerable ability, was heavily influenced by Western socialist and democratic ideas. But for Hatta, a modernist Muslim renowned and respected for his integrity and religious devotion, these Western ideas and approaches were perfectly compatible with Islam. Sukarno was much more traditionally syncretic in his approach. He happily endeavored to reconcile the three seemingly irreconcilable streams of political philosophy that had begun to divide the movement, publishing in 1926 an influential essay entitled *Nationalism, Islam and Marxism*.[5] Sukarno is usually regarded as the principal exponent of Indonesian nationalism, yet clearly he was influenced greatly by Marxist ideas and also saw himself as a modernist Muslim. Indeed he became a lifelong member of Muhammadiyah in the late 1930s and was active in SI until 1922.

Since boundaries between ideas were so rubbery in this period, it is no surprise that the boundaries between organizations were highly porous. As individuals tried out ideas, they tried out the organizations associated with them, often moving freely among them (except between Muhammadiyah and NU) and often holding simultaneous memberships. This factor, combined with the amorphous nature of the early SI, explains how it was that all the principal political currents that were swirling around in the early nationalist movement came to find themselves facing off within SI in the early 1920s. Hitherto, when organizations had been small and engaged in little more than discussion, the gestating political differences and the lack of organizational discipline had not mattered. But when SI exploded into a mass movement with apparently considerable political potential, it suddenly mattered a great deal who its leaders were and what policies they would adopt.

Political differences within SI in its heyday decade, roughly 1915–25, were extraordinarily complex, involving sharp ideological differences, disagreements over tactics and strategy, as well as clashes of personality and ambition. Most important, SI became a battleground between two political ideologies: Islamism and communism. In 1916, ISDV members began to join SI as a strategy to obtain the mass base needed to pursue their revolutionary goals. A wave of militant actions, such as strikes and burning of sugarcane fields, swept parts of the country around this time, mostly attributable to people associated with SI. There was even a secret "Section B" faction established within SI by some militants with the apparent intention of organizing a revolt. In this atmosphere, ISDV members were able to garner considerable support and gain control of many SI branches. From the pool of militants thus generated, ISDV recruited more members and, influenced by the Bolshevik success in Russia, formed the Communist Association of the Indies in 1920 with Semaun (whom the Dutch exiled in 1923) as chairman. It soon became the Indonesian Communist Party (PKI), the first communist party in Asia.

Determined opposition to the communists within SI came from those Muslims for whom Islam was an exclusive and holistic belief system encompassing a complete political ideology as well as laws governing spiritual and social matters. Mostly modernists, including many Pan Islamists and Muslim businessmen, they regarded communism as anathema and, while opposing Dutch colonialism, also opposed most radical activity because it smacked of class warfare. Thus on crucial votes, they won support from all moderate SI members, not necessarily because the latter generally endorsed Islamist principles but because they were concerned about the organization's radical direction and the mounting state repression it incurred. The crunch came when a measure was forced through the 1921 SI Congress, preventing dual membership of SI and other organizations, a measure principally applied to PKI. The result was a split within SI, the communists taking the militants and creating Sarekat Rakyat (People's Union), which continued to engage in militant action for a few years while the rump SI slowly declined in importance. Militancy continued for some years in the face of mounting repression from the colonial authorities, culminating in a mad attempt at rebellion by the underground PKI remnants between November 1926 and January 1927. By this stage, with most of the leadership under arrest or in exile, there was very little Marxist influence remaining on those who carried out the rebellion, which owed more to the tradition of Islamic messianic rural revolts than to Bolshevism. The resultant repression weakened the PKI so much that it barely existed for the next 20 years.

For SI, the expulsion of the communists proved a Pyrrhic victory. In the process, SI lost most of its militants and was abandoned by much of its disillusioned mass base. Many less Islamist-inclined Muslim intellectuals also left or lapsed into inactivity, partly from disappointment and disgust with the political disputes and machinations, but also in response to increasing repression from the colonial authorities. Nevertheless SI, which became the Sarekat Islam Party in 1923, continued to exist and to exert considerable influence for some time to come. Some of those who parted company with SI in the mid-1920s, such as Sukarno, were instrumental in developing a different political perspective, one in which neither Islam nor Marxism occupied the central place. Usually the members of this new wing of the broad nationalist movement are referred to as the "secular nationalists" because their central ideal was Indonesian nationalism and because they advocated an independent Indonesian state that was religiously neutral. The secular nationalists wanted an Indonesia in which all Indonesians could feel an equal sense of belonging irrespective of whether they were Muslim, Christian, Hindu, or Buddhist. Also important, but less emphasized explicitly, Muslim secular nationalists opposed an Islamic state because they were disinclined to follow a rigorous practice of Islam. Those for whom Islam remained at the center of their politics, such as SI, are often dubbed "Islamic nationalists."

This reflects a division that had emerged among Indonesian Muslims, especially in Java, probably in the late nineteenth century. Using Javanese terms later borrowed by scholars, Indonesian Muslims have often been categorized as either *santri* or *abangan*. Whether modernist or traditionalist, Muslims for whom Islam is their central focus of identity are *santri* Muslims. Typically, they are much more inclined to practice Muslim religious observances, such as prayer and fasting. Politically they are generally much more sympathetic toward the ideal of an Islamic state and toward political organizations that highlight an Islamic identity and so can also be considered as Islamist. *Abangan* Muslims are usually no less religious, but their Islam is more syncretic, including many ideas and practices that are technically pre-Islamic. Typically, they are more relaxed about formal Islamic religious observances, more inclined toward mysticism, and resistant to Islamist political ideas. It is debatable whether or not the *santri-abangan* cleavage remains influential in contemporary Indonesia. Certainly it has much less force and clarity than it once did. Even when it was undeniably an important factor, too much ought not to be made of its explanatory value. The distinctions and divisions between *santri* and *abangan* were never as clear cut as the idea suggests, and many other factors and complications were always involved.

Secular nationalism, already politically active in the Netherlands as Perhimpunan Indonesia (PI) under Hatta's leadership, first acquired organizational expression in Indonesia in the form of study clubs in the early 1920s. As their name suggests, they were very much the preserve of the young Western-educated elite. One of these, the Bandung Study Club formed in 1925, was transformed in 1927 into the Indonesian Nationalist Association and a year later under Sukarno's leadership into the Indonesian Nationalist Party (PNI). Many other secular nationalist organizations were formed during the last decade and a half of colonial rule, some to replace those banned by the Dutch, and others because of political differences.

THE INDONESIA IDEA

Before continuing, it is worth pausing to consider how the "idea" of Indonesia emerged—how it was that the broad nationalist movement became predominantly one for the independence of a new nation called Indonesia. Clearly, there was widespread sentiment in favor of independence from the Dutch, but the ideas of an Indonesian national identity and of a single nation-state to contain it was not an automatic choice. Nor was it automatic that the nation-state in question should comprise the territory of the Netherlands Indies.

An independent nation-state of Indonesia was not the ultimate objective of either the communists or the Islamists. Neither movement, in their purest forms at least, acknowledged the legitimacy of nationalism and nation-state boundaries. Both envisioned and championed a political community that transcended such limitations. For the communists, their political community was that of the global proletariat, for the Pan Islamists that of the global Muslim community. With a few exceptions, however, proponents of these two causes were forced by practical considerations to adopt a more achievable goal, if only as a step toward attainment of their respective utopias. For both, throwing off the colonialist yoke was desirable, but much more so if the independent state that resulted was under their control and encapsulated their respective political visions. Thus for the communists, the immediate goal became the establishment of a socialist Indonesian state and for the Pan Islamists an Islamic state of Indonesia. In deference to the force of the Indonesia idea they both adopted Indonesia as the name of the state they envisioned, and both included Indonesia in their organizational names, the communists (PKI) as early as 1924. The Sarekat Islam Party felt compelled to follow suit in 1930, becoming the Sarekat Islam Party of Indonesia (PSII).

In effect, the Islamists and communists had been forced to make concessions to a more successful ideology: nationalism. But why did this nationalism take the Indonesia form? Several distinct nationalist movements could have developed, each striving for separate homelands. As noted several times, many different peoples inhabited the territory of Indonesia, many of which existed within independent states only a decade or so earlier. Indeed, some sentiments in favor of resurrecting former independent states did exist, but such ideas found little support at the time. Much more in favor for several years were ideas that could have evolved into movements for new independent nation-states of Sumatra, Java, Ambon, and so on. Thus members of the emerging Western-educated elite founded organizations with names such as "Young Java," "Young Sumatrans Union," and "Young Ambon," mostly in the 1910s. But the identity ideas behind such organizations, usually founded on ethnicity, withered quickly in favor of a broader nationalist vision. To some extent, these earlier visions constituted conceptual stepping-stones. For example, the notion of Sumatra as a national entity was one that necessarily embraced numerous ethnic groups and many former states. But there was no historical precedent for this idea. Never had there been a state that encompassed the whole island of Sumatra. The only possible exception was Srivijaya, but if indeed it did hold sway over all of Sumatra (a dubious proposition) it only did so as part of a bigger empire that also included much of Malaya and Java. Thus, once the leap of imagination necessary to envision Sumatra as an entity that could evolve into a nation-state had been taken, it was only a small step to imagine an even broader national framework. Indeed, the latter was more logical because the legal, institutional, and economic framework already existed in the form of the colonial state. But something less tangible than such practical considerations lay behind the success of the Indonesia vision: it was the indispensable sense of community necessary for a sense of nationalism to exist. Inadvertently, this was something the colonial state created among the younger generation of Western-educated Indonesians who then went on to spread the idea to the masses.

The Western-educated indigenous elite were drawn from hundreds of ethnic groups with different languages, customs, and histories. Most had Islam in common, but they all shared something else—their common experience of Dutch colonial rule. There were a number of aspects to this experience. To each other they were Javanese, Minangkabau, or Sundanese, but to the Dutch they were all *inlanders* (natives). This racial categorization was superimposed on all of them equally, giving them a common identity vis-à-vis the state with profound implications. It determined their access to education, their rates of pay, their legal rights, and a broad range of other conditions of life. Moreover, the native category to which they were allotted was subordinate legally not only to that of the Europeans, but also to that of the Eurasians, Chinese, and other Asians. A more positive aspect of their common experience was their shared exposure to the Dutch educational curriculum, which gave them a language in common and a host of common philosophical, historical, and literary reference points. Moreover, this shared language and outlook also distinguished them from their fellow Indonesians, pushing them together as a group. There was also an experiential element to this forging of a sense of common identity among the Western-educated Indonesian elite. From all over the archipelago, they came to Batavia and Bandung, some on to Leiden, to attend the same educational institutions and work at the same jobs, ones usually below what they were educationally qualified for. Together, they studied, labored, and lived under the same regulations, restrictions, and accompanying frustrations and suffered in the same prisons when their efforts to bring about change landed them in trouble with the authorities.[6]

All of these shared experiences encouraged them to see their common condition and to forge a common identity and then to imagine it as a national identity inhabiting its own nation-state (thereby joining the modern world). But this was an identity generated within the legal and territorial framework of the Netherlands Indies. For the nationalists, much of the framework could stay, but along with the Dutch, the name had to go. The name *Indonesia*, originally a geographer's term coined in the nineteenth century, caught on. Among the first times it was used in the new political sense was in 1922 when Hatta used it to rename the Indies Association as the Indonesian Association (PI). By 1928 it was firmly established, a fact reinforced by the Youth Congress held in Batavia in October of that year at which the famous Youth Pledge was taken: "One nation: Indonesia; one homeland: Indonesia; one language: Indonesian."

COLONIAL RESPONSES TO THE NATIONALIST MOVEMENT

Initially, the colonial authorities responded with a cautious welcome to the early manifestations of the nationalist movement. The formation of Budi Utomo and then of Sarekat Islam was tolerated, the latter more coolly. But as we have seen, the authorities displayed no hesitation in dealing firmly with the more radical Indies Party formed around the same time. Dutch inhabitants of the colony, especially those with business interests, were more inclined to react with hostility and fear. Their attitude is revealed in a job advertisement that appeared in Indies newspapers in 1913:

> Required with an eye to the rising unrest among the native populace in Java, a capable Netherlands-Indies military officer, willing to advise the management of several large enterprises concerning the preparation of their installations against attack.[7]

To some extent, these fears were borne out as the incidence of strikes and other militant actions rose sharply. With an eye to this powerful interest group, but still broadly sympathetic to the Ethical Policy goals, the authorities responded in what they regarded as a measured way, attempting to channel the movement away from militancy. They continued to tolerate indigenous organizations and allowed them some latitude to express Indonesian grievances, provided they did not engage in activity regarded as threatening to the colonial status quo. Whenever the state deemed this line to have been crossed, it took action against the offenders. Individuals were jailed or exiled, newspapers were censored or banned, and organizations had their activities restricted or were banned outright. The colonial state maintained this approach throughout the remainder of the colonial era, but the levels of supervision, surveillance, and repression increased sharply in the mid-1920s. By the 1930s, Ethical Policy ideas had been abandoned, even repudiated, by the colonial authorities.

One measure of the trend is provided by the nationalists' encounters with the judicial system. At first, sentences were relatively light and acquittals were possible, but later, sentences increased sharply and acquittals were unheard of. For example, SI leader H.U.S. Tjokroaminoto was imprisoned in 1921 and jailed for seven months before being acquitted in 1922. Hatta was arrested in September 1927 but acquitted at his trial in the more liberal Netherlands in March 1928. Sukarno was arrested in December 1929 and imprisoned until December 1931, serving two years of a four-year sentence. Arrested again in August 1933, this time Sukarno was not afforded the luxury of a trial but was sent into indefinite internal exile first to Flores from 1934 to 1938 before being transferred to Bengkulu. In February 1934, Hatta and Sjahrir were sent to the infamous prison camp at Bovun Digul in Papua (where over a thousand participants in the 1926–27 rebellion languished) before being exiled to Banda in 1936. In 1941 even the respected nationalist cooperator, H. Thamrin, the leader of the Betawi community (the indigenous inhabitants of Batavia), was arrested.

The ambiguity inherent in the Dutch response to the nationalist movement is aptly revealed in the following measures: the creation of the Volksraad (People's Council) in 1917 and the promulgation of the "Guru" and "Wild Schools" Ordinances in 1925 and 1932. Establishing the Volksraad was an Ethical Policy measure, albeit a cautious and limited one. It conceded a small, essentially advisory voice in the colonial government to indigenous Indonesians as well as to other Indies inhabitants and might have evolved into a genuinely democratic parliament. Some tiny steps were made in this direction through incremental reforms to its composition. But as the Ethical Policy winds subsided, the Volksraad was left adrift and all but irrelevant, transformed from a symbol of hope for change into a monument to the colonial regime's resistance to even the most moderate of nationalist aspirations.

The Volksraad began with 19 elected members, 10 of whom were Indonesians, and another 19 appointed members, 5 of whom were Indonesians. Not only were Indonesians in a minority, but also since only Indonesians who paid a high level of income tax and were literate could vote for Volksraad members, this ensured that those elected were predominately staunch defenders of the status quo. By 1931 there had been only a slight improvement, with 30 seats for Indonesians, 25 allocated to Europeans, and 5 to "foreign orientals." Thus the Volksraad far from fulfilled nationalist hopes. Yet indicative of their initial desire for a genuine dialogue with those espousing nationalist aspirations, the colonial authorities appointed some quite radical Indonesians to the Volksraad in 1918, including Tjokroaminoto and a former Budi Utomo leader, Tjipto Mangoenkoesoemo. Although the Volksraad was a limited measure, many nationalists responded positively at first, taking the government's action as a sign of goodwill and hoping that the authorities would be encouraged to move further. Thus the SI decided to participate in the Volksraad in 1917. But by 1924 the frustrated SI had reversed this decision and most nationalists had adopted the principle of noncooperation and boycotted the Volksraad. Only the more patient of the cooperators were still prepared to participate, but even their moderate efforts evoked no significant concessions from the Dutch. When in 1936 the Volksraad narrowly voted in favor of a petition calling for implementation within 10 years of Indonesian autonomy within a Dutch-Indonesian Union, the petition was flatly rejected by the Netherlands government.

If the Volksraad experiment symbolized the hesitant half-gesture toward accommodating Indonesian nationalism, then the Guru and Wild Schools Ordinances represented the colonial government's impulse to control and constrict the development of nationalist sentiments. The government provided nowhere near enough educational facilities to meet demand, prompting an explosion of nongovernmental educational institutions. The authorities became very concerned at the capacity this created for the propagation of ideas deemed harmful to the colonial state. Their reactions were heavy handed and probably induced far more anticolonialist sentiments than they prevented. The Guru Ordinance required religious teachers to formally notify the authorities of their intentions to teach and to submit both the curriculum and student names. The Wild Schools Ordinance stipulated that private schools required government permission to exist. Both policies excited considerable controversy, partly because the measures were regarded as inter- ference with religion. A wave of protests from across the entire nationalist spectrum was evoked by the Wild Schools Ordinance, prompting even the moderate Volksraad to reject the education budget in symbolic protest. Although the Wild Schools Ordinance was modified slightly in 1933, the government persisted with its policy and responded to the protests with a new round of arrests and bannings.

By the eve of the Second World War, all significant noncoopera- tor nationalist leaders were detained, exiled, or had been cowed into inactivity. Limited activity by the most moderate of the nation- alist cooperators was all that stirred. What would have happened if the war had not intervened can never be known, but in 1940 none but the most optimistic nationalists dreamed that the Dutch would grant independence before many decades had passed. Perhaps eventually the Dutch would have relented and worked with the moderate nationalists. Had they done so earlier, a very different Indonesia might have emerged, one with more links to the Netherlands perhaps, and with a federal rather than a central form of government. Or perhaps the Dutch would have remained recalcitrant, like the French in Vietnam, prompting a more violent road to independence. As it happened, due to the war, the road was violent, but far shorter than anyone had expected.

JAPANESE OCCUPATION

Raw materials from Indonesia had been in great demand in industrializing Japan for several decades prior to the 1940s. This significant economic relationship was severed in the middle of 1941 when the Netherlands Indies joined the economic embargo imposed on Japan by the United States and its allies. The embargo was intended to dissuade Japan from its alliance with Germany and Italy and to pressure it into retreating from its militaristic adventures in Asia. The embargo succeeded only in making a reckless Japanese government covet Indonesia's resources all the more, especially the materials necessary for war such as rubber and oil. Immediately after the attack on Pearl Harbor in December, the Japanese swept south through Southeast Asia, winning easy victories and receiving the surrender of Dutch forces on March 8, 1942.

The subsequent Japanese occupation of Indonesia was a painful period in Indonesia's history. The standard of living for Indonesians had already declined greatly due to the Great Depression and was now to fall far further. This was partly a byproduct of the almost complete cessation of international trade during the war. But the Japanese military occupation added immensely to the burden, as the Japanese authorities squeezed Indonesia ruthlessly for the raw materials, food, and labor to assist their increasingly desperate war effort. Indeed, so much rice was requisitioned that toward the end of the war there was famine in many areas. The most infamous measure implemented to mobilize Indonesian labor was the *romusha*, labor battalions in which at least two hundred thousand Indonesians served, most of whom were worked to death. In addition, many thousands of Indonesian women were forced into sexual slavery as "comfort women" for the Japanese troops. Yet from the painful occupation emerged the opportunity for independence. Inherently, the removal of the Dutch colonial regime provided a potential opportunity for Indonesian independence, either with Japanese support or in spite of it. It turned out to be a bit of both. Although the Japanese posed as liberators and were initially received as such by most Indonesians, their plan for Indonesia was far from full independence. Their long-term intention was to allow Indonesia a degree of self-governance but firmly within the Japanese political and economic orbit. In the interim, the Japanese were in no more hurry than the Dutch had been to implement political progress toward even this limited form of independence. Quite quickly, however, the circumstances facing the Japanese compelled them to take steps leading in this general direction and then to go further as the exigencies of their military situation obliged them to make greater concessions to the nationalists.

The Japanese needed cooperation from the general Indonesian population and from civil servants. Otherwise, their occupation would have required much greater levels of manpower and would have delivered far less to the war effort. Potentially, without considerable cooperation, the Japanese could have become bogged down in suppressing resistance. Indeed, there were some revolts, all of which the Japanese crushed, as well as some passive resistance, but the incidence of such resistance was low, a fact largely attributable to Japanese policies designed to elicit cooperation. To this end, they were prepared to work with the nationalist leaders, drawing them into roles within the Japanese occupation regime, and to utilize Indonesians in administrative positions at much higher levels of authority than the Dutch had been prepared to sanction.

Islamic leaders, long treated with barely concealed disdain and regarded with suspicion by the Dutch, were also wooed for roles in the Japanese regime. Clumsiness on the part of the Japanese obstructed these efforts at first. The prime example was the Japanese insistence that Muslims bow towards Tokyo, a gesture much too similar to Muslim prayers that involve prostration towards Mecca for Muslims to accept. But the Japanese soon rectified such mistakes and were able to win at least grudging cooperation from Indonesian Muslims.

The Japanese were also prepared to arm, train, and mobilize hundreds of thousands of Indonesians, in marked contrast to Dutch policy in this regard. Even on the eve of war, the Dutch had only implemented a relatively modest increase in the number of Indonesians in their colonial army. Among an array of organizations established to mobilize Indonesian youth by the Japanese, two stand out in this context: Peta (Defenders of the Homeland), formed in October 1943, and Barisan Hizbullah (Forces of God), formed in early 1945. The members of Peta were heavily indoctrinated, irregular troops, trained with the primary purpose of conducting guerrilla operations in the event of an Allied invasion. Barisan Hizbullah was also an irregular, armed force trained for guerrilla warfare but drawn explicitly from the *santri* Muslim population.

Although implemented to meet Japanese objectives, these measures nevertheless ensured that Indonesia was much better placed and prepared for independence. Thus when the opportune moment came at the end of the war, the nationalists were politically ready to seize it, civil servants were ready to administer the new nation, and, crucially, there were Indonesians with the military training to defend it. There was also a crucial psychological dimension to these developments. Indonesians in the bureaucracy discovered that they could do the jobs formerly reserved for their Dutch "superiors." Individual Indonesians given military training gained confidence through their acquisition of military skills and through the knowledge that there were many more like them. Their confidence was further bolstered by Japanese training methods, which included heavy emphasis on martial spirit and promoted ideas of Asian superiority. Perhaps of even greater importance psychologically, however, and for all Indonesians, was the mere fact of the Dutch colonial regime's removal, particularly because of the manner of its demise. Seemingly so permanent and powerful, it had been swept aside in weeks with little hard fighting at the hands of an Asian army, dispelling forever the aura of power and superiority that had surrounded the colonial state and the Dutch people.

Dutch removal also provided the political space within which the Indonesian nationalist movement could develop. Although its development was subject to Japanese-imposed constraints, the context was still vastly more conducive than had pertained under the Dutch. It was for this reason, combined with a general recognition that history potentially had suddenly provided a golden opportunity, that most nationalists agreed to work with the Japanese. No doubt their release by the Japanese from a decade or more of imprisonment and internal exile at the hands of the Dutch was persuasive. But there is little question that their decision to do so was based on largely rational considerations, made in the best interests of Indonesia's independence struggle. On Sukarno's part there was little hesitation. For Hatta and Sjahrir, committed antifascists, the decision to cooperate with the Japanese was more difficult. They decided that Hatta would cooperate while Sjahrir would keep his distance from the Japanese administration and seek to make clandestine contact with the Allies. As it happened, this division of labor worked to the independence movement's advantage. Sukarno and Hatta were able to use the Japanese to achieve Indonesia's independence, while a nationalist leader of Sjahrir's stature remained sufficiently untarnished by the Japanese brush in order to negotiate with the victorious Allies.

The Japanese did not initially make much use of the likes of Sukarno and Hatta. Indeed, Sukarno was not brought to Jakarta from Sumatra until July 1942. Thus early efforts by the Japanese to mobilize the Indonesian masses behind their war effort, first through the "Triple A Movement" and later through an organization known as "Putera," were of limited success. But as the war worsened for the Japanese, they acceded to the repeated requests from Sukarno and Hatta for a mass organization in which they would be far more than mere figurehead leaders. Accordingly, the Jawa Hokokai was established in January 1944, a mass organization for everyone over 14 in Java, to be organized through the existing civil administration down to village level.

Sukarno and Hatta used their respective skills effectively in utilizing the Hokokai to promote the nationalist cause, in the process cementing their places as the movement's indispensable dual leadership. Sukarno traveled widely throughout Java on speaking tours, ostensibly to rally support for Japan's war effort, but his real purpose was to generate enthusiasm for Indonesian independence. This was possible because the Japanese recognized the necessity for his speeches to appeal to Indonesian nationalism to some extent. They of course wanted the nationalist message fused with and subordinated to Japan's cause. Sukarno, a mesmerizing and brilliant speaker, was able, through voice modulation cues and use of clever references only fully understood by his Javanese audiences, to make Indonesian nationalism the central message. Crucially, Sukarno's speeches were also broadcast over the radio, reaching a wide audience through the Japanese network of loudspeakers installed in the center of every village. In this way, the idea of Indonesia and the Indonesian nation penetrated mass society to a far greater extent than had been possible during the Dutch era. Hatta meanwhile concentrated on managing the Hokokai, effectively drawing into his hands the threads of the administration structure, to whose personnel his quiet, rational style usually appealed more than did the flamboyant Sukarno. Less visible than Sukarno's efforts, Hatta's work was nevertheless vital, positioning the nationalists to quickly seize functioning reins of power at the moment they slipped from the Japanese grasp.

DECLARATION OF INDEPENDENCE

Not until September 1944 did the Japanese publicly promise independence for Indonesia, although without specifying a date. By this juncture, the Japanese knew that to stand any chance of averting defeat they needed maximum cooperation from the Indonesians, which partly explains the promise. It was also made because, if Japan were to lose, the Japanese much preferred to see an independent Indonesia than for the Dutch to regain their former colony. Nevertheless, a further six months elapsed before any meaningful steps were taken. Finally in March 1945, the Japanese announced the creation of an Investigating Committee for Preparatory Work for Indonesian Independence. Its Japanese-selected membership included mainly older-generation, secular nationalists. Clearly the Japanese intended to retain control over the process to ensure an outcome that suited their interests and timetable. The cautiously worded title of the investigating committee indicates that the Japanese authorities believed there was no need to hurry. Indeed they expected that the committee would be bogged down for months in acrimonious debate. To their surprise, having begun meeting in May, the committee had drafted an interim constitution by mid-July.

This was no mean feat. There were real difficulties involved in reaching agreement. As we have seen, during the last three decades of the Dutch colonial era the nationalist movement was riven by numerous bitter disagreements, causing it to splinter into ever-smaller organizations. The divisions were over strategy, principles, and goals, exacerbated by personal differences and jealousies, as well as by regional sentiments and cultural, religious, and ethnic differences. Some of these divisions, such as those between cooperators and noncooperators, were rendered redundant with independence at hand and under circumstances over which the committee members had no control. Other divisions and differences paled in light of the opportunity that all recognized might not come again for decades and so were either resolved or readily set aside. One question, however, remained as a sticking point: the basis of the independent state. The committee membership, selected by the Japanese, contained very few Islamic nationalists, but everyone knew this was an artificial situation and that the Islamic nationalists represented a significant social group that could not be ignored. Without their agreement, the constitution and any government based upon it would lack legitimacy. The demand for a state based on Islam was a statement of fundamental principle that the Islamic nationalists could not abandon but was a position equally unacceptable to the secular nationalists. It appeared that there was no way forward, but in reality the few Islamic nationalists present wanted a way out of their dilemma, not wanting to be the cause of a failed attempt at independence. Sukarno obliged, offering a compromise that he made easier for everyone present to accept by presenting it, using all his oratorical skills, not as a compromise but as a lofty ideal.

Sukarno's "Pancasila" (five principles) speech, delivered without notes, was a virtuoso performance.[8] He asserted that there were five principles that united them all and could therefore serve as the basis of the Indonesian State. They were (in his order) nationalism, humanitarianism/internationalism, social justice, representational government, and belief in God. The principles were expressed in sufficiently vague terms as to render them unobjectionable and could be viewed through quite different ideological prisms. Nevertheless, it was clear that the Pancasila was essentially an expression of secular nationalist principles with the concept of an Indonesian nation at its unspoken center. Many Islamic nationalists remained uncomfortable with nationalism, but the battle had long been won in favor of the Indonesia idea. All but the most rigid Islamists had retreated to the more tenable position of advocating Indonesia but with an Islamic content. Secularism was more problematic, but the inclusion of the belief in God principle provided a sufficiently proportioned fig leaf to make plausible the claim that Indonesia's constitution would not make Indonesia a secular state. This concession was not difficult for the secular nationalists. Few if any of them did not believe in God. Their opposition was to a theocracy in principle and, more practically, to the creation of a situation in which Christians, Hindus, and Buddhists felt discriminated against and in which the state decreed the form that Islam should take. The unspecified nature of God in the principle averted these problems.

To persuade the Islamic nationalists to accept the Pancasila, Sukarno pitched a further clever argument. He urged them to accept it as a temporary measure for the sake of attaining independence. After all, he argued, once independence had been won, then the democratic process would deliver an Islamic state if Indonesians desired it. Since the Islamic nationalists claimed to represent the majority of the population, this was a difficult argument to refute. Nevertheless, they extracted three further concessions in subsequent discussions. First, the draft constitution was amended to stipulate that the president had to be a Muslim. Second, the principle of belief in God was shifted from the last to the first place in the Pancasila, which became the prologue to the constitution. Third, this principle was rephrased to read, "Belief in the One God with the obligation for Muslims to implement Islamic law." The agreement to insert the words after *God*, seven (ambiguous) words in Indonesian, was termed the Jakarta Charter and was to generate decades of controversy, one that still plagues Indonesia today.

Only during the last days of the war did the Japanese step up preparations to grant independence, establishing the Preparatory Committee for Indonesian Independence on August 7, 1945, with representatives from the outer islands as well as from Java. Japan's leaders now knew that defeat was inevitable and clearly intended to bestow independence on Indonesia, including all the territory previously contained in the Netherlands Indies. But time ran out. The dropping of atomic bombs on Hiroshima and Nagasaki prompted Japan to surrender unconditionally on August 15. The Japanese were ordered to maintain the status quo until authority could be handed over to Allied troops, which meant no transfer of power by Japan to the Indonesians and the imminent return of Dutch control. Younger-generation nationalists pressured Sukarno and Hatta to declare independence unilaterally, going so far as to kidnap them during the night of August 15. But Sukarno and Hatta, not unreasonably, feared the consequences of such a step and refused to acquiesce to the demands of their kidnappers. If the Japanese authorities had acted on their orders, a declaration of independence could have resulted in a bloodbath and the crushing of the Indonesian independence movement before the Dutch arrived. Their bluff called, the young hotheads released Sukarno and Hatta unconditionally the following day.

After their release, Sukarno and Hatta pursued an unofficial agreement whereby the Japanese would turn a blind eye to a declaration of independence and the establishment of an Indonesian government. Through the good offices of Vice Admiral Maeda Tadashi, a sympathetic Japanese officer who occupied a pivotal position in Jakarta responsible for army-navy liaison, Sukarno and Hatta were able to secure the gentleman's agreement they sought. They spent the night of August 16 in Maeda's house, where, in discussion with a handful of colleagues, they framed and signed a brief declaration of independence in the name of the Indonesian people. The following morning, outside Sukarno's house a short distance away, Sukarno read out the declaration of independence in front of a small crowd. The Japanese did not recognize the declaration of independence, and the Allies did not even know of it for some days. But August 17 is the date that Indonesians celebrate as the birth date of their Republic of Indonesia, taking the view that it is their declaration of independence that should be celebrated rather than the date it was accepted.

DIPLOMATIC AND ARMED STRUGGLES FOR INDEPENDENCE

With tacit Japanese approval, the nationalist leaders set about constructing a government. The preparatory committee met to acclaim Sukarno and Hatta as president and vice president, respectively, and to adopt the interim constitution drafted by the investigating committee. In doing so, it made the important political decisions to remove the Jakarta Charter from the Pancasila and the stipulation that the president had to be a Muslim. This was done in recognition that, otherwise, many areas of Indonesia inhabited by non-Muslims were likely to prefer the return of Dutch rule to joining the republic. The preparatory committee also entrusted Sukarno and Hatta with the task of forming an Indonesian National Central Committee (KNIP), which, although unelected, soon assumed the functions of a parliament. For the most part, the rest of the government, which theoretically spanned all of Indonesia, was constructed by the simple expediency of assuming (albeit discreetly) all Indonesians in the Japanese administration to be under the republican government's authority. There was no practical alternative to this step under the circumstances, but consequently, the republican administration was politically conservative from the outset. Apart from the nationalist members of KNIP and other nationalists appointed to key positions, those Indonesians who now occupied positions of power, down to the village level, were mostly the same people who had done so under the Japanese and the Dutch.

There were no Dutch or Allied forces for the republic to contend with for several weeks, except in parts of eastern Indonesia, providing a brief opportunity for the fledgling Indonesian government to consolidate its authority. For the most part, the Japanese assisted by ignoring the activities of the "illegal" republican government, but the Japanese presence impeded republican access to the machinery of government, including offices, records, and the vitally important means of communication. Among other consequences, this meant that news of the declaration of independence and the establishment of the republican government was slow to spread. Arguably, the Japanese struck a major blow to the republican cause in late August by demobilizing the Indonesian military forces they had trained. This prevented the republican government from inheriting something akin to a standing army, which would have allowed it to wield more authority from the outset and would have bolstered the capacity to resist the Dutch. The Japanese took this step to avoid confrontation with these Indonesian forces, a wise precaution perhaps as growing resentment toward the Japanese had already generated a number of clashes, including a revolt by a Peta unit at Blitar in February 1945. Had a major conflict broken out in August between the Japanese and Indonesian troops, it is likely the Japanese would have crushed the republican government along with its fledgling army, so perhaps the Japanese decision was in the republic's best interests. As it happened, there were numerous clashes between the

Japanese soldiers and zealous nationalist youth, particularly where the latter sought to acquire Japanese arms. In most instances, however, conflict was avoided and significant amounts of Japanese military equipment were quietly handed over to local republicans.

Having been occupied by Germany for most of the war, the Netherlands was not immediately able to reoccupy Indonesia. Thus the principal Allied force confronting the republic was British. Under the terms of agreements made among the Allies, the British forces were to accept the Japanese surrender, release and repatriate prisoners of war, and hand Indonesia back to the Dutch. But this assumed that Indonesia was in Japanese hands, which to a significant extent was no longer the case. Much of Indonesia was in the hands of the republic and was becoming more so with each passing day. Under the circumstances, the British confined themselves to the first two tasks. Moreover, they were prepared to negotiate with the Indonesian authorities to achieve these objectives and to avoid becoming embroiled in conflict with republican forces. The Dutch complained bitterly about this policy because it amounted to de-facto recognition of the republic and allowed it valuable breathing space. Despite the best efforts of both the British and republican leaders, conflict did break out between their respective forces, notably in Surabaya. Here, an extremely bloody battle raged throughout November, leaving thousands of Indonesians dead before the republican forces were driven from the city. Militarily, this was a significant defeat for the Indonesians, but it provided emphatic proof to the British and Dutch, as well as to the Indonesians themselves, that there was committed mass support for the republic.

The battle of Surabaya made the Dutch realize that to regain their colony they effectively needed to reconquer it. But they remained undaunted, convinced that their military superiority would prevail over what they saw as scattered rebels led by Japanese puppets. They also believed that the bulk of the Indonesian population would welcome their return. Their perspective was not entirely delusional. The Dutch did enjoy significant Indonesian support, particularly from among traditional rulers who saw the republic as a threat to their personal interests. Some parts of Indonesia, especially parts of eastern Indonesia where a significant proportion of the population was Christian, were staunchly pro-Dutch. Wariness of the potential for Javanese domination of Indonesia under republican rule also provided the Dutch with a useful political wedge from which they could extract grudging support, or at least neutrality, in other parts of the country. In the military sphere, too, Dutch confidence was not entirely misplaced. They enjoyed a clear superiority in conventional warfare. Nevertheless, their confidence was founded on a gross underestimation of the degree to which the situation had changed during the Japanese occupation.

Recognizing the military reality, the republican government abandoned Jakarta in January 1946, transferring the capital to Yogyakarta, where its young sultan, Hamengkubuwono IX, had declared for the republic. Also in recognition of the profound military gap, republican forces, a motley collection of brave but ill-disciplined, poorly trained, and lightly armed volunteers, generally avoided set-piece battles. Instead, after the costly experience of the battle for Surabaya, they opted to fight a guerrilla war. As the Dutch built up their forces, including navy and air force assets, they were able to push the Indonesian forces back with little difficulty. But for all their wishful thinking, the nature of the opposition was quite different from anything the Dutch had experienced before. Its logistics and communications were poor and its army weak, but the republican government was the central leadership of an unprecedented Indonesia-wide resistance against the Dutch. That the republic meant quite different things to different groups of Indonesians in different parts of the country mattered little in terms of the difficulty confronting the Dutch. To all those supporting the republic, it meant ousting the Dutch and then shaping a new future for themselves. For the Dutch, the consequence was a war on multiple fronts, one that was ultimately beyond their capacity to win. Even in the most pro-Dutch areas, there were republican sympathizers, and even after Dutch forces captured territory, its inhabitants remained predominantly pro-republican. Moreover, the Dutch could no longer utilize mostly Indonesian troops to do the fighting, as had been the case throughout the colonial era. Dutch troops were needed now, and in large numbers. In essence, the problem was this: the Netherlands is a small country with a small population. Indonesia, on the other hand, is many times larger and with a much bigger population. That hadn't mattered before, when the Indonesians were easily divided into manageable conquests. Now that the Indonesians were largely united, it was crucial.

The Dutch were able to win sweeping victories over the four years of conflict. Progressively, they squeezed the republic into smaller areas, culminating in a lightning airborne assault on Yogyakarta in

December 1948, during which they captured the principal republican leaders, including Sukarno, Hatta, and Sjahrir. Thus by the end of 1948, the republic's political leadership was in Dutch hands, as was almost every city and almost all the territory of Indonesia. The supreme commander of the republican army, General Soedirman, remained at large. But he was a harried invalid dying from tuberculosis being carried from village to village through the mountains of East and Central Java to avoid capture. But things were not as bleak for the republic as they seemed. The Dutch could win any set-piece battle, but they were rarely offered any. Instead, they were subjected to incessant and widespread guerrilla pressure and could only move freely through the countryside in daylight and in force. Even in the cities, they were not immune from attack as a surprise raid with fighting in the center of Yogyakarta for several hours in March 1949 demonstrated to the world. And while Soedirman remained at large, he remained a symbol of the republican army's defiance. Moreover, its military operations continued under the capable central command of his Dutch-trained deputy, A. H. Nasution. Worse perhaps, the capture of the republican leadership proved a major diplomatic setback to the Dutch cause rather than the masterstroke it had seemed at the time. The Dutch had grossly underestimated the degree to which the United States and the United Nations (UN) would be offended by the Dutch snub to their diplomatic investment in a solution to the Indonesia issue.

In tandem with the fighting, there had been negotiations from the beginning. In part, this reflected international pressures on the Dutch from Britain, Australia, the United States, and the UN, where the Indonesia matter was raised as early as January 1946. Negotiations were also motivated by the costs of the war for both sides. But a settlement was difficult to achieve. The federal arrangement offered by the Dutch, which involved continued association with the Netherlands and limited genuine autonomy, would have been attractive to many nationalists had it been offered in the 1930s. But it was now far from acceptable, and republican cabinets that conceded ground in this direction during negotiations found their domestic political position weakened. Both sides also entered negotiations because of their military weakness. But while republican military weakness was constant, for the Dutch it was variable, reflecting temporary logistical problems encountered in their military buildup. Thus the Dutch abandoned negotiations and reverted to military conquest whenever they judged the conditions right, referring to their operations as "police actions." This belligerent behavior (a function of strength) was in stark contrast with the consistent conciliatory negotiating approach from the republic's representatives (a function of weakness).

The contrast was to prove very costly for the Dutch in the court of world opinion. In the late 1940s, the world was weary of war, and decolonization, not recolonization, was the spirit of the age. The Dutch appeared out of step—the more so because the continuing military resistance seemed to show that the Dutch were merely prolonging the agony and that Indonesian nationalism could not be denied in the long run. In the aftermath of the Dutch capture of Yogyakarta, the UN Security Council demanded that the Dutch release the republican leadership, implement a cease-fire, and fulfill the terms of the Linggajati agreement arranged with the republic in November 1946. The Dutch were reluctant to do so because this meant effectively handing back to the republic control over Sumatra, Java, and Madura, the territory allotted to the republic within the agreement's proposed federal United States of Indonesia. But it seems that the Dutch were beginning to recognize that the military solution had failed. Certainly their determination to reconquer Indonesia vanished when the United States applied serious pressure in April 1949, insisting that the Netherlands must come to terms with the republic or lose the massive reconstruction funds offered under the Marshall Plan. Shortly afterward, the republican leaders were returned to Yogyakarta, and negotiations in the Hague began to hammer out the details of a settlement.

Among Indonesians, the popular perception was that armed struggle rather than diplomacy was primarily responsible for Indonesia's triumph, an interpretation assiduously promoted by the army for its own political ends and one that continues to have considerable currency. A more sober assessment indicates that both diplomacy and armed resistance were indispensable, indeed that they complemented each other. Less widely acknowledged is the role of shifting international circumstances, which prompted the crucial change in United States policy in light of the looming Cold War. Continuing armed struggle for Indonesian independence risked providing an opportunity for the Soviet Union to exploit a region that straddled vital world trade routes. Especially after the republican government demonstrated its aversion to communism through crushing a PKI revolt in 1948, the United States concluded that supporting an independent Indonesia was a better policy than bankrolling the protracted and probably futile Dutch efforts to turn back the clock.

In appearance, the final settlement resembled the terms of the Linggajati agreement. It was agreed to form a Republic of the United States of Indonesia (RUSI) in association with the Netherlands. The structure was essentially federal, and the republic was only one of the member states. But three crucial factors ensured that in reality the republic would dominate. The republic contained the overwhelming bulk of the population, Sukarno was president of RUSI and Hatta both vice president and prime minister, and the republican army formed the core of RUSI's army. Predictably, an end was put to this unbalanced arrangement within months of the formal transfer of sovereignty on December 27, 1949, as all of the other RUSI member states were absorbed into the Republic of Indonesia, which thereby transformed itself into the centralist state that essentially it remains today. Few of the Dutch-created states displayed much reluctance, and only in Ambon was their any serious resistance with a declaration of independence by the "Republic of the South Moluccas," thus generating Indonesia's first separatist rebellion. Effectively, therefore, the republic's triumph was merely slightly delayed. There were some bitter pills to swallow however, notably that Papua remained in Dutch hands pending future negotiations, and the republic had to accept the Netherlands Indies' debt, a crippling sum. The Papua issue and Indonesia's heavily indebted condition at its troubled birth were both factors that impeded Indonesia as it set out to meet the many challenges of independence at the conclusion of its revolutionary war for independence.

NOTES

1. Takashi Shiraishi, *An Age in Motion: Popular Radicalism in Java, 1912–1926* (Ithaca: Cornell University Press, 1990).

2. R. M. Soewardi Soerjaningrat, "If Only I Were a Netherlander," in *Indonesia: Selected Documents on Colonialism and Nationalism 1830–1942,* Chr. L. M. Penders (St. Lucia: University of Queensland Press, 1977).

3. Rudolf Mrazek, *Sjahrir: Politics and Exile in Indonesia* (Ithaca: Cornell University Press, 1994), p. 112.

4. The political career and ideas of Misbach are best recounted in Shiraishi, *Age in Motion.*

5. Soekarno, *Nationalism, Islam and Marxism,* tr. Karel H. Warouw and Peter D. Weldon (Ithaca: Cornell University Press, 1970).

6. The argument raised in this paragraph reflects the ideas contained in Benedict Anderson, *Imagined Communities: Reflections on the Origin and Spread of Nationalism* (London: Verso, 1983).

7. Cited in Ruth T. McVey, *The Rise of Indonesian Communism* (Ithaca: Cornell University Press, 1965), p. 7.

8. An excerpt of the speech in English is contained in Herbert Feith and Lance Castles, eds., *Indonesian Political Thinking 1945–1965* (Ithaca: Cornell University Press, 1970).

4

The Sukarno Era
(1945–1967)

When he proclaimed Indonesia's independence in August 1945, Sukarno had been the leading Indonesian nationalist for two decades. As the movement's indispensable figurehead, he became Indonesia's first president, almost without question, a position he occupied for more than two decades. His presidency spanned a difficult and painful period in Indonesia's history, first as the new country fought for its very existence, and then as it grappled with the many challenges of independence. As president, Sukarno was at the epicenter of Indonesia's turbulent political life. He often played a pivotal role in events, increasingly stamping his personality and political values, if not always his authority, on an Indonesia that struggled to resolve the competing and often incompatible visions held for its identity and destiny.

GOVERNMENTS DURING THE REVOLUTION

In August 1945, Sukarno was uniquely placed to make the declaration of independence. His authority within the nationalist movement and his popularity with the masses were unequalled. He also enjoyed good personal relationships with the Japanese authorities and with key *santri*-Muslim leaders. These factors allowed him to make a crucial contribution during the delicate and dangerous early weeks of the republic's life. A famous example of the value of Sukarno's unique personal authority at this juncture occurred on September 19. He persuaded a massive, excited crowd, gathered in what is now Medan Merdeka (Independence Square) in central Jakarta, to disperse quietly and thus avoid a disastrous clash with the Japanese. Yet only a few weeks after the Medan Merdeka incident, Sjahrir, with Hatta's support, effectively sidelined Sukarno. This abrupt decline in Sukarno's political position was possible because what was a major political asset in August had become a liability by October. Sukarno's association with the Japanese worked against him at this point as anti-Japanese sentiments came to the fore among the Indonesian masses. The Japanese taint also reduced Sukarno's utility to the nationalist cause at this time because of the republic's need to deal with the victorious Allies, for whom Sukarno was a war criminal.

In October the Indonesian National Central Committee (KNIP) took power into its own hands, ending the period of extraordinary presidential powers and effectively setting aside the 1945 constitution. KNIP entrusted the exercise of its power to a working committee, effectively a cabinet responsible not to the president but to KNIP. A parliamentary system of government, or at least something closely resembling one, had been established, an impression reinforced by the new government's invitation for the free formation of political parties. That events should have taken this turn is somewhat surprising, given the dire circumstances confronting the fledgling republic. An often-violent social revolution threatened a collapse of the tenuous governmental structure. At the same time, the republic's survival was threatened by the buildup of Allied troops on Indonesian soil and the imminent return of the Dutch in force. Usually, circumstances such as these generate an authoritarian government, one able to take decisive action to deal with the emergency, rather than prompting formation of a more democratic political system. Somehow, Sjahrir, the principal architect and immediate political beneficiary of these reforms, was able to ride this crisis to power and install his preferred political system with himself as prime minister. The key to this feat was Sjahrir's rare dual credentials as a nationalist and leftist figure of considerable stature and as an antifascist who had abstained from collaboration with the Japanese.

With considerable exaggeration, Sjahrir was able to pose as an anti-Japanese "resistance" leader to the Allies, an image that was convenient for them to accept. This image, combined with the form of government that accompanied Sjahrir's ascent to power, made it easier for the British to have expedient dealings with the republican authorities. The same applied to the Dutch for whom, despite their belligerent bluster, it was also convenient to have an acceptable republican leader to negotiate with. His acceptability to the Allies raised Sjahrir's political stocks in Indonesia. He also benefited from a rising tide of youthful impatience with the older-generation republican leadership. With the aid of considerable misunderstanding on their part as to his political views, Sjahrir was cast (albeit briefly) as the champion of the zealous nationalist youth and others who wanted radical action and drastic change (although they were generally unclear as to its precise nature).

Sjahrir's prime ministership only lasted until June 1947. In this period, political circumstances and alliances shifted quickly so that during his brief tenure he led three different cabinets. Sjahrir's policies of resisting social revolution and the more extreme manifestations of Indonesian nationalism quickly lost him popular support in an atmosphere in which radicalism and the nobility of "the struggle" had far more appeal than caution and a cool head. Even less popular in this context, particularly after it quickly became apparent that negotiations were proving unfruitful, was Sjahrir's willingness to continue to negotiate and even to make unpalatable concessions to the Dutch. Sjahrir's impossible political problem (high public expectations combined with the absence of means to meet them) was shared by all the governments that succeeded his during the revolution. Not surprisingly, under these circumstances, political stability proved elusive. It was not until Hatta's government's formation in January 1948, an emergency cabinet responsible to the president rather than to KNIP, that a modicum of political unity and cohesion was achieved. Although by this point the revolutionary impulse had waned, this did not mean that the government's political authority was no longer challenged—on the contrary. But most political forces were now prepared to rally around the government if only to avoid weakening the republican cause.

REVOLUTIONS WITHIN THE REVOLUTION

During the revolution, considerable conflict raged within republican ranks. While all desired independence, there were sharply contrasting visions as to the nature of the Indonesia to be built, once independence had been achieved. In the midst of the revolution, elections were not possible. Therefore, apart from interelite negotiations and "parliamentary" debates, there was no peaceful mechanism whereby political disputes could be resolved, even if everyone had been so inclined. Some political differences proved so sharp that the protagonists were not prepared to wait until victory over the Dutch to settle them. Moreover, because all political tendencies quickly came to be linked to armed groups, the temptation to resort to force often proved difficult to resist. There were two serious, armed revolts against the authority of the republican government during the period of the revolution and a number of failed coup attempts (as well as what some regard as the successful Sjahrir "coup" of October 1945 discussed above). Many smaller "incidents" also occurred, including acts of insubordination by military commanders, which could be construed as mutinies or rebellions but were settled through negotiation. There was also the so-called social revolution that convulsed many parts of Indonesia for several months following the independence declaration.

Although larger political forces and issues occasionally became involved, the "social revolution" was essentially local and episodic, connected only in the sense that certain patterns were discernable. Many grievances had accumulated over the preceding decades in most local areas. The Dutch policy of forced village amalgamations had often pitted rival local elites against each other, and in many places, there were serious tensions flowing from religious change, notably from issues associated with Islamization. A myriad of other socioeconomic changes and pressures generated significant friction, including the growth of antifeudal sentiments linked with ideas of modernity and nationalism, as well as interethnic conflicts. With the departure from power of the Dutch and Japanese, these grievances and frictions could be given expression. Traditional and village elites were often targeted, especially where they had become closely associated with Japanese rule. In this period, many local officials were removed, sometimes violently. Some particularly violent social revolutionary episodes occurred in parts of Sumatra where either leftist republicans or local Muslim leaders overthrew traditional aristocratic elements. The "three region's affair" is the best-known Javanese case. The same strange but potent blend of communists and Islamists that carried out the ill-fated 1926–27 rebellion was responsible for the removal of local and regional government officials on the northern coast of Java in late 1945. Here and elsewhere, republican troops intervened to suppress the social revolution. If the bulk of the existing local and regional government apparatus were to be successfully grafted onto the central republican government, then its personnel and their interests had to be protected. For the most part, even where the old elite were not reinstated, there was little real change to the social structure. The new elites quickly assumed the habits and outlooks of those they had replaced.

The social revolution phenomenon soon fizzled out, but much greater challenges to the government's authority were posed by two major revolts. Both represented visions for Indonesia that were impossible to reconcile with any other, and both were bound up with the vexatious politics associated with Indonesia's army.

As noted above, because the Japanese disbanded the Indonesian military forces they had established, the republic did not inherit a standing army. Into this vacuum poured anybody who was so inclined with a following and access to arms. For the most part, those who did so were the leaders of youth organizations mobilized by the Japanese. Unfortunately, they were imbued with militaristic attitudes but rather less military training. Many Peta and Hizbullah commanders also reformed their old units as best they could. This self-forming army was a haphazard collection of local forces comprising small-sized units with widely varying experience, training, armaments, and discipline. There was no central command, little cohesion among the various components, and little sense of any obligation to obey government orders or to remain politically neutral. On the contrary, most armed bodies were formed on the basis of a particular political outlook, or soon acquired one, depending largely on the inclinations of their commanders. Beginning in October 1945, efforts were made by successive governments to remedy this situation. But pushing these fluid and self-contained armed bodies into one centralized military structure with a defined chain of command and common ethos proved very difficult. Even more difficult was subordinating them to the government.

Problems of this sort have persisted long beyond the revolution. Well into the 1960s, army personnel tended to owe their primary loyalty to their immediate commanders rather than to the army as a whole, let alone to the state. Similarly, the phenomenon of regional and ethnic identities associated with particular units also continued to impede central control for decades. To some extent, these characteristics of the Indonesian army continue to the present, in particular a considerable degree of institutional independence from civilian government controls. The independent origins of the army in the 1945 context are the major source of the problem. The strength and pervasiveness of traditional patron-client relationships as a primary means of social organization made such a form of development natural and highly resistant to external pressure. The experience of the revolution reinforced these characteristics. That commanders were obliged to supply their units themselves inculcated "entrepreneurial" habits among the officer corps and reinforced the patron-client relationship between commanders and their soldiers. Similarly, the nature of the struggle meant that units were obliged to operate largely independently of formal chains of command and logistical support. The army's collective sense of political independence from the government was also reinforced by events during the revolution. Disdain developed for civilian politicians who appeared self-serving and weak for their pursuit of negotiations and their preference for captivity over continued resistance in the mountains.

Not surprisingly, under these circumstances, the government was rarely able to impose its will. For example, the central commander appointed by the government, Urip Sumohardjo, was replaced with Soedirman at a senior officers meeting in November 1945, a fait accompli that the government was forced to accept several weeks later. Sometimes individual units or groups of units defied both government and central military authority. Usually such internal disputes were resolved through negotiation, but occasionally arrests, kidnapping, and even armed clashes occurred. Twice, such internal army disputes degenerated to the point at which they developed into a serious rebellion, always an indication that other intractable political issues had become involved.

The commander of the Hizbullah forces in the Garut region of West Java, S.M. Kartosuwirjo, rejected the Renville Agreement (signed in January 1948), under which terms republican forces would abandon West Java to the Dutch. Kartosuwirjo elected to remain and wage a guerrilla struggle, a stance that little concerned the republican government or the army central command. But Kartosuwirjo went much further. In May, he declared himself head of the "Islamic State of Indonesia" and refused to recognize the republican government. Known as the Darul Islam Rebellion, this conflict continued until the early 1960s. Its main center remained in West Java, though other Islamist-tinged rebellions linked up with it in South Sulawesi, South Kalimantan, and Aceh. The affair left an institutional legacy of bitterness and distrust toward political Islam in the Indonesian army that has only recently declined.

A similar effect was created with respect to the opposite end of the political spectrum by the events known as the Madiun Rebellion. The withdrawal of republican forces from West Java was again the catalyst. The main force withdrawn was the Siliwangi Division, the best-equipped and best-organized republican force, partly because it contained a significant proportion of Dutch-trained soldiers, such as its commander, Nasution. Its senior officers largely supported the Hatta government's efforts to rationalize the army through demobilizing excess units and implementing the principles of chain of command. The arrival of the Siliwangi Division in Central Java altered the balance of power within republican politics, strengthening the government's hand vis-à-vis its leftist opponents, who enjoyed considerable influence among local Javanese military units. Other factors added to these tensions. The Siliwangi Division was mainly Sundanese. Local units were almost exclusively Javanese and resented the Sundanese presence in "their country," all the more so because the Siliwangi appeared privileged in terms of equipment and government favor. These feelings were accentuated by the shortages of rice and other basic necessities in the remaining republican-held territory where most republican forces were now concentrated and from which each unit needed to extract its own supplies.

Friction was inevitable and clashes escalated between rival units. Matters boiled over in September when leftist units associated with the Indonesian Communist Party (PKI) seized the East Javanese town of Madiun and issued a grandiose announcement that they had established a new national government. At this point, Musso, the new leader of PKI who had spent most of the previous 20 years in Moscow, made a massive miscalculation. Musso endorsed the rebellion and raced to Madiun to lead it. The government reacted with vigor, dispatching the Siliwangi Division to deal with the rebels. Sukarno threw his political weight decisively behind the government, denouncing what he carefully termed the "PKI-Musso." Within weeks, the leftist forces were defeated and their leaders either captured or killed, including Musso. Thereafter, leftists, PKI in particular, were regarded with extreme hostility by the majority of the senior officer corps who saw them as having "stabbed the republic in the back" during the war for independence. The Madiun

Rebellion left another significant legacy. During their brief period of control of Madiun, leftist forces killed many *santri* Muslim civilians in the vicinity. In the wake of the leftist defeat, revenge killings of *abangan* civilians took place. The left in Java had become significantly associated with the *abangan* community, a phenomenon that was to have dire consequences later.

The period of the revolution established or reinforced a number of important social and political themes that continued after independence was won. Established elite groups were displaced, but only to be replaced or joined by others, and seldom did this process entail any real change to the social structure. The religious-cultural differences between *santri* and *abangan* Muslims in parts of Java hardened and became sharply politicized as the socioreligious cleavage became entangled with national political affairs. Governments struggled for political stability and to control the army while grappling with a host of serious problems. The army central command struggled to exert control over its divisions and yet strove simultaneously to retain its political and operational independence from government. The army itself was a political battleground, and its political divisions intersected with many that also rent Indonesian society. The army's institutional inclination toward resolute opposition and suspicion toward PKI and toward Islamist politics crystallized, along with its self-ascribed duty as the paramount defender of the republic against internal as well as external threats. Perhaps most important, the principal competing visions for the future of Indonesia remained unresolved; indeed, they acquired additional sharpness as a consequence of the blood spilled on their behalf.

PARTIES AND PARLIAMENTARY DEMOCRACY

For several years after the formal recognition of independence, Indonesia (within the framework of another provisional constitution) persisted with parliamentary democracy. Elections for parliament, the People's Representative Council (DPR), and a constituent assembly, intended to produce Indonesia's permanent constitution, were expected to be held within a year or two but did not take place until 1955. The delay was partly due to technical and logistical difficulties, but lack of political will was the main reason. In the interim, the DPR continued with members appointed roughly in accordance with their parties' presumed levels of support. All parties complained bitterly about their allotted proportion of seats. Without an election, the accuracy of their claimed levels of support could only be guessed at, but in hindsight, it is clear that DPR membership did reflect a reasonable effort at inclusiveness under the circumstances. The DPR's tardiness in making arrangements for the elections probably indicates a collective fear that the parties' support bases were smaller than they claimed. The 1955 elections proved most of these fears to be justified.

Retrospectively, it is clear that there were nine significant parties. Masyumi (Consultative Council of Indonesian Muslims) had an unpromising beginning as an artificial Japanese creation into which all Muslim organizations were dragooned in October 1943. Despite the practical political advantage of remaining unified and the emotional appeal of Muslim unity, Masyumi remained intact only briefly after independence. Sarekat Islam Party of Indonesia (PSII), proud of its past glory, broke ranks in July 1947, unable to reconcile itself to a subordinate role within Masyumi. A few years later, in July 1952, Nahdlatul Ulama (NU) also split from Masyumi, bitter over its reduced influence within the organization. Masyumi's refusal to allocate to NU the religious affairs ministry, which NU had come to regard as its own, was the final straw. Despite these breakaways, Masyumi continued to be a major force. Among them, Masyumi, PSII, and NU constituted the main *santri* parties. Masyumi and NU, respectively, provided the principal political representation for modernist and traditionalist Muslims.

The Indonesian Nationalist Party (PNI) saw itself as the reconstitution of the old PNI founded by Sukarno in 1927. Ideologically, as a secular nationalist organization, this claim was largely accurate, but in membership terms there were important differences. Alongside the radical, nationalist, educated elite who had been its original membership, now joined many senior civil servants and large landowners, including much of the established elite favored under Dutch and Japanese rule. The Indonesian Communist Party (PKI), its new leadership having successfully distanced itself from Musso and the Madiun Rebellion, won support from workers and poor peasants, as well as from intellectuals. It operated more cautiously than hitherto and publicly emphasized a radical, nationalist, anti-imperialist stance, suitably cloaked in Marxist terminology. PNI and PKI were the two main secular parties that drew their support from *abangan* Muslims. In addition, there were four other small parties that exerted considerable influence despite low levels of mass support. The Socialist Party of Indonesia (PSI) formed by Sjahrir in November 1945 also espoused a secular ideology tinged with Marxism, but not of the Leninist variety. Its social democracy appealed largely to intellectuals and those attracted to rational and pragmatic policies, including influential individuals in the officer corps and bureaucracy. The Murba (Proletarian) Party comprised the followers of the charismatic revolutionary Tan Malaka, a PKI founder who broke with Moscow in the 1920s and was killed (by hostile republican troops) during the revolution. Between them, the Catholic Party and Parkindo (Indonesian Protestant Party) represented Indonesian Christians, a relatively wealthy and educated community, well represented in elite circles.

A striking characteristic of the party structure that emerged following independence was the importance of "identity politics." Almost all of the parties relied upon primordial loyalties (religious and ethnic affiliations) for their respective support bases. To varying degrees, they all promoted themselves as representing the interests of a particular primordial identity, although they often posited it as being the only authentic national identity and presented it as having far more "members" than was actually the case. For example, Masyumi saw itself as the genuine voice for all Indonesian Muslims, although in practice (after 1952) its supporters were overwhelmingly modernist-inclined *santri* Muslims. Its support was also strongest among certain ethnic groups, such as the Sundanese and Minangkabau. This primordialist phenomenon added greatly to the political tensions of the postindependence period, especially because all the parties established their own party-linked social and cultural organizations, including trade unions, peasant associations, youth groups, women's organizations, and artistic groups. Thereby, primordial identities were further politicized, and the politicization was embedded deeply into society.

The delay in conducting elections proved costly for those who hoped Indonesia's fledgling democracy would be consolidated. The temporary parliament lacked legitimacy, and the longer it delayed elections, the less authority it enjoyed. Governments in this period were necessarily made up of large and unwieldy multiparty coalitions, cobbled together with many compromises over policy, ministerial personnel, and the prizes of office. They generally retained office for relatively short periods before the complex deal unraveled.

Following Hatta, Mohammad Natsir of Masyumi became prime minister in September 1950 with PSI support. PNI was excluded from

Natsir's cabinet, a recipe for trouble that led to the disgruntled PNI forcing Natsir's resignation within seven months. One of Natsir's main leadership rivals within Masyumi, Sukiman Wirjosandjojo, formed the next cabinet in June 1951, a Masyumi-PNI coalition that excluded PSI. Sukiman proved better able to work with the PNI leaders and with Sukarno than had Natsir. Perhaps this was because Sukiman was Javanese and Natsir was Minangkabau, but personality probably played a bigger role. Natsir was principled to the point of stubbornness and had clashed with Sukarno frequently in the 1930s in a celebrated exchange of articles about Islam and nationalism. The Sukiman government was also short lived, falling due to a foreign policy regarded as too pro-American. (Neutrality was strongly equated with independence by Indonesians in this period.)

Another Masyumi-PNI coalition formed the next cabinet in June 1952, but this time the PNI's Wilopo was prime minister. The Wilopo cabinet lasted somewhat longer than its predecessors, dissolving itself in June 1953 before a vote could be taken on a no-confidence motion. Tensions between Masyumi and PNI had grown over several policies, including economic austerity measures and efforts to reduce the size of the army and the swollen bureaucracy. Generally, Masyumi supported these measures, but PNI was at best unenthusiastic. The government also lost authority due to the failure of its efforts to reduce the size of the army. After PNI shifted to the left at its December 1952 congress, Wilopo increasingly came under attack from within his own party and resigned. The deaths of several squatters at the hands of police in Sumatra provided the emotive issue that would have allowed the PNI left to support the no-confidence motion had it come to a vote.

After several weeks of difficult negotiations, the left-wing PNI leader, Ali Sastroamidjojo, became prime minister, leading a cabinet that excluded Masyumi and PSI but included NU. The willingness of NU to enter a government with PNI that excluded Masyumi reflected how far relations between NU and Masyumi had deteriorated. Naturally, this move exacerbated the bitterness. The Ali government enjoyed a degree of longevity far exceeding that of its predecessors, holding office for two years until July 1955 when NU withdrew its support. In August 1955, Burhanuddin Harahap of Masyumi became prime minister, heading a cabinet coalition of Masyumi, NU, and PSI. Now it was PNI's turn to be on the outside, and at a crucial time, as the Burhanuddin government came to office just before the 1955 elections. The new government was able to reverse many Ali-government measures that would have benefited PNI in the elections. Many PNI-aligned civil servants in strategic positions were replaced with Masyumi or PSI sympathizers.

The constant instability of governments during this period further undermined the DPR's legitimacy and with it the parliamentary system. Parliament seemed only to bicker, and much of the bickering seemed motivated by the benefits of office, including the attendant opportunities for corruption. Meanwhile, Indonesia continued to experience serious problems associated with underdevelopment and the legacies of almost a decade of war. Export industries were slow to recover, impeded by damage to infrastructure and the lack of capital and expertise, and much of the earnings were lost to smuggling and corruption. Education levels were extremely low, and enormous effort was expended to rectify this problem. But the brake on development caused by a population's low educational levels takes decades to remove. Population growth, despite the high death rates due directly or indirectly to the decade of war, continued its rapid rise. It placed great strain on limited government resources, as well as on the country's supply of food, land, and employment. In tandem with the population increase, a massive influx of people to the cities exacerbated many social problems and added to the government's difficulties. These were huge problems, and the weight of expectations was unreasonably high, but governments and parliament did far less to tackle them than they could have. Most members of the elite seemingly preferred the pursuit of short-term political interests to the hard grind of tackling Indonesia's problems.

Not everyone was disappointed by the shortcomings of the parliamentary system. Darul Islam benefited greatly from the weakness and distraction of governments of this period. Although PKI flourished during parliamentary democracy, it did not wish the system's success, otherwise its arguments for a communist Indonesia would have carried little force. The army, with little regard for civilian politicians, chafed at the political constraints imposed upon it under parliamentary democracy. The possibility of a military government was often canvassed in army circles. Indeed, ineffectual moves to bring the army to power were made on more than one occasion in this period, foundering largely due to factionalism within army ranks. Sukarno also had reasons to be pleased by the course of events. He had always been attracted to the idea of a one-party state; indeed, he had promoted this vision immediately after the declaration of independence but had been rebuffed. As weak governments in quick succession floundered in the face of Indonesia's difficulties, Sukarno found his political stocks were rising. Time had reduced the stain of his Japanese associations, and he had remained the indispensable figurehead of the republic throughout the revolution. Moreover, his constitutional role to name cabinet formateurs proved to be a pivotal position. Cabinet formateurs were responsible for conducting the delicate negotiations between party leaders necessary for the construction of a government with a working parliamentary majority. Since they often became prime minister in the new government whose creation they had facilitated, it was a highly prized assignment. Thus in circumstances where governments changed frequently, Sukarno was often placed in a position to bestow this favor on a politician of his choosing. Not only did he thereby earn the gratitude of those he chose, but it allowed him to influence the political outlook of governments through his choices, the more so because formateurs often consulted him as they worked. The frequency with which governments fell also served to emphasize his position as the one to whom all turned in a crisis.

THE 1955 ELECTIONS

The long-promised general elections for a new DPR were finally held in September 1955. Elections for the constituent assembly (a separate body elected purely for the purpose of producing a permanent constitution) took place several weeks later. All adult Indonesians were entitled to vote, including women. The Kartini-inspired campaigns for women's rights and the active role of women in the nationalist struggle had borne some fruit. It was hoped that the outcome of the parliamentary elections would produce a stable government with the legitimacy and authority to take the necessary steps to overcome Indonesia's problems. Similarly, it was hoped that the elected constituent assembly would succeed in its mission and produce a constitution with broad support, in the process resolving the thorny issues that lay at the heart of Indonesia's instability. Unfortunately, the results of these elections were not conducive to fulfilling these hopes, and subsequent political developments soon further undermined Indonesia's fragile democracy and added to Indonesia's political instability.

The widely held assumption that fewer parties would obtain seats from the elections than the 20 parties represented in the appointed parliament proved false. Twenty-eight parties won sufficient votes to gain representation in the DPR. The widely expected clear "winner" also failed to materialize. While few had expected that any party would gain more than 50 percent of the vote, it was thought that either Masyumi or PNI would emerge with a substantially larger proportion of the vote than any other party. Such an outcome would have provided a "winner" with the moral authority to form the government and determine fundamental policies. In fact, the margin between PNI with 22.3 percent of the vote and Masyumi with 20.9 percent was too small for PNI to wield the "winner's" expected authority over the "losing" Masyumi. Moreover, there were two other parties not far behind: NU and PKI with 18.4 percent and 16.4 percent of the vote, respectively. Several other parties also gained a respectable vote (PSII 2.9%, Parkindo 2.6%, Catholic Party 2%, PSI 2%, and Murba 0.5%). A significant 11.7 percent of the vote was divided among the remaining 19 parties.

The good showings by PKI and NU were the biggest surprises. Most Masyumi leaders had been rather dismissive of NU. They downplayed its level of support and were contemptuous of the quality of its political leadership. They were shocked to see that NU was barely behind Masyumi in terms of support. In fact, the NU and PSII votes combined were greater than the votes achieved by Masyumi, revealing just how costly the splits had been that the Masyumi leadership had been unable or unwilling to prevent. PKI's strong showing shocked everybody, not least the army. Only seven years had passed since the Madiun Rebellion, and yet in terms of popular support, PKI was apparently stronger than it had ever been.

The pattern of the election results indicated starkly just how fractious the Indonesian polity was. There were four large parties separated by only a relatively small margin of votes but also by wide ideological and primordial gulfs. It was difficult to see how a stable coalition could be formed among them unless they were willing to make major compromises. The large number of smaller parties commanding varying proportions of significant support further impeded the building of potential coalitions. Not only did their sheer presence complicate matters, but they also brought with them into the DPR additional sharp divisions. The elections also revealed another dimension to the intractable political divisions confronting Indonesia. Generally speaking, PNI, NU, and PKI gained most of their support in Java, whereas Masyumi was most heavily supported outside of Java. It was this Java versus "outer islands" cleavage that, mixed with other contentious political issues, generated the national political crisis that led to the demise of parliamentary democracy for more than three decades.

REGIONAL REBELLION AND THE DEMISE OF PARLIAMENTARY DEMOCRACY

The new postelection government was established in April 1956 (the Burhanuddin cabinet having remained in office in the interim). Ali Sastroamidjojo returned as prime minister to lead a PNI–NU–Masyumi coalition. But apart from their shared antipathy toward PKI, these parties could find little common ground. Neither their disdain for PKI nor the threat of military rule if they failed proved sufficient inducement to mount a common and concerted effort to overcome Indonesia's mounting problems. Within a year, the second Ali cabinet was dissolved by Sukarno and martial law proclaimed. A complex series of events at the center and at the periphery, some the bitter fruit of factors that had been gestating since the revolution, interacted to produce this outcome.

Although the 1948 events had removed most of the Islamist and leftist elements from within the army, there yet remained many internal divisions. Some senior officers harbored personal political ambitions, and others shared the outlooks of particular parties. There were also structural tensions. Dutch-trained officers were resented by those trained by the Japanese or who were "self-taught" through their experience during the revolution. The former were generally far better educated and possessed more technical military skills, whereas the latter saw themselves as more "nationalist." Those in the latter group also tended to be more closely tied to their troops and to "their" regions and were averse to the establishment of a strong central command and to professional military principles. Many local commanders had forged business empires, usually in alliance with local elites and local business interests. The alliances were often cemented through marriage, as the "new men" of the army were welcomed into the families of the establishment. From the business proceeds, commanders provided for their troops' needs since central funding remained far from adequate. Naturally, most commanders also lined their own pockets and those of subordinate officers and relatives.

A strong central command threatened these cozy, local arrangements. The imposition of officer rotation and the assertion of central command authority would mean that local commanders would be monitored more closely, limiting their latitude and thus weakening the business advantage that accrued to their positions (more likely, perhaps, a large cut would be demanded). These were powerful disincentives for local commanders to cooperate with efforts to create a strong central command. Moreover, the Dutch-trained officers would be at a considerable advantage in competing for central command posts as well as generally in a context in which posts and promotions were to be determined by merit. The sensitivity of this issue was exacerbated by the recurrent inclination of the central command and government to demobilize excess troops, including excess officers.

Nasution's efforts in 1952 to augment central command authority and to "rationalize" the army had failed. Indeed, his failure had cost him his position. But by November 1955, political conditions had shifted sufficiently to see him restored as army chief of staff and ready to launch another attempt at army reform, this time with the backing of the government and the president. Ironically, many of the politicians who had previously supported such efforts, and with whom Nasution shared a broadly similar political outlook, were now among his opponents. Similar shifting on this and related issues had also taken place within the army, an effect produced by the combination of two separate developments: a significant shift to the left at the political center and the scale of economic interests that had become entwined with many regional commands.

While in many areas the business activities of local commanders were relatively modest, in export-producing regions outside of Java, the scale of these operations had grown to massive proportions. In these instances, the illegal business activities of local commanders involved large-scale smuggling, conducted so openly from local ports that the term *smuggling* seems inappropriate. The massive smuggling of the nation's scarce export products robbed the central government of desperately needed revenue and impeded imposition of any central economic policy. Clearly, the smuggling could not be brought under control without reining in the power of regional military commanders, and so the interests of the central command and those of the central government coincided. Objectively, this had been the case for several years. But hitherto, the left, including Sukarno, had generally sympathized with the "revolutionary" officers and protected them against the rationalizing efforts of soldiers like Nasution and politicians like Natsir. In the wake of the elections, however, power at the center had shifted to the left. As it did so, the left inherited the centralizing impulse formerly associated with the right, while many of the latter were now loath to see Jakarta acquire more power. These shifting outlooks were strongly reinforced by the politics of ethnicity and regional economic interests. Densely populated but with little export industry, Java's interests would be better served by a central economic approach, whereas the regions with important export industries benefited from the status quo, a de facto economic and political autonomy. Those who benefited most were the new regional elites, pivoted upon the local military commanders. But now the election results had delivered a national government that favored Javanese interests.

Sukarno had always resented the restrictions imposed upon him as a figurehead president. Although he largely complied with the constitutional niceties in the early 1950s, he gradually found opportunities to intervene in the course of political events. In truth, he did not need to search for them. The succession of political crises and the increasing willingness of political groups to appeal to him for intervention presented him with ample opportunities. At the same time, his lack of formal responsibility for government and policy meant that he escaped blame for Indonesia's problems and was not tarred with the brush of corruption and the pursuit of self-interest that were attached to the parties. (PKI, excluded from all governments in this period, acquired a similar exaggerated image of purity.) Under these circumstances, Sukarno's reputation increased further, and with it his influence. It was also fortuitous for him politically that the Papua issue remained unresolved. It was an issue almost tailor-made for him to exploit.

Negotiations with the Dutch over the future of Papua proved most unsatisfactory from the Indonesian perspective, and the issue quickly became an extremely emotional one. Sukarno's slogan of Indonesian sovereignty "from Sabang to Merauke" (the former an island off the northern tip of Sumatra and the latter on the far eastern border of Papua with Papua New Guinea) resounded very effectively. This issue fit well with Sukarno's lifelong political stance: the generally popular theme of promoting national unity and deploring divisiveness. In the postindependence period, Sukarno modified his theme to imply that Indonesians were to blame for their country's ills only in allowing themselves to be divided. He laid ultimate blame on the "neocolonial" forces, a popular diagnosis and one that neatly connected with the Papua issue. Sukarno was also successful in exaggerating his stature as an international statesman. His prominent role in the Asian-African Conference of April 1955 (which gave birth to the Non-Aligned Movement), held at Bandung in West Java and attended by most Asian leaders, was instrumental in this regard.

In tandem with Sukarno's increasing popularity and political importance, certain political forces deemed it advantageous to move closer to him. PKI acquired presidential protection in exchange for supporting Sukarno, an arrangement made possible by its assumption of a public posture barely distinguishable from radical nationalism. Nasution also hitched himself to Sukarno. After being blocked by Sukarno in 1952, Nasution had concluded it was much better to have Sukarno as an ally than as an opponent because no substantial political change was possible without his acquiescence.

As Indonesians became increasingly dissatisfied with parliament in the middle of the 1950s, Sukarno's speeches began to talk of "burying the political parties" and to call for an alternative political system called "guided democracy."[1] Vehement opposition to Sukarno's ideas came from Masyumi, the Catholic Party, and PSI, but varying degrees of lukewarm political support came from PKI, PNI, Parkindo, and NU, with warmer support emanating from Murba and Nasution. Those who represented the interests of the export-producing outer islands, together with those inclined toward the right, worried that their enemies would acquire greatly increased influence over central government policies. The resignation of Hatta from the vice presidency on December 1, 1956, added to their fears, removing as it did a powerful outer-island and moderate voice in Jakarta. Those hoping for a compromise solution to the looming crisis acceptable to outer-island interests promoted the idea of a Hatta emergency cabinet. Frustrated that PNI and NU cabinet members would not resign to facilitate this proposal, Masyumi unilaterally resigned from the Ali cabinet in January 1957. This protest, like that of Hatta beforehand, had no chastening effect on Sukarno and his allies. If these gestures of principle made any difference to the course of events, it was only to further reduce the influence of outer-islanders and moderates in Jakarta and to close channels of communication between two polarizing sides.

Against this political backdrop, Nasution's army-reform measures met with much foot-dragging by officers ensconced in lucrative regional commands. As pressure mounted, a coup was attempted in August 1956, led by Nasution's cousin, deputy, and long-term rival, Lieutenant Colonel Zulkifli Lubis. Nasution foiled the plot with ease. In December, matters escalated when "army councils" were formed in Sumatra. Effectively thereby, regional commanders had seized power in their areas, a move that was generally popular with the local civilian populations. Similar army councils were established in Sulawesi, Kalimantan, and Maluku. Neither Jakarta nor the "rebel" army commanders chose to deem these actions as rebellion at this point, and so negotiations and intense political maneuvering took place as all concerned looked for ways to attain their objectives peacefully. Even after the army rebels in eastern Indonesia issued a Universal Struggle Charter (Permesta) on March 8, 1957, effectively an open declaration of rebellion against the center, there was no immediate recourse to violence. It was the event, however, that triggered the resignation of the Ali cabinet and Sukarno's declaration of martial law (which remained in effect until May 1963).

Sukarno announced a "business cabinet" in April 1957. The respected nonparty politician Djuanda Kartawidjaja became prime minister, a choice that offered some reassurance to the right and outer-islanders. On the other hand, several of Sukarno's radical protégés were given ministerial positions, including Chaerul Saleh and Dr. Subandrio. Ostensibly, the cabinet was nonparty, but it contained mainly NU and PNI figures as well as PKI sympathizers. The cabinet's reflection of the political shift was further underlined by the exclusion of PSI and the Catholic Party. Sukarno did extend Masyumi a small olive branch by offering cabinet positions to selected Masyumi figures. But Masyumi expelled the two members who accepted.

The political temperature continued to heat up throughout 1957, and the leftward drift continued. Provincial elections in 1957 revealed further significant PKI gains in many parts of the country, especially on Java. Workers led by PKI and PNI unions seized Dutch enterprises in November and December in protest against the UN's failure to pass Indonesia's motion calling on the Netherlands to relinquish Papua. (Control over the enterprises was subsequently assumed by the army, providing it with significant economic resources.) An assassination attempt was made on Sukarno at the end of November, leaving Sukarno unhurt but killing and injuring many. In December, Natsir and other Masyumi leaders fled Jakarta for Sumatra, citing intimidation by leftist youth groups. Matters came to a head in February 1958 when prominent PSI leader and former cabinet minister, Professor Sumitro Djojohadikusumo, together with Natsir and other Masyumi leaders, met with the rebel Sumatran military commanders (including Lubis) in Padang and issued a three-part ultimatum to the central government. They demanded the dissolution of the cabinet, formation of a new business cabinet by Hatta and Sultan Hamengkubuwono IX pending new elections, and the return of Sukarno to the position of a figurehead president. Following the ultimatum's predictable rejection, the Sumatran rebels announced the establishment of the Revolutionary Government of the Republic of Indonesia (PRRI) and were immediately joined by the Permesta rebels. There could be no further ambiguity. The Indonesian central government was confronted with rebellion.

Despite sympathy from several neighboring countries including the Philippines, Malaya, Singapore, and Australia, and support from the United States that extended to the supply of arms and other clandestine assistance, the rebellion was easily defeated by firm military action organized by Nasution. The rebellion's defeat allowed Sukarno to consolidate his system of "guided democracy," established the authority of the army central command and the central government, and apparently confirmed Indonesia on a leftward course.

GUIDED DEMOCRACY

Guided democracy was touted as a modernized, authentically Indonesian method of governance as practiced in traditional villages. Essentially, it was imagined to be a native form of democracy whereby villagers assembled as equals to discuss an issue until a consensus emerged that everyone could accept. There is only the flimsiest historical basis for this highly idealized vision of how traditional villages were governed. Moreover, it is a vision that completely ignores enormous regional variations and the historical reality of rajas and sultans who ruled the state above the village. Nevertheless, the guided-democracy idea was extremely seductive. The nation's governance problem could be blamed on the inapplicability of the Western-style democracy model that had been "imposed" on Indonesia. And the solution to the problems was as neat as it was nationalistic: simply revert to an Indonesian model. For Sukarno personally, the concept had particular appeal. It sat well with the persistent authoritarian streak to his political ideas that the Japanese experience seemed to have crystallized. Perhaps most important, it fit his image of himself as the "guide" who could discern and articulate the "consensus" for the people with whom he fancied he had an almost mystical connection, knowing their minds and their needs better than they did themselves.

Some were not seduced. Hatta, in an article banned at the time, offered a far less romantic explanation of guided democracy, describing it bluntly as "a dictatorship supported by certain groups."[2] He was correct up to a point. It was an authoritarian regime that some political forces supported, and Sukarno's position as the system's linchpin bore a passing resemblance to that of a dictator. But it is clear that guided democracy was also an unstable political compromise. Furthermore, far from being an iron-fisted dictator, the variable authority Sukarno exercised was derived largely from the political space he could negotiate as the indispensable balancer of contending political forces. In truth, he had few cards to play other than his considerable prestige and his equally considerable ability to manipulate people and situations. Thus, while guided democracy was supposedly an enduring system of government, it is better seen as an uneasy truce held together by Sukarno. It should also be understood as being Sukarno's government, despite his penchant for delegation and inattention to detail. Of course, the underlying fragility of guided democracy helps to explain the heavy-handed insistence on its authenticity as an indigenous political system and also why so many were prepared to go along with it. Thereby, it could be presented as a noble endeavor of cooperation for the national good, and the pain of resolving Indonesia's deep political cleavages could be postponed.

The army's defeat of the PRRI-Permesta Rebellion left the it far more united and with a much-enhanced reputation. It was easily the strongest political (and administrative) institution in the country. But it dared not seek to rule alone, preferring to embrace a "middle way," a concept advanced by Nasution in December 1958 whereby the army would not abstain from politics as in a (Western) democracy, but neither would it establish a military dictatorship. Like so much else to do with guided democracy, this was a rationalization justifying a position made necessary by circumstances. The army still had many weaknesses, not the least of which that it remained factionalized. It also lacked legitimacy, and an attempt to seize power would have generated considerable opposition, including that from powerful opponents such as PKI and Sukarno. The solution was to rule in partnership with Sukarno, who could provide the necessary legitimacy to add to the army's muscle and organizational capacity. Sukarno was agreeable, although he intended to be the dominant partner, a feat he was largely able to pull off through political acumen and shrewd use of his personal authority.

In this situation, Sukarno recognized that without his own party, he needed to exert influence over the existing parties to obtain organized civilian support, without which he would be in danger of becoming the army's puppet. Most parties were prepared to cooperate in exchange for a place in the system and Sukarno's protection against the army. PKI was the most valuable for Sukarno in this regard because of its unparalleled mass mobilization capacity. It was also highly vulnerable and thus perhaps the most reliable of his allies. The army made no secret of its antipathy toward the PKI; indeed, on more than one occasion, Sukarno's intervention was needed to secure the release of PKI leaders detained by the army and to lift restrictions imposed upon its activities. The other parties were also important, however, and also had powerful motivations for supporting Sukarno. While many members of the civilian elite benefited from close links with influential army figures, most increasingly found themselves in competition with the latter for wealth and power. Both in Jakarta and in the regions, martial law bestowed a significant advantage on army officers in the practice of favor-trading and manipulation of the bureaucracy vital for business success and wealth accumulation. For the civilian elite, their places in government and Sukarno's favor provided them with vital leverage in their business-politics competition with the army. Thus, most of the other parties were also willing to lend Sukarno their more modest mass mobilization capacities and the legitimacy they enjoyed through their proven civilian support. Though less potent than PKI, their support was still welcome, all the more so because thereby Sukarno was not solely reliant on PKI as a counterbalance to the army.

In addition to Sukarno's use of civilian political forces to balance against the army, he also exploited divisions within the army. Thereby, he was able to outmaneuver Nasution, "promoting" him to the figurehead position of commander of the armed forces in June 1962 and replacing him as army chief of staff with the more malleable Ahmad Yani. Sukarno also cultivated the police, navy, and air force, seeking to take advantage of their jealousies of the army, which very much regarded itself as the dominant service. The air force proved the most conducive in this regard, its commander Surjadi Surjadarma and his successor Omar Dhani (from 1962) were both supporters of Sukarno. In return, the air force, and to a lesser extent the navy, received the bulk of the new military equipment Indonesia was able to secure.

The mechanism whereby the army could be accommodated in the guided-democracy political system was provided by returning to the 1945 constitution, a solution suggested by Nasution. The 1945 constitution provided for an authoritarian political system with a strong executive president to whom ministers were responsible rather than to parliament. It also provided for two representative bodies (whose powers were weak and ill defined): a standing parliament (the DPR) and a People's Consultative Assembly (MPR), to which the president was theoretically accountable but which met only occasionally. It also suited the guided-democracy concept because particular passages could be interpreted as allowing for "functional groups" to make up the membership of the representative bodies. According to the "functional groups" concept, society is composed of identifiable groups who perform a particular function for society, such as farmers, fishermen, academics, artists and so on. This fitted the guided-democracy vision of Indonesian society, according to which ideological conflict (which political parties were seen to articulate) was culturally alien. Moreover, by deeming the army a functional group it could be given a formal place in the system. An added attraction was the nationalist legitimacy attached to the 1945 constitution because of its association with the revolution, a factor that dovetailed neatly with the nationalist garb in which guided democracy was cloaked. But how was the return to the 1945 constitution to be carried out? There was the small matter of the directly elected constituent assembly already working on a permanent constitution.

Considering the political circumstances, the constituent assembly had made considerable progress on its task but predictably had become bogged down over the issue of the philosophical basis of the state. The two main contenders still were Islam and the "secular" Pancasila. This was a difficult question to resolve because essential principles were at stake, which few were willing to abandon. Nor could the question be resolved by a vote because neither side could muster the required two-thirds majority since the election result for the constituent assembly had closely resembled that for the DPR. The "secularists" combined were in the majority, but the *santri* Muslim minority was well over the proportion needed to block any measure on which its constituent parts were united. After intense pressure was applied to NU, it appeared that a two-thirds majority could be obtained in favor of the proposed return to the 1945 constitution. But the deal unraveled on the old Jakarta Charter issue. When the constituent assembly voted to exclude the Jakarta Charter from the 1945 constitution, NU could no longer support the proposal. Its members in the constituent assembly voted against it, together with the other *santri*-based parties. But Sukarno, urged on by Nasution, was not prepared to remain entangled by constitutional and democratic niceties. He dissolved the constituent assembly, and returned Indonesia to the 1945 constitution (without the Jakarta Charter) by the highly constitutionally dubious method of a presidential decree in July 1959.

With the 1945 constitution in place, Sukarno encountered only a little further resistance. DPR rejected the government's budget in March 1960, to which Sukarno also responded by dissolving it by decree. In June 1960, Sukarno appointed a new parliament. He called it the DPR Gotong Royong (DPR-GR), a Javanese term meaning something like "mutual cooperation," which Sukarno frequently invoked as containing the essence of Indonesia's village community spirit. The DPR-GR contained many of the same party leaders (minus those of Masyumi and PSI) who had sat in the elected parliament, although now many of them were included supposedly because they represented "functional groups" rather than their parties. Of course, they were all now present at Sukarno's pleasure, not because they had been elected. In September, Sukarno appointed a Provisional People's Consultative Assembly (MPRS), of similar composition to the DPR-GR, completing the construction of guided democracy's principal government structures. Niggling remnants of opposition were also dealt with. Masyumi and PSI were banned in August 1960, and in April the following year, all but the 10 largest remaining parties were also dissolved. In January 1962, Natsir, Sjahrir, and others, including the bulk of the Masyumi leadership, were imprisoned, ostensibly because of their alleged support for the PRRI-Permesta Rebellion.

COUP, KILLINGS, AND THE FALL OF SUKARNO

Guided democracy soon proved incapable of solving Indonesia's pressing economic development problems. It also failed to contain the growing political friction for more than a few years. There were, however, some initial successes. The defeat of the PRRI-Permesta Rebellion was followed by settlement of the separatist rebellion in Aceh in May 1959, achieved through conceding a substantial degree of local autonomy. Then in 1962, the Darul Islam Rebellion in West Java was defeated, following the capture and subsequent execution of Kartosuwirjo. The Darul Islam—linked rebellion in South Sulawesi continued until the death of its leader, Kahar Muzakkar in 1965, but it had declined to the level of an irritant long beforehand. Thus by the early 1960s, the internal security problems that had plagued the republic since its inception seemed settled. Capping off these successes was Indonesia's attainment of sovereignty over Papua. Anxious to prevent Indonesia from slipping further toward the orbit of either Beijing or Moscow, the United States had pressured the Netherlands on the issue. Finally in 1962, the Dutch agreed to surrender the territory to the UN, which handed over administration to Indonesia with the proviso that "an act of free choice" be held within a few years to ascertain the will of the Papuans. This was not the only instance in the early 1960s in which Indonesia benefited from being able to play its Cold War suitors—Washington, Moscow, and Beijing—off against each other, acquiring thereby economic aid and arms supplies.

The combination of economic aid, a relatively benign internal security situation, and Jakarta's control over the economic resources of the outer islands ought to have facilitated significant economic improvement, which in turn might have eased political tensions. But the opportunity was squandered, and Indonesia lurched toward disaster. To be fair, the fleeting opportunity was not easy to grasp. While boosting national pride, the seizure of Dutch enterprises had proved economically disastrous, leading to massive falls in production in Indonesia's principal export industries. The army's assumption of control over these enterprises, as well as over those previously controlled by the regional rebels, only made matters worse, since most of the profits had been siphoned off by the army. Probably the greatest obstacle, however, was the continued focus by most political forces on the looming political showdown rather than on economic development. Under these circumstances, economic conditions soon worsened, and declining living standards (for most) added to the political tensions.

Against this background, Indonesia continued to shift leftward both domestically and internationally. Within months of getting its way on Papua, Indonesia became embroiled in another international dispute with the West, one that also involved Indonesia's neighbors. The proposal to add the British territories of Singapore and northern Borneo (Sarawak, Sabah, and Brunei) to Malaya (a former British colony) to create Malaysia was declared unacceptable by Indonesian Foreign Minister Subandrio in January 1963. When Malaysia was created over these objections, Indonesia launched a low-level conflict labeled *Confrontation* (Konfrontasi) against Malaysia, a policy that also brought Indonesia into conflict with Malaysia's military backers, Britain and Australia. That there was little actual fighting but an abundance of bellicose Indonesian threats contributed to suspicions that Indonesian feelings had been to some extent deliberately whipped up. Certainly the issue served various domestic political ends. For the Sukarno regime, it provided a new external enemy to distract Indonesians from their economic misery and their internal conflicts. For the army, it provided an excuse for more arms purchases and for extending martial law. For PKI, it provided a "safe" issue allowing it to mobilize supporters and to loudly confirm its credentials as the most nationalist and most radical political force. It also scuttled any moves toward economic stabilization, reduced American influence while promoting that of Beijing, consolidated Indonesia's international leftist drift, and distracted the army from repression of PKI.

Up until this juncture, since its near destruction after the Madiun affair, PKI had generally avoided open confrontation with its domestic enemies. It had also sought to build the biggest mass membership possible and the broadest possible coalition of allies. This strategy had been spectacularly successful. Through welfare activities in the villages and the assiduous construction of a plethora of social and cultural organizations, PKI had embedded itself deeply into society and attracted millions of supporters. It had also established a good relationship with Sukarno and, although not part of the government, was influential in Jakarta. The PKI leadership recognized, however, that the party still had some serious weaknesses. The number of members and supporters was large, but relatively few were committed. They could be relied on to vote for PKI but not to fight for it. Second, PKI lacked an armed fighting force and thus was perpetually vulnerable to the army, which was dominated by vehemently anticommunist generals. There was also a looming danger. While Sukarno was in power, PKI was protected and there was some slight prospect that it could inherit power from

Sukarno peacefully. But Sukarno could not live forever, and the best-case scenario of power falling gently into PKI's lap could not be relied upon.

In response to its weaknesses and emboldened by its dramatic growth and the radicalized political climate, the PKI leadership apparently decided to implement two measures. Clandestine efforts to win supporters in the army were stepped up, and a more aggressive domestic political strategy was embarked upon, aimed partly at hardening the membership for possible struggles to come. A land-reform bill had been passed in 1960, but very little land had been redistributed because the local authorities that were meant to implement the law were captive to landowning interests. In 1963, PKI launched a campaign of "direct action," in which local PKI leaders organized land-poor peasants to seize land to which they felt entitled. The campaign was an abject failure. PKI lost many fair-weather supporters, and its weaknesses were exposed. Worse, the air of unstoppable momentum that had come to surround it was punctured, and PKI's enemies discovered their strengths. In most places, the landowners and local authorities, often supported by the police and the army, more than matched local PKI forces. PKI's campaign proved especially unsuccessful in areas with a large *santri* Muslim population. Many *santri* community leaders were large landowners, and the *santri* communities themselves were largely impervious to PKI's blandishments. This was partly due to religious convictions that made Marxist ideology unacceptable, but it was also due to *santri* antipathy toward the PKI's *abangan* associations, both in terms of personnel and organizational culture. PKI had won many supporters in a short time, but overwhelmingly they were *abangan*, thus further entangling the party in this deep-seated socioreligious cleavage and further politicizing it.

During 1965, Indonesia's political situation seemed to be rapidly escalating toward a crisis. In this year, Indonesia's radical foreign policy drift was confirmed emphatically when Sukarno withdrew Indonesia from the UN, the International Monetary Fund (IMF), and the World Bank and announced the Jakarta–Phnom Penh–Hanoi–Beijing axis. Indonesia's economy neared collapse with hyperinflation. As political tensions rose, PKI, having been defeated in its land-reform campaign, pushed for the creation of an armed "fifth force" (alongside the police, army, navy, and air force) ostensibly to pursue Confrontation. Its creation would have provided PKI with a fighting force that would have reduced the

army's advantage over it, a development that the army was determined to prevent. Tensions approached the breaking point over
this issue in September, as it appeared that Sukarno intended to
back PKI's proposal. Tensions also rose significantly at this time
as Sukarno's evident ill health (he had collapsed briefly in August,
for example) raised fears that his imminent death or incapacitation
would trigger a violent struggle for power.

What happened next continues to be the subject of considerable
controversy among Indonesians. In the early hours of October 1,
1965, six senior generals, including Yani, and an adjutant apparently mistaken for Nasution (who escaped) were seized and taken
to Halim air force base outside Jakarta. They were all killed and
the bodies buried in a disused well. These actions were carried out
by soldiers from the Presidential Guard (a military unit responsible for protecting the president), supplemented by members
of a PKI youth organization. Similar forces took control of the
national radio building, the Presidential Palace, and other key
sites around Merdeka Square. Later that morning, Colonel Untung
of the Presidential Guard announced over national radio that the
"September 30 Movement" (G30S) had foiled a plot by generals
working for the American Central Intelligence Agency (CIA) to
overthrow the government. Untung stated that Sukarno was safe
and that the G30S had taken temporary control. Exactly what the
plotter's intentions were will probably never be known, as their
action was quickly foiled. Within hours, General Soeharto, who
commanded Indonesia's crack troops, the Army Strategic Reserve
(Kostrad), assumed command of the army and mobilized to defeat
the G30S, a task he accomplished in Jakarta by nightfall. The Halim
air base was taken the following day, and G30S forces elsewhere
(mainly in Central Java) were mopped up within days.

PKI was blamed for the plot, and hundreds of thousands of its
members and supporters were killed by the army and its civilian
allies during 1965 and 1966. A similar number were imprisoned for
years without trial, including the well-known author Pramoedya
Ananta Toer. Prominent among those involved in the killings
were *santri* Muslim youth groups. The killings were spurred on by
virulent anti-PKI propaganda, including a ludicrous but widely
believed fabrication alleging that members of the PKI-affiliated
Indonesian Women's Movement (Gerwani) had tortured the generals to death at Halim then mutilated the bodies after engaging in a
frenzied sexual orgy.

The 1965 coup attempt, if such it was, remains one of modern history's great mysteries. Like the opening of a classic "whodunit" mystery, there is little hard evidence and plenty of potential culprits, all with strong motives and the means to act. That a military coup by senior generals was planned for early October, as the G30S claimed, is plausible. If so, or if the leadership believed it to be so, the fact that PKI would attempt a preemptive coup using its supporters in the army is equally plausible. That Sukarno might have initiated or acquiesced to the G30S actions is also credible, either because as he aged he wished to bequeath power to the PKI or simply because he wished to remove the generals who obstructed his policies. It is also possible that (as they claimed) the G30S was a group of staunchly Sukarnoist officers acting on their own initiative. That Soeharto, the ultimate beneficiary, was the true culprit is also possible, as is the claim that the CIA engineered the whole affair, given U.S. interests in a change of regime in Indonesia. All of these theories (and numerous variations) have been advanced, and with the limited available evidence, a good case can be advanced for them all.

The most likely explanation is that the affair was cooked up between Sukarno and a few of his closest confidants, including D.N. Aidit, the leader of PKI. It was intended to be a delicate and limited operation that would allow Sukarno to rid himself of the senior generals who were impeding his political objectives without himself appearing to take the initiative. The operation was not intended to bring PKI to power, at least not immediately, but to create a political environment whereby Sukarno could bequeath power to a like-minded, radical, nationalist regime in due course. The plan was for the G30S group to act, ostensibly without Sukarno's knowledge, out of selfless loyalty to him and devotion to the "higher" duty of the revolution and Indonesia. They would arrest the senior generals deemed disloyal to Sukarno and provide evidence of their complicity in a plot with the CIA to seize power. Sukarno, his hand thus forced, would be obliged to remove the generals, perhaps pending an investigation, in the process naturally selecting replacements more sympathetic to his objectives. Whether in fact the generals were planning an imminent seizure of power may never be known. But it would have been extraordinary if they did not at least have a contingency plan to do so in the event of Sukarno's sudden death or incapacitation. After all, there was no vice president (Hatta had not been replaced) and no clear constitutional process for succession. If this were the plan, then the overzealous behavior of those responsible for arresting the generals sent it awry, but the actions of Soeharto were what made it unsalvageable.

That Soeharto was both blissfully unaware of the plots (as he claimed) and fortuitously left off the list of generals to be arrested is difficult to believe. He was one of the most senior generals and, as Kostrad commander, had at his disposal Indonesia's elite troops, the best-equipped and most combat-ready troops in the capital. The claim made by one of the key G30S plotters, Lieutenant Colonel Latief, an old comrade of Soeharto, both at his defense trial and upon his release from prison after Soeharto's fall, provides a plausible explanation.[3] Latief maintains that, acting on behalf of the G30S plotters, he made Soeharto aware of their plans to secure his acquiescence. Soeharto, according to Latief, agreed to remain neutral but then took advantage of his unique position. He allowed the G30S actions to go ahead, which rid him of his rivals for command of the army. He then used the superior military forces at his disposal to crush the G30S and was able to pose as Indonesia's savior in the process.

Without the emergence of more incontrovertible evidence, it is impossible to be certain if this interpretation is correct or if some other account is to be preferred. Nevertheless, the historical consequences are clear. The G30S affair and the subsequent destruction of PKI and the overthrow of Sukarno ended Indonesia's leftward drift decisively and ushered in the long-running regime of Soeharto.

NOTES

1. Sukarno, "Let Us Bury the Parties," in *Indonesian Political Thinking 1945–1965*, ed. Herbert Feith and Lance Castles (Ithaca: Cornell University Press, 1970).

2. Mohammad Hatta, "A Dictatorship Supported by Certain Groups," in *Indonesian Political Thinking*, Feith and Castles.

3. Latief's trial did not take place until 1978, and none of the key details of his account were published in the Indonesian press at the time. See W. F. Wertheim, "Whose Plot?—New Light on the 1965 Events," *Journal of Contemporary Asia* 19 (1979), pp. 208–209.

5

The Soeharto Era
(1966–1998)

Having risen to power in the wake of the G30S affair, Soeharto remained at the apex of Indonesian politics for over three decades. The regime he constructed, known as the "new order," ushered in an era of economic development and modernization lauded by many as one of Asia's most profound economic miracles. Others, while acknowledging that economic development and social stability experienced during the new order brought many benefits to Indonesia, have criticized the regime on several grounds, not least for the stifling and repressive political environment it maintained. Until the Asian economic crisis of 1997–1998 brought Indonesia's long boom to a shuddering halt, perhaps most observers, including most Indonesians, pardoned the new order for its failings and excesses as the price to be paid for economic development and political stability.

SOEHARTO CONSOLIDATES POWER

The new order represented a sudden and far-reaching alteration of political and economic policy direction for Indonesia. Significant policy changes were made within months of the G30S events, signaling an unmistakable shift in the locus of political power from the left to the right. Nowhere was this shift more apparent than in the realm of international relations as Indonesia abandoned its hyperradical, nonaligned posture. (Indonesia under Sukarno proclaimed itself to be the champion of the "new emerging forces," beholden neither to Moscow nor Washington. Indeed Sukarno declared these "old forces" to be of declining historical relevance.) Indonesia rejoined the UN and the IMF, ended Confrontation with Malaysia, and broke off diplomatic relations with China. Indonesia was also one of the founding members of the Association of Southeast Asian Nations (ASEAN), initially a grouping that emphasized its anticommunist posture. While maintaining its active membership of the nonaligned movement, Indonesia had effectively become a Washington ally in the Cold War. Similarly dramatic was Indonesia's new economic policy, also oriented firmly toward the West and market capitalism. The extent and speed of these shifts, implemented or begun during 1966 and 1967, has often disguised the degree to which Soeharto's new-order prospects hung in the balance at the outset.

In retrospect, we can see that the G30S affair provided the stepping-stone to power for Soeharto, but in its immediate aftermath and for several months afterward, this eventuality was far from a foregone conclusion. For several months, there was a real struggle for power with a weakened but still formidable Sukarno. There were also potential rivals to Soeharto among the surviving senior officers, and there were other visions contending to construct a new order according to their own ideas. That Soeharto did come to power and proved able to stamp his personality and preferences so firmly on the new order can now be seen as largely attributable to his deft political skills. At the time and for long afterward, the degree to which Soeharto manipulated the circumstances and forces that pertained in the late 1960s was under appreciated. This perception was aided by the fact that Soeharto before 1965 was not a prominent political figure; indeed, his reputation was that of a competent career soldier lacking personal political ambition and strong political views. This image was perpetuated throughout 1965–67 by his seeming reluctance at every point to take the necessary next step in his progress to power until compelled by circumstance and his sense of duty. Yet for all the feigned reluctance, his every step was decisive and there were no missteps. It was only as the years (and then the decades) of his presidency passed and his power grew to unprecedented proportions that the extent of Soeharto's political skills became widely recognized. It is now clear that the successful camouflage of his political acumen was a vital and intrinsic dimension of his political armory.

Sukarno proved powerless to halt PKI's destruction but nevertheless clung to the presidency for a further 18 months. Without PKI, Sukarno's political position was much weaker than before, a weakness compounded by suspicions that he was involved in the G30S plot, which alienated a broad range of erstwhile supporters, military and civilian alike. Sukarno's position was also weakened by Soeharto's control of the army. Before, Sukarno had usually been able to bend the army to his will through exploiting divisions and through browbeating or charming its commanders. But Soeharto's grip on the army was greater than that of any of his predecessors, and he worked assiduously to consolidate it throughout this period. Suspect regiments were transferred or purged, as were leftist or Sukarnoist officers. Some of the latter were eased into lucrative and honorable retirements as ambassadors or businessmen. Soeharto loyalists were promoted and moved into strategic posts. Moreover, Soeharto was not intimidated by Sukarno and was immune to Sukarno's blandishments. Nevertheless, Sukarno retained a considerable bank of political capital. He was still popular in some quarters and commanded considerable respect as the president and proclaimer of independence, even among many of his critics. Therefore, Soeharto could not immediately move against Sukarno; indeed, after the initial shock, Sukarno appeared to be reestablishing his authority in early 1966.

Soeharto's strategic sense had not deserted him. Coolly he bided his time and allowed Sukarno to overreach himself by making a number of provocative statements and cabinet appointments. These actions galvanized Sukarno's opponents and energized the anti-Sukarno student movement. With quiet support from army forces loyal to Soeharto, these students launched a series of unruly demonstrations in the capital that created the impression of disorder and chaos. Pressure on Sukarno was increased by crack pro-Soeharto troops moving on the Presidential Palace during a cabinet meeting on March 11, 1966. Probably the objective was to arrest the leftist ministers. Hearing of their approach, Sukarno was sufficiently unnerved to flee by helicopter to his presidential retreat at Bogor in the mountains south of Jakarta. There, a few hours later, he was visited by three generals, emissaries of Soeharto, who persuaded

Sukarno to sign a document known as the March 11 Order authorizing Soeharto to take all necessary measures to restore security. Despite Sukarno's, protests Soeharto treated this document as if it were a transfer of power and relegated Sukarno to a figurehead president. Troops loyal to Soeharto curtailed Sukarno's movements, controlled his communications, and vetted his visitors. Sukarno was not astute enough (or was too proud) to accept this political setback and await an opportunity to recover some ground. On the contrary, he continued to play into Soeharto's hands by making more provocative statements (such as defending PKI) at every opportunity. Combined with revelations from show trials of G30S figures convened by Soeharto in late 1966 that seemed to implicate Sukarno, the effect was to further alienate the middle ground and to stiffen the resolve of Sukarno's enemies. Ultimately, a stacked MPRS emergency session removed Sukarno from the presidency and anointed Soeharto acting president in March 1967. Kept under house arrest and allowed few visitors, Sukarno died in June 1970.

CONSTRUCTION OF THE NEW ORDER

In addition to the army, many other political forces felt they had contributed to the overthrow of Sukarno and were keen to assume a significant political place in the post-Sukarno era. Prominent among them was a broad spectrum of student and youth groups and the "parent" organizations to which they were affiliated (often loosely), such as Muhammadiyah, NU, PSII, the Catholic Party, and PNI's right wing, as well as the outlawed PSI, Masyumi, and Murba. Precisely what these civilian organizations each envisioned for the new order varied enormously, but it was widely assumed that the destruction of Sukarno's "old order" would result in a return to democracy. The most deluded believed the army would quickly retire from the political scene, once it had established security, and hand power over to the civilians. Others accepted that the process might take some time and would likely involve the army governing in partnership with the parties until security was assured and the worst of the economic mess and corruption cleaned up. While avoiding specific commitments, Soeharto encouraged these optimistic assessments. They were not entirely baseless, as many of Soeharto's supporters within the army were genuinely committed to an eventual restoration of some form of democracy, or at least to the construction of a much more open political system than that which Soeharto went on to create.

Promises of a general election were made as early as 1966, but various pretexts were employed to delay it until June 1971. This allowed Soeharto and the group around him time to consolidate their grip on the army and the machinery of government and to create the circumstances whereby the election result would confirm them in power. To these ends, an ingenious political system was constructed, one that included the appearance of a genuine electoral process while ensuring that the regime could be the only winner. A key feature was a generous proportion of reserved DPR and MPR seats to be filled principally by members of the army and other presidential appointees. These arrangements would provide the army with a significant, ongoing place in the political process, something most pro–new order civilian politicians could accept. Their acceptance was predicated on the assumption that, since a majority of seats remained open for electoral contest between the (approved) political parties, a considerable degree of democracy was preserved. Accordingly, right up until the election, most political party leaders were convinced that the outcome would be an army-civilian governing partnership. Even when, as the election date approached, it seemed that the army intended to dominate the imagined partnership, the principal concern of the party leaders shifted to merely seeking to ensure that their party would be the one chosen as the army's subordinate partner.

In fact, the Soeharto group had no intentions of sharing power with anyone. Also contesting the election was a new party created by Soeharto army loyalists called Golongan Karya (Functional Groups/ Golkar). Golkar comprised the nation's permitted functional groups, all of which were quickly brought under army control. Crucially, Golkar also came to include all civil servants, eventually right down to the lowest village officials, a factor that gave Golkar enormous political and economic leverage. Golkar's leadership was imposed from above, consisting of committed Soeharto loyalists; thus, primarily it represented the interests of the regime rather than those of the functional groups' members. Using the tight grip that the regime had acquired over the security forces and the machinery of state, massive pressure and inducement were brought to bear to generate a large vote for Golkar while the other parties were hampered and their leaders intimidated. The outcome, which shocked the other party leaders together with most observers, was an emphatic victory for Golkar with 62.8 percent of the vote, leaving the other parties to share just over a third of the votes among them. NU did the best with 18.7 percent, while the once-mighty PNI received less than 7 percent. When Golkar's elected representatives in DPR and MPR were added to the appointed members, the Soeharto regime had a massive majority of 82 percent in the MPR and 73 percent in the DPR.

Its legitimacy and political power enhanced, however dubiously, by the election victory, the Soeharto regime set about completing its political system. The political parties represented the principal unfinished business in this regard. A start had been made with the army's intervention into PNI's affairs at its April 1966 congress, which ensured that the party's right-wing faction gained control. Masyumi represented more of a challenge, although the outcome was the same. Supporters of Masyumi expected it would be restored immediately to legality after Sukarno's removal from power. Soeharto did release Masyumi's leaders from jail in the middle of 1966 but resisted calls for Masyumi's rehabilitation. Eventually in February 1968 he allowed the creation of a new party, Parmusi, to replace Masyumi, but on the condition that the government vet the Parmusi leadership to ensure that it comprised only acceptable figures, a category that excluded all of the former Masyumi leaders. When, despite these precautions, Parmusi began to show an unexpected independent streak overly reminiscent of Masyumi, regime loyalists planted within the Parmusi leadership engineered an internal party coup in October 1970. The government then stepped in and foisted a new leadership on Parmusi, after which Parmusi became the tamest of all the parties. Similar but less-successful intervention took place in NU in this period; indeed, government meddling in the internal affairs of political parties to ensure compliant leaderships remained a hallmark of the new order.

The regime had demonstrated its determination and capacity to limit the political independence of political parties and equally its capacity to ensure itself a handsome election victory. But these measures had required enormous effort, and clearly the parties remained an irritant that was likely to recur. Several parties still proved troublesome. NU had demonstrated its resilience by obtaining a vote marginally better than its result in 1955 despite the government's pressure. PSII, weak and internally divided, was nevertheless anything but malleable, and even the purged PNI had campaigned with unexpected vigor. The problem at its heart was that the parties, despite their venality and top-down approach, did each have a genuine base in society. In this light, some voices within the regime proposed banning all the parties, leaving Golkar as the sole political party and thereby transforming Indonesia into a one-party state. Such a drastic step would not have sat well with the outside world, however, and ran the risk of increased civilian resistance. Instead, a lesser measure was implemented, one that nevertheless increased the regime's grip while preserving a democratic appearance. The parties were forced in January 1973 to amalgamate into two new parties: the Islam-based parties were obliged to merge and become the United Development Party (PPP), and the rest were obliged to merge as the Indonesian Democratic Party (PDI). The parties were thereby effectively robbed of their particular identities and condemned to endless additional faction fighting, both factors likely to further weaken their limited electoral prospects.

This system, dubbed "Pancasila democracy," functioned very effectively. PDI and PPP constituted a safety valve for oppositional pressures, and their participation in the regular elections provided the new order with a credible democratic facade. National elections took place in 1977, 1982, 1987, 1992, and 1997 and never threatened Soeharto's grip on power. Golkar's vote ranged between 62 and 74 percent, PPP's best result was 29.3 percent, and PDI's best was 14.9 percent. MPR dutifully endorsed Soeharto as president after each election; indeed, a rival candidate never stepped forward. The regime's grip on power was so secure and pervasive that many politicians, including many who had once adopted an oppositional stance, reinvented themselves and joined the Golkar fold. Similarly, many emerging community leaders who might have been expected to pursue politics through another political vehicle, or else to remain outside the formal political process, opted to join Golkar. In this way, over time, Golkar came to incorporate a broader range of social elements, affording them a limited voice in the decision-making process in exchange for their support and with the tacit understanding that they had to limit their aspirations to within bounds acceptable to the regime.

Not only was the political sphere tightly controlled to the regime's advantage, but Indonesian society was also closely monitored. This was achieved through two principal mechanisms. First, the incorporation of functional groups into Golkar automatically ensured that most organized expressions of society were under the regime's control. Thus, for example, there were neither free trade unions nor any independent bodies representing business interests. These and other similar organizations existed (legally) only within Golkar or not at all. Second, tightly linking village and neighborhood government to the state also served to control society. The army's territorial command structure that paralleled the civilian bureaucracy made this especially effective. Thus, the army, whose security role was directed primarily at internal "enemies," monitored all levels of government administration and, in theory at least, was aware of everything that happened even in the smallest communities. Indeed, village officials were charged with keeping elaborate records of village affairs and reporting to the local military authorities. These records included such details as when people left the village or moved into it. Even short-term visitors were obliged to report to village authorities. This more intrusive, supervisory role of the army was justified by the ideology of "dual function," an extension of Nasution's doctrine of the "middle way" alluded to previously in chapter 4. According to the army's new ideology developed in April 1965, it had a dual role, a military role and a sociopolitical role, which took it into the realms of ideology, politics, society, culture, economy, and religion.[1]

The only significant elements of civil society that retained a measure of independence from the state were religious organizations, although they too were subject to scrutiny and were obliged to operate within prescribed boundaries. Anything that smacked of politics on the part of religious organizations was likely to be viewed as inappropriate, and politics was interpreted so broadly by the authorities that the traditional community advocacy role of religious organizations was often perceived in this light. Indicative of the degree to which religious organizations were viewed with suspicion was the measure Soeharto introduced in 1983 obliging all social organizations to nominate the Pancasila as their sole ideological basis. Naturally, this was quite problematic for organizations whose raison d'être was their respective religious beliefs. Ultimately, after considerable agonizing, all the religious organizations managed to concoct a formula of words that satisfied the "sole basis" requirement, while simultaneously reaffirming their particular religious identities. In reality, the measure was largely of symbolic importance only, but thereby it served to underline the regime's expectations of absolute loyalty to the state.

Restriction and control were key aspects of the new-order regime's success; but Soeharto's acute political judgment, which rarely failed him, was perhaps even more important. Indeed, the clever calibration and targeting of the restrictions and control, as well as of the rewards and incentives, was crucial to Soeharto's continuing grip on power. Soeharto well understood that there were political currents that he needed to crush and others that he needed to monitor and constrain. But crucially, he also understood that, among the latter, there were always elements that were prepared to accommodate themselves to his regime in exchange for a little more room to breathe and a minor place at the table of power. He appreciated that in order to benefit from these "accommodationist" tendencies, he needed to make some accommodations in return. He was also flexible enough in his thinking to recognize the value of allowing back "into the fold" those who shifted toward an accommodationist stance. Why force them to remain his enemies? He displayed similar awareness to shifts among his allies and flexibility in his stance toward them.

A good example of this political subtlety on Soeharto's part occurred in the late 1980s and early 1990s. Having asserted the regime's authority over Islamic organizations with the "sole basis" measure, Soeharto found ways to make peace offerings with a number of concessions to rising Islamic sentiments in society. For example, he ended the restriction on Muslim girls wearing the *jilbab* (a Muslim headdress covering the hair) in state schools. Of even more significance, he allowed the creation in 1990 of a new Muslim organization, the All Indonesia Association of Muslim Intellectuals (ICMI). Thereby, an influential pool of opponents and critics, behind which was a swelling social change, were converted into allies. This broadening of Soeharto's base at this juncture was particularly useful because, in tandem with steps to tighten his personal grip on Golkar, he was able to rest more weight on civilian supporters and so needed to rely less on the army. This maneuver significantly increased Soeharto's personal power and authority over the new-order regime.

ECONOMY AND SOCIETY DURING THE NEW ORDER

When the new order came to power, Indonesia's economy was bordering on collapse. Economic growth was either negative or negligible. The government was unable to service its debts (projected foreign exchange earnings for 1966 were less than the scheduled debt repayments),[2] and a massive 63 percent of government expenditure was being financed by deficit, fueling an annual inflation rate of almost 600 percent.[3] Output from the export sector had declined sharply due to neglect, shortage of capital, and lack of expertise, and much of the little that was produced continued to be smuggled abroad, depriving the government of desperately needed revenue. The manufacturing industry, already underdeveloped, technologically antiquated, and producing almost exclusively for the domestic market, had almost come to a standstill. It was simply unable to afford spare parts and essential inputs due to the soaring cost of imports, or else could not procure them due to bottlenecks at the ports caused by a mixture of red tape, corruption, and deteriorating infrastructure. Naturally, these extremely poor economic circumstances were reflected in the poor standard of living. Per capita income declined during the 1960s, and the percentage of the population classified as very poor was 61 percent on Java and 52 percent elsewhere.[4]

Soeharto's government improved Indonesia's economic circumstances remarkably quickly. Following the advice of Indonesia's American-educated economists, dubbed the "technocrats," the government adopted a rigorous, orthodox, economic prescription. Inflation was swiftly brought under control with a balanced budget policy, falling to 15 percent by 1969.[5] A battery of exchange-rate and trade restrictions and other regulations that provided incentives for outer-island smuggling and blocked foreign capital entry were dismantled. Indeed, the new regime operated a very liberal policy toward foreign investment, actively encouraging major investments on extremely favorable terms to international oil and mining companies. Simultaneously, debts were rescheduled and arrangements made for the receipt of significant and ongoing injections of aid funds. Fortuitously, at this juncture came the dramatic rise in the international oil price of the 1970s, providing the government with a massive surge of revenue. Oil exports, joined in the late 1970s by liquefied natural gas exports, have remained a major source of foreign exchange ever since. Partly in response to declining oil and gas prices in the 1980s, the government implemented a further round of liberalizing measures, making for a more diversified economy that was less reliant on oil and gas. The new policies stimulated an export-oriented manufacturing sector in which electronics, clothing, footwear, and woven fabrics were prominent.

Considerable effort was also put into expanding Indonesia's tourism industry. The combination of aid funds and healthy export revenues allowed the government to make massive, badly needed investments in infrastructure, dramatically improving Indonesia's transport, communications, and power networks.

Indonesia's economic growth rate fluctuated during the new order, largely in response to international conditions, but it was usually around a healthy 6–7 percent. But the economy did not only grow impressively; it was also transformed. The proportion of Gross National Product (GNP) contributed by agriculture declined from more than 50 percent at the beginning of the new order to only 19 percent by the early 1990s.[6] Though agriculture still provided around 50 percent of employment, this was down from 73 percent.[7] Similarly, as a proportion of GNP, industry rose from 11 percent to 40 percent, and manufacturing from a tiny 8 percent to 21 percent in the same period.[8] A significant improvement in living standards accompanied the process of growth and transformation. Daily caloric intake per capita rose from 1,816 to 2,605, the proportion of the population that had not attended school dropped from over 68 percent to less than 19 percent, and the proportion of the very poor in Java dropped from 61 percent to 10 percent and outside of Java from 52 percent to 7 percent.[9] Even without statistical indicators such as these, the dramatic increase in general prosperity that occurred during the new order was obvious to any casual observer. Over just two decades, high-rise buildings and freeways transformed city skylines, and a new middle class numbering in the millions, clutching all the latest electronic gadgets, flooded into massive new and glittering shopping malls.

Despite the transformation of the economy and the surge in urbanization, the new order did not ignore the agricultural sector—on the contrary. Indonesia, the world's largest rice importer, became self-sufficient in rice by the middle of the 1980s, despite an 80 percent rise in consumption per capita over roughly the same period.[10] This was achieved through the introduction and heavy subsidization of the much higher-yielding "green revolution" rice varieties, along with the accompanying fertilizers and pesticides, supplemented by significant state investment in irrigation works and other production facilities. From an economic rationalist perspective, the resources devoted to attaining rice self-sufficiency would have been better expended elsewhere. But from a political and welfare perspective, it was an effective and popular achievement, ensuring that the effects of Indonesia's economic prosperity were felt tangibly in rural areas where the bulk of the population still lived. Much less attention was paid to the cash-crop sector, where outcomes accordingly were relatively poor, though with some patchy success with particular products such as palm oil. Nevertheless, many of the long-established cash crops such as rubber, tea, cocoa, coffee, coconuts, cloves, and tobacco continued to be important, many continuing to earn significant but declining proportions of foreign exchange. Other agricultural products were also important during the new order, especially timber and fish, including a rapidly growing fish-farming industry producing prawns and shrimp. But the success of the timber and fishing industries is offset by serious environmental concerns over their operations as well as by fears that grossly excessive rates of extraction mean that these industries are not sustainable. The new rice varieties also involved environmental costs due to the heavy associated use of pesticides and fertilizers.

Frequently, the new order was lauded for its economic record by international development agencies such as the World Bank. But the new-order government did not always follow the orthodox, free-market economic prescriptions promoted by such agencies and Indonesia's technocrats. There remained a powerful attraction to the economic nationalist and state ownership policies associated with the Sukarno era and a widespread distrust of the market and little genuine embrace of capitalism. Such attitudes are deeply ingrained, reaching back at least to the anticolonial movement, when socialist ideas and the idea of cooperatives became popular. Cooperatives remain an important and popular economic mode of organization in Indonesia, although to outside observers, they appear anachronistic and in practice they rarely perform in accordance with the original ideal. The traditional *priyayi* disdain for commercial activity and a widespread Islamic association of capitalism with the West also support the persistence of statist inclinations in Indonesia. It is noticeable that the new order's liberalization measures were not extended to privatization of state companies, as commonly occurred elsewhere in the world in the same period. Instead, there was a de facto compromise. A lot of new, private enterprise was allowed to develop alongside the existing state sector, and there were efforts (not markedly successful) to make the state sector perform more efficiently and to compete with the private sector.

Examples of the new order's economic nationalist inclinations abound. As noted above, the new order's initial approach toward attracting foreign capital was extremely liberal. But when the exigencies of the economic situation eased as oil revenues began filling government coffers, some restrictions on foreign capital were introduced. Only when economic circumstances deteriorated was there a renewed wave of liberal reforms in the 1980s. In the interim, the government also took the opportunity of the oil bonanza to direct revenue toward implementing strategic industrialization policies within the state sector. Many of these endeavors proved to be ill conceived, just as the technocrat detractors had insisted they were. Moreover, there was considerable "leakage" in the form of corruption. The massive squandering associated with the state oil company, Pertamina, in the 1970s is only the most infamous example. Even after Pertamina was reined in and a chastened government adopted the 1980s liberalization reforms, economic nationalist efforts continued, especially projects associated with the influential minister for research and technology, Professor B.J. Habibie. A frequently cited example of Habibie's ill-fated efforts to have Indonesia leapfrog to a higher stage of development was his almost single-handed creation of an Indonesian aircraft industry. This industry proved a classic "white elephant," completely unable to compete in the international arena and thus reliant on generous state subsidies.

In addition to these economic rationalist criticisms of the new order's economic record, several others were frequently voiced, all with some degree of validity. Critics allege that Indonesia's economic success during the new order relied heavily on the overexploitation of nonrenewable resources, such as oil, gas, and timber. It was feared that once these resources ran out Indonesia would be in trouble—that not enough had been done to promote diversification away from reliance on these few high export-earning products. Other critics expressed concerns with regard to the high level of indebtedness, fearful that it left Indonesia vulnerable if the capacity to service such debts should suddenly decline.

Another persistent criticism was related to the distribution of the economic benefits. Some regions of Indonesia did not benefit as much as others; in particular, eastern Indonesia seemed to have been left behind. Clearly also some people benefited much more than others. Critics claimed that far too much of the benefit was confined to a tiny, super-rich elite, while the mass of the population only benefited marginally. In this context, the degree to which the Soeharto family and friends were able to become dominant economic players was often cited. There was often a racist dimension to such distribution complaints. A significant proportion of the conglomerates that came to dominate the private sector were owned by Chinese Indonesians, often in partnership with members of the Soeharto family or with other politically powerful indigenous Indonesians. Finally, a related criticism was that, however impressive the new order's economic record, its rampant corruption and nepotism and the related market distortions meant that the possibility of even more impressive progress was squandered.

Social changes during the new order were no less rapid and far reaching than the economic. Although still a small minority, the proportion of Christians in the population rose from 7.39 percent in 1971 to 8.92 percent in 2000, compared with a much smaller rise (proportionally) to 88.22 percent from 87.51 percent for Muslims over the same period.[11] The explanation lies only partly in a higher population growth rate for Christians. It is also attributable to a much greater proportion of people with no official religion, living mainly in Papua and Kalimantan, converting to Christianity rather than to Islam.[12] This trend, which was often rumored to be much greater, is partly responsible for a heightened sense of animosity toward Christians among some Muslims. But far overshadowing this trend was a major shift among Muslims toward *santri* forms of Islam and toward overt expressions of Islamic practice. The number of mosques rose greatly, mosque attendance increased significantly, and the number of Indonesian Muslims performing the *haj* and wearing traditional Islamic dress increased greatly. These changes seemed most apparent among young Muslims who were exposed to religious education to a much greater extent than before. This was due to a combination of factors. As young people entered the state education system in much greater numbers and stayed much longer than before, then automatically more of them encountered qualified religious instruction. The expansion of State Institutes for Islamic Studies (IAIN) operated by the Department of Religious Affairs was an important element in fostering this trend, as was the heavy emphasis on *dakwah* (proselytizing) activities that many modernist Muslims associated with Masyumi turned to when their political activities were blocked. But to a large extent, this "Islamization" phenomenon in Indonesia was simply the local manifestation of a phenomenon that has been taking place throughout the Muslim world. The new-order regime, although wary of political manifestations of Islam, was not at all averse to these religious developments; indeed, the state devoted considerable resources to support the building of mosques and other Islamic religious activities.

For women, the Soeharto era was a mixed experience. There were significant changes in the lives of Indonesian women during this period, not always as a direct consequence of government policies. In political terms, the new order quite deliberately sought to restrict the capacity of women to organize independently in pursuit of their interests. It also actively sought to reinforce what it conceived to be traditional gender roles, including an emphasis on women as mothers and wives. In fact, historically, women in Indonesia generally enjoyed a high status with quite varied social and economic roles, including important roles in farming and trade. Under the new order, however, women were corralled into official organizations such as the Family Welfare Movement (PKK) and Dharma Wanita, an organization for the wives of civil servants in which leadership and status mirrored that of their husbands. On the other hand, the new order showed no inclination to restrict women's social roles to the degree desired by some Islamic organizations. Nor did the government's interpretation of traditional gender roles exclude women from the public sphere, including participation in the economy, education, and even politics, although it remained more difficult for women than men to participate in such fields. Class, of course, continued to affect the degree to which women could overcome obstacles to their participation in the public sphere and shaped the kinds of choices open to them. Nevertheless, in general terms, economic prosperity, modernization, and the expansion of education and health facilities under the new order indirectly contributed to a number of positive developments in women's lives and to the gradual expansion of their range of options.

Thus, overall, the gap between males and females in educational achievements narrowed appreciably during the new order, especially at primary and secondary levels of schooling. More than 20 percent of females completed secondary school in 1990 compared with just over 29 percent for males, while the comparable figures for primary school were 28.1 percent and 32.2 percent.[13] The gap remained widest at the furthest ends of the spectrum of educational attainment: in 1990, there were twice as many males (2.1%) as females (1.0%) with a tertiary education and twice as many females (25.4%) as males (12.2%) who had received no schooling at all. In absolute terms, however, these figures still represent significant improvements. In 1961, almost 80 percent of females had received no schooling, and women with tertiary qualifications were almost nonexistent. Similarly, civil service remained male dominated, but the proportion of males declined from almost 82 percent to less than 67 percent between 1975 and 1992.[14] It is noticeable, however, that the proportion of males in the senior ranks barely declined in the same period, from 91 percent to 89 percent.

A good example of how new-order policies had a mixed impact on women is provided by the government's highly successful family planning program. The campaign involved encouraging people to marry later (in their midtwenties) and to use contraception (which the government subsidized) to restrict the number of children to two per couple. While women continued to bear primary child-care responsibilities, having fewer children and having them later provided them with more time to pursue other activities as well as reduced the incidence of adverse health problems associated with pregnancy and birth. Similarly, the prominent role women played in the campaign, while on the one hand reinforcing stereotypical gender roles, also empowered women in their communities and provided avenues whereby other issues of concern to women could be pursued.

OPPOSITION TO THE SOEHARTO REGIME

Despite the Soeharto regime's tight grip on power and the high risks involved, there was always opposition. It took various forms and had a variety of goals, ranging from reform to revolution, and included those who merely wanted to take Soeharto's place.

Among those disappointed by the new order were members of the student movement that had campaigned so vigorously against PKI and Sukarno. The continuing corruption, the apparent lack of progress in social welfare, and the lack of democracy quickly disillusioned many students. Even before Sukarno had been removed from the presidency, they were dealt a harsh lesson in the limits to their freedom of political action when a student demonstration was dispersed violently by Soeharto's troops in October 1966. Although student demonstrations over issues such as corruption continued, they were increasingly met with force and their message received with indifference or irritation. The last major action of the early new-order student generation came in January 1974 with mass protests that degenerated into riots, the so-called Malari affair (an acronym meaning *January disaster*). The occasion for the protests was the visit by the Japanese prime minister, Tanaka Kakuei. The grievance was the flood of Japanese capital and products into Indonesia that offended Indonesian economic nationalist sentiments. Memories of the harsh Japanese occupation of Indonesia during World War II were still fresh enough to add to the resentment. To a large extent, however, this issue was merely the convenient focus for a number of connected popular grievances that the student demonstrators and urban rioters expressed. The fruits of the orthodox economic policy were not yet apparent, while the costs to small-scale indigenous business interests were obvious, as was the rampant corruption of those in government positions. The government responded by cracking down harshly, discarding the last shreds of the formerly close relationship it had fostered with the student movement.

Student protest actions continued spasmodically throughout the new order, despite meeting frequently with harsh repression, including arrests and occasional long jail terms as well as beatings and occasional deaths and "disappearances." Students and other social activists often associated with various nongovernment organizations protested over issues such as political censorship and corruption but particularly over cases of social injustice perpetrated against the poor and powerless. A common issue was land appropriations in the name of development, all too frequently with little or no compensation reaching those dispossessed. But after 1974, there were no protests on the scale of the Malari affair until 1996.

Another kind of opposition to Soeharto also manifested itself during the Malari affair. The facts remain elusive, but it seems that General Soemitro, then head of Kopkamtib (Operational Command for the Restoration of Security and Order) attempted to ride the popular dissent to power. If so, his maneuvering was unsuccessful and he was relieved of his command. Soeharto himself took control of Kopkamtib. From that point on, Soeharto was careful to ensure that all positions from which it might be possible to launch a coup against him were occupied by people whose loyalty to him was unquestioned. For example, his son-in-law General Prabowo Subianto was made deputy commander of Kopassus (Special Forces) in 1983 and its commander in 1995. Similarly, Soeharto often promoted to such positions those who would be unable to move against him even if they were tempted to do so, such as General L. B. (Benny) Murdani, who was made commander of the army in 1983. As a Catholic, Murdani could never aspire to the presidency.

Soemitro was not the only opposition to emerge from within the new-order elite. A number of other senior officers prominent in establishing the new order either fell out of favor or became disillusioned with Soeharto's rule. Some became "outside" critics quite quickly, unhappy with the level of corruption and the degree to which the regime maintained its authoritarian posture. Others moved to a similar position much later, apparently having accepted a need for continuing tight control for an extended period but not indefinitely. Some who shifted to an oppositional posture felt that the nature of the regime had changed, becoming increasingly personalized around Soeharto and increasingly corrupt, with Soeharto's family notorious in this regard. An important manifestation of such disgruntled former insiders was a group known as the Petition of Fifty, which included such former new-order luminaries as Nasution and Ali Sadikin, the former Jakarta governor, as well as a number of prominent intellectuals and former politicians such as Natsir. Signed in May 1980, the petition protested the degree to which the army had become a tool of the regime rather than being politically neutral. Most famously, it also accused Soeharto of misusing the Pancasila by insisting on his interpretation over all others. The Petition of Fifty group continued to issue similar complaints throughout the remainder of the new order and to meet in defiance of the regime to discuss political issues. Although members of the group experienced varying degrees of "payback," their stature, both domestically and internationally, provided them with a degree of protection enjoyed by very few other regime opponents. Although never a serious challenge to Soeharto, this group provided an outlet for views and complaints that few others could voice and served as a conduit for the exchange of ideas for reform.

Some Muslim groups were a major source of opposition to the regime, or at least to many of its policies. Many modernist Muslims, particularly those associated with Masyumi, were very disappointed by the new order's stance toward Islam, the more so because they felt that their contribution to the defeat of Sukarno's "old order" had been significant. As Natsir vividly expressed, "we have been treated like cats with ringworm."[15] Essentially, the new-order regime took a stance similar to that of the colonial government, happily endorsing Islamic religious and social activities but barely tolerating any political activity conducted in the name of Islam. Not tolerated at all were any political activities or statements indicating support for an Islamic state, including calls for the restoration of the Jakarta Charter. This attitude partly reflected the regime's composition. It was dominated by senior officers such as Soeharto whose attitude was largely a product of their bitter experiences combating Darul Islam and other rebellions against the unitary state with an Islamist dimension. Personal religious tastes were probably also a factor as many key regime figures practiced an *abangan* form of Islam. Soeharto himself was attracted to *kebatinan,* before apparently becoming more *santri* in the 1990s, a shift marked by performing the *haj* in 1991. Moreover, many senior generals were Christians, a factor that no doubt stiffened the government's approach with respect to Islamist tendencies as much as it caused consternation among *santri* Muslims who saw the early new order as overly Christian influenced.

A small minority of Islamist militants was prepared to use violence against the regime and those whom they regarded as enemies. In the early new order period, there were numerous arson attacks against churches, and in March 1981, Islamist extremists hijacked a Garuda (Indonesia's national airline) flight. All except one of the hijackers were killed when Indonesian commandos stormed the aircraft. Then, in 1984–85, a renewed wave of bombings and arson attacks occurred, largely in response to the September 1984 shooting of dozens of Muslim demonstrators in the Jakarta port district of Tanjung Priok. Details still remain murky concerning this affair, but key issues raised by the demonstrators were the Pancasila "sole principle" issue and the corruption and collusion intrinsic to the business practices of those favored by the regime, for which they mainly blamed wealthy Chinese. For much of the extremist activity, the regime blamed a shadowy group called Komando Jihad that it claimed to have discovered in 1977 (somewhat conveniently just before the 1977 elections). As always, the government response was to crack down firmly, arresting large numbers of suspected Islamist activists on each occasion. The government also took the opportunity to implicate some of its other enemies in these extremist actions, including a prominent signatory of the Petition of Fifty, Lieutenant General Hartono Dharsono, a former commander of the Siliwangi Division and former secretary general of ASEAN. Dharsono was jailed for seven years for his alleged involvement. Such blatant political opportunism led many to suspect that the regime itself was behind much of the violence perpetrated in the name of Islam, either directly through shadowy security agencies or through agent provocateurs.

The overwhelming majority of *santri* Muslims who were involved in political activity against the new order never resorted to violence of course. Nor was their opposition always ineffectual. For example, measures proposed by the government in 1973 (a secular marriage law and recognition of *kebatinan* as a religion) were abandoned due to the vehemence of *santri* opposition. Also, of some surprise to regime strategists was the degree to which PPP managed to win a significant vote in the 1977 and 1982 elections despite the handicaps the regime had placed upon it. But PPP's strong showing, together with the persistence of occasional militant Islamist actions, only served to reinforce the regime's hard-line stance toward all Islamist political activity at this juncture. In turn, this prompted most mainstream *santri* leaders to shift toward a less confrontational stance or to seek alternative means to advance their interests and to oppose the regime in more subtle ways.

Organizations such as Muhammadiyah and NU had always been primarily oriented toward socioreligious activities, and most of the leaders they produced were comfortable with cooperating with the government. NU reinforced this posture in December 1983 when Abdurrahman Wahid (popularly known as Gus Dur) assumed its leadership. Wahid's policy was ostensibly to withdraw NU from politics by ending its institutional membership of PPP and to concentrate on NU's socioreligious activities. Much like Muhammadiyah, however, which despite temptation had never assumed a formal political role, this did not really mean that NU had no further political involvement. What it did mean was that NU as an organization was less subject to state scrutiny, interference, and restriction. Nor was it any longer constrained by the factionalism rampant within PPP. At the same time, NU was still able to exert considerable political influence (perhaps paradoxically even more than before) because Soeharto could not ignore an organization of 35 million members. Nor could PPP or Golkar ignore it since individual members of NU were free to engage in the formal political process, now either in PPP or Golkar, naturally bringing with them the votes of the NU members who supported them when they did so.

SEPARATIST MOVEMENTS DURING THE NEW ORDER

From its inception, Indonesia has been plagued by armed insurgencies fighting to achieve independence for those parts of Indonesia where a strong sense of separate national identity exists. Usually this sentiment is linked to a powerful sense of economic grievance derived from a perception that the fruits of economic development largely flow toward Java and that "outsiders" are the primary beneficiaries of the region's wealth. The new-order government was confronted by three such separatist insurgencies in Papua, East Timor, and Aceh.

In accordance with the settlement achieved in 1962, Jakarta administered Papua from May 1963, but the territory's inclusion in Indonesia required confirmation through an "act of free choice." In reality, the Papuans were given no choice. Instead of a free and fair general referendum, the Indonesian authorities selected 1,022 community leaders in September 1969 and with Indonesian soldiers looking on asked them to endorse joining Indonesia. Not surprisingly, they obliged, but equally unsurprisingly, many Papuans did not accept this incorporation into Indonesia and, where possible, pursued the goal of independence. Some took up arms as the Free Papua Movement (OPM). With limited resources, hampered by disunity and with very little external sympathy, OPM waged a small-scale, spasmodic, guerrilla campaign against the Indonesian army. The Soeharto regime cracked down hard on all expressions of Papuan independence and launched periodic military operations against OPM. The extremely difficult terrain made eradicating OPM impossible, but the repressive measures ensured that the independence movement made no apparent political progress. Meanwhile, the government's transmigration policy, whereby large numbers of Javanese and other Indonesians were resettled in Papua (named Irian Jaya upon its inclusion in Indonesia), seemed partly designed to block the future possibility of independence by eventually transforming the Papuans into a minority.

Due to a strange quirk of the colonial era the island of Timor was divided between the Netherlands and Portugal, the latter occupying the eastern portion and a small enclave on the northwest coast. With independence, Indonesia inherited the Netherlands' portion (West Timor), but Portugal remained in control of the rest of the island (East Timor). From the Indonesian perspective, the continued existence of a small, European colony surrounded by Indonesian territory was clearly an anomaly eventually to be rectified by the entire island becoming Indonesian. The matter was not considered pressing, however, and little was said on the subject until 1974 when Portugal abruptly began to decolonize. Indonesia was not prepared to accept an independent East Timor and formally annexed the territory in July 1976 after invading in December 1975. Indonesian motives went beyond merely "tidying up" the map. A left-leaning regime had been about to consolidate itself in East Timor, an outcome that was anathema to the new-order regime that had only just destroyed leftist political forces in Indonesia. Probably of more concern, though this was not emphasized publicly, was the possibility that an independent East Timor could encourage separatist sentiments in Indonesia. Largely due to the Cold War context, international protests at Indonesia's actions were relatively muted. Indonesia had recently become a valued de facto Western ally, and the communist victories in Indo-China in 1975 had renewed Western fears of communism in Asia.

It was widely expected that the surprisingly fierce resistance offered by the East Timorese during the Indonesian invasion would not last and that East Timor's incorporation into Indonesia would soon become a fait accompli. But these expectations were not fulfilled. Stubborn resistance continued, including that from a small but effective guerrilla force known as Falantil (Armed Forces of National Liberation of East Timor). Frustrated, the Indonesian army responded with brutal repression and large-scale military sweeps of the island's mountainous terrain, but these measures did not succeed in eradicating the resistance. The Indonesian government's development measures in the areas of health, education, transport, and industry also generally failed to win East Timorese hearts and minds—all the more so because considerable wealth was being siphoned out of East Timor by corrupt officials and generals. In the outside world, meanwhile, the plight of the East Timorese became a significant human rights issue, creating for Indonesia a persistent and irritating diplomatic problem.

Aceh's provincial status and the local autonomy granted it as a "special area" at the end of the 1950s did not long placate the Acehnese, who soon came to view these arrangements as mere window dressing. In the mid-1970s, major oil and gas projects located off the Acehnese coast began to earn significant amounts of foreign exchange. Few of the benefits appeared to be flowing to the Acehnese, either in terms of development funds or the associated economic opportunities that these projects provided. On the contrary, the beneficiaries appeared to be the central government and those individuals, mostly non-Acehnese, in a position to exploit their political connections. It was against this background that Hasan de Tiro proclaimed Acehnese independence in December 1976 and the Movement for Acehnese Independence (GAM) began its struggle. GAM was unable to defeat the Indonesian army but had sufficient support and military capacity to wage a guerrilla campaign. As GAM appeared to be gaining political support, the Indonesian authorities responded with increased levels of repression. In 1990, Aceh was declared a Military Operations Area (DOM), a form of martial law that allowed the army to impose curfews, house-to-house searches, checkpoints, and arbitrary detention. These measures and worse, including torture and summary executions, did not defeat GAM. But they imposed much suffering on the Acehnese, adding to Indonesia's poor human-rights reputation and, ironically, adding to the level of popular support within Aceh for independence.

THE OVERTHROW OF SOEHARTO

By the mid-1990s, the new order seemed an impregnable permanent political fixture. Through a mixture of design and accident, its creators had arrived at a highly successful formula, one that had spanned three decades and delivered Indonesia political stability and unprecedented economic development. No doubt the regime's enduring capacity to manage and, where necessary, crush political dissent had much to do with its longevity and air of solidity, but two other factors were equally important. First, great wealth was certainly channeled into the hands of the country's tiny elite, but many more people further down the social scale also enjoyed tangible benefits. The millions of people who joined Indonesia's middle class during the new-order decades were obvious beneficiaries, but many ordinary people also found reasons to support or at least tolerate the regime that represented stability and order as well as gradual material improvements in their lives. As noted above, there were always regime opponents who worked, insofar as they could, for its removal or radical reform. But the lack of widespread and strongly felt discontent was probably a greater obstacle to their efforts than the fear inspired by the regime's repressive capabilities.

Second, another impediment lay in a different fear; fear not of the regime but of what might replace it. The dissatisfaction with the new order felt by many *santri* Muslims was tempered, particularly in the 1960s and 1970s, by the bulwark it constituted against communism or other radical secular political forces that might emerge. Others opposed to the left, including many with aspirations for a more democratic Indonesia, were comforted by similar rationalizations. For Christians, Hindus, and Buddhists, the new order for all its deficiencies was tolerated because it provided a firm barrier to their worst nightmare: an Islamic state of Indonesia. This sentiment was shared with only a little less vehemence by many *abangan* Muslims. There was also a general fear of the chaos and violence that could accompany any regime change. Conceivably, matters could get out of hand to the point of national disintegration or a civil war. Such fears were given credence by the collective national trauma associated with the events of 1965–66, which provided a powerful disincentive to support far-reaching political change. There was also an understandable aversion to risking the current prosperity, again a fear underlined by recent historical memories. The new order played very effectively on such fears to bolster its legitimacy and to deflect calls for change.

Also by the mid-1990s, however, the pressures for change were growing significantly. There was a new international context in which the new order, with its authoritarian controls and rampant corruption, seemed increasingly out of step. The Cold War was over, and democratic reforms were taking place around the world, including in regional neighbors Thailand, the Philippines, Taiwan, and South Korea. In this light, Indonesians were becoming increasingly impatient for a similar reform process and less fearful of the prospect of change, especially as the proportion of young people with higher levels of education and awareness of the outside world rose. Against this background, a new generation of activists, students, women, labor, and the rural land-poor rose to push for change and human rights. Less affected by the trauma of the past, and conscious that their aspirations were part of the global political trend, they pressed forward with growing confidence despite the beatings, arrests, heavy jail terms, and occasional brutal deaths that they risked.

Nevertheless, there still seemed no reason to expect the new order's imminent demise. On the contrary, most observers expected that it would be perpetuated long beyond Soeharto, perhaps evolving into a somewhat more open and less personalized political system after his passing. Only in retrospect can it be seen that the regime contained the seeds of its own demise. Among other problems, it turned out that effecting the transition from Soeharto to another leader posed far more difficulties than had been realized. This was a consequence of the extraordinary degree to which the regime in its later years became embodied in Soeharto, accompanied by weakness in its institutions of governance. It was difficult to conceive of any potential successor commanding the degree of personal authority possessed by Soeharto necessary to inherit all the levers and threads of power unchallenged. And with the other institutions of government so weak, no smooth transitional mechanism existed. Naturally, this situation suited Soeharto because it enhanced the security of his own political position, but it posed a collective threat to the ruling elite and to the system's viability after Soeharto. The personalized rule of an aging Soeharto brought a related problem. The sense that he had been in power too long was palpable by the early 1990s, giving added impetus to the growing desire for change. That Soeharto stubbornly turned his back on reform after flirting briefly with the possibility in 1990–91 added to the growing frustration with his rule. Unwittingly perhaps, Soeharto had begun to fritter away the grudging goodwill he had accrued from his regime's achievements by staying too long, by blocking change, and by failing to prepare for a succession.

A manifestation of the growing aspiration for change and the first clear sign that the old methods of control were losing their effectiveness came in 1996 when the regime intervened in PDI. Much to the chagrin of Soeharto, Megawati Sukarnoputri had ascended to the PDI leadership. In symbolic terms, as the daughter of Sukarno, this was a personal challenge to Soeharto that captured too much of the popular imagination for his liking. As PDI leader, Megawati said and did little, but this only encouraged the projection onto her of myriad aspirations for reform. Soeharto feared that her campaign during the looming 1997 elections would provide a platform for an unprecedented demonstration of mass discontent. It was likely that PDI campaign rallies would draw massive and enthusiastic crowds and that the PDI vote would rise, phenomena that would at the very least be highly embarrassing for Soeharto and could potentially undermine his grip on power. The usual remedy was employed. Pressure was brought to bear on the PDI leadership to oust Megawati and replace her with former leader, Soerjadi. But Megawati refused to concede the legitimacy of her defeat, and her supporters occupied the PDI headquarters in Jakarta. The site became an instant pole of attraction for all the regime's opponents, a permanent rolling demonstration and space for free speech. The remedy having produced the opposite to the desired effect, the regime turned to another familiar and more drastic cure. Hired thugs and soldiers out of uniform posing as PDI members besieged and stormed the building. In the process, the building was destroyed by fire and many of the occupants were killed. But again, this did not produce the desired effect. These actions provoked an unprecedented level of outrage that erupted into several days of rioting and demonstrations on such a scale that it took several days to restore order.

The repercussions from the clumsy PDI intervention continued to be felt. The May 1997 elections were won handsomely by Golkar, but this outcome met with great skepticism under the circumstances. Another indication of the regime's loosening grip was provided by the campaign period. It was marred by violence, and there was an embarrassing absence of enthusiasm at Golkar rallies. In sharp contrast, the atmosphere at PPP rallies was buoyant as many of Megawati's young PDI supporters attended and fraternized ostentatiously with their PPP counterparts. This was not supposed to happen. The Islamist PPP and the secular nationalist-Christian PDI occupied opposite ends of the legal political spectrum. Their mutual antipathy was supposed to ensure that the opposition to Golkar was perpetually weak and divided. The pitiful PDI showing (only 2.6% of the vote) further drove home the message that there was a shift in the wind. Megawati's call for PDI supporters to boycott voting for PDI in protest over her ousting from the leadership was effective, proving that the overwhelming majority of PDI voters supported her. The cumulative effect of these events demonstrated a shift in the national mood away from the grudging acquiescence that had prevailed for so long and toward growing and more defiant expressions of the desire for change. Nevertheless, the Soeharto regime still seemed in firm control. But at this juncture, in the middle of 1997, dramatic external events provided the catalyst that set in motion the regime's dramatic collapse several months later.

In tandem with many other countries in Asia, Indonesia had been experiencing a surging economy for several years, fueled by an apparently endless flow of cheap foreign capital. Then came the Asian economic crisis. Beginning in Thailand in July 1997, it quickly spread around the region as spooked investors suddenly began withdrawing their capital from most Asian countries, in the process dramatically reducing the currency values and thereby drastically undermining the economies of the countries concerned. Indonesia was one of the worst affected. In June 1997, the rupiah was trading at 2,400 to US$1. As the crisis bit, the rupiah began to slide, dropping to Rp 17,000 to US$1 at its lowest point in January 1998. This was an economic crisis of major proportions. Thousands of businesses failed or suspended operations, millions lost their jobs, and all the social indices associated with poverty that had been falling steadily for decades rose significantly. The government floundered for a solution, appearing inept, incapable, and utterly venal as those in and close to power appeared concerned only with securing their own wealth from the unfolding catastrophe. The regime's legitimacy, founded above all on the economic prosperity it had delivered, ebbed away as the months passed with no end to the crisis in sight.

Discontent rose sharply, expressed through episodes of violent social disorder and frequent political protests. Ineffectual repression targeted primarily at the political protests seemed to be the regime's only response. A consensus began to grow that the visibly ailing Soeharto could not solve the crisis, even that he posed a major obstacle to its solution, giving rise to hopes that he would bow to the inevitable and not seek another presidential term at the MPR session in March 1998. But Soeharto dashed these hopes and had himself sworn in for a seventh term. Indeed, he signaled his intentions to preserve his position and that of his family and friends above all other considerations by having Habibie sworn in as vice president, a man who had long been treated as if he were Soeharto's adopted son. Soeharto also named a cabinet bereft of even the usual sprinkling of moderate reformers and respected figures; instead, it consisted of only his closest cronies. In response, protests spearheaded by the students escalated and began to receive more open support from several established political figures. Prominent among the latter was Amien Rais, the former leader of Muhammadiyah. Then, on May 4, controversial price increases, part of the painful remedy insisted upon by the IMF in exchange for economic assistance, came into force, prompting a renewed round of popular protests. At one such protest at the elite Trisakti University in Jakarta, army snipers shot dead several students. It appears that regime insiders ordered this action with the intention of provoking more widespread and indiscriminate disorder. This, apparently it was expected, would force the reluctant army leadership to respond with drastic repressive measures, crushing the protests and thereby preserving the Soeharto regime.

If this were the plan, then it proved an abject failure. Certainly, it caused the students to redouble their efforts but did not provoke them to violence; moreover, it greatly increased the general sympathy for their cause. Perhaps most significantly, it proved the last straw for many wavering regime supporters who it seemed did not have the stomach for the blood spilling that the increasingly desperate regime was in danger of provoking. The elite were beginning to come to the conclusion that their interests would be best served by facilitating the peaceful and immediate removal of Soeharto. To ratchet up the pressure on Soeharto, the army looked the other way when several thousand students occupied the parliament building on May 18, 1998, and made no move to oust them. On May 20, the cabinet resigned en masse, and later that evening, army commander (and Soeharto loyalist) General Wiranto visited Soeharto. Presumably, Wiranto reiterated the message that Soeharto had no option but to resign, a message that numerous regime stalwarts and moderate reformers alike had conveyed over the preceding days. Presumably also, certain promises were made with respect to how he and his family would be treated. The following morning in an atmosphere of high drama, Soeharto made a brief statement on national television announcing his resignation. The long-running Soeharto era was over, but did this also mean the end of the new-order regime he had constructed? This would depend on whether the impetus for change could be sustained in conjunction with the degree to which the elite establishment would rally to defend its interests.

NOTES

1. Harold Crouch, *The Army and Politics in Indonesia* (Ithaca: Cornell University Press, 1978), pp. 24–25.

2. Hal Hill, *The Indonesian Economy Since 1966* (Cambridge: Cambridge University Press, 1996), p. 65.

3. Hill, *The Indonesian Economy*, p. 3.

4. Hill, *The Indonesian Economy*, pp. 3–5.

5. Hill, *The Indonesian Economy*, p. 32.

6. Hill, *The Indonesian Economy*, p. 5.

7. Hill, *The Indonesian Economy*, p. 22.

8. Hill, *The Indonesian Economy*, p. 5.

9. Hill, *The Indonesian Economy*, p. 5.

10. Hill, *The Indonesian Economy*, pp. 123–28.

11. Leo Suryadinata et al., *Indonesia's Population: Ethnicity and Religion in a Changing Political Landscape* (Singapore: ISEAS, 2003), p. 105.

12. Suryadinata, *Indonesia's Population*, pp. 105 and 115.

13. These figures, and those cited in the following two sentences, are from a table in Hill, *The Indonesian Economy*, p. 207.

14. Hill, *The Indonesian Economy*, p. 120.

15. Cited in Muhammad Kamal Hassan, *Muslim Intellectual Responses to "New Order" Modernization in Indonesia* (Kuala Lumpur: Dewan Bahasa dan Pustaka Kementerian Pelajaran Malaysia, 1980), p. 122.

6

Indonesia after Soeharto (1998–)

Soeharto's fall from power opened up several possibilities. Most Indonesians, especially those who had struggled against his regime, hoped for an era of democratic reform. But this was by no means a foregone conclusion. Many observers believed that without Soeharto there was a real prospect of Indonesia descending into chaos, perhaps even leading to the country's disintegration or to civil war. Others predicted that the military would assume power, a prospect that was even more likely if the chaos scenario began to unfold. Some wondered just how far the Islamization of Indonesia had proceeded during the preceding decades; perhaps now, an Islamic state of Indonesia would emerge. There was also a distinct possibility that the new-order regime would quickly regain its equilibrium and carry on much as before, making only a few cosmetic concessions to the reformers.

Compounding the difficulty inherent in predicting the likely course of events was the degree of control over Indonesian society that Soeharto's regime had exercised. This control, including decades of political censorship and little freedom of speech, made it difficult to gauge the degree and nature of social change that Indonesia had undergone over the new-order decades and its likely

political consequences. There was clearly some sentiment in favor of
establishing an Islamic state, some in favor of democracy and political
openness, and in some areas a desire to separate from Indonesia. But
no one knew how much support these respective sentiments commanded. Similarly, it was impossible to know whether interreligious
and interethnic frictions would pose a serious threat to Indonesia's
stability if not kept in check through the authoritarian methods the
new order had always maintained were necessary. Church burnings
and related incidents, mainly in East Java in the early nineties, and
the violence perpetrated against Chinese Indonesians in Jakarta and
elsewhere during the overthrow of Soeharto suggested that a potentially serious threat of this nature did exist.

These questions could only answered by the course of events
themselves as various forces maneuvered to impose themselves on
the post-Soeharto era. Time would also tell if those who came to
wield power after Soeharto could deal successfully with Indonesia's
many pressing problems. The biggest problem was the economic
crisis, but interethnic and interreligious conflict and separatist insurgencies were also prominent, as was the construction of a new political system if reform was to be pursued.

THE HABIBIE PRESIDENCY

In accordance with the constitution, following Soeharto's resignation, Vice President Habibie was sworn in immediately as
president. This was the first time in Indonesia's history in which
a regime change was effected through due constitutional process,
surprising many observers and not only those who were expecting
an army takeover if Soeharto was toppled. Because Habibie was
unpopular and commanded little support from key power brokers,
there had seemed little prospect that the constitutional process
would be followed so strictly. Most reformers regarded Habibie
as Soeharto's man and thus an integral part of the system they
wished to eradicate. The army disliked Habibie for his role in the
All Indonesia Association of Muslim Intellectuals (ICMI), which
had assisted Soeharto in resisting army influence in the 1990s, and
for his interference in army equipment purchases. It was Habibie's
"bright" idea for instance for Indonesia to purchase the redundant
East German navy following reunification of Germany. The vessels
were cheap, but the refit expenses were enormous and Indonesia
still finished up with antiquated naval assets. No one doubted

that Habibie was very clever, but it was widely believed that he was prone to making impulsive decisions that could easily result in disaster. He did have some support within Golkar and among intellectuals, though not from the technocrats who abhorred his economic nationalist tendencies. Habibie's strongest support came primarily from *santri* intellectuals and business interests associated with ICMI. But this was a narrow political base. That he nevertheless gained the presidency was probably because none of the others who coveted it had enough support at that juncture to make an unconstitutional move to seize it. They preferred to allow Habibie to become president rather than any of their other rivals, confident that he would not succeed in consolidating his grip on the prize.

The national mood in favor of major reform was at its height in the immediate aftermath of Soeharto's resignation. Large demonstrations demanding various reforms and promoting a range of political demands were frequent. The media broke free of its former straitjacket and gave expression to a broad range of criticisms and aspirations. People lost their fear of the security forces, to the point where traditional landowners began reoccupying land they regarded as having been stolen from them by powerful interests during the Soeharto era. To stand against this tide would have required a major army crackdown, likely to result in large-scale popular resistance and considerable bloodshed. Few among the elite favored such a course. Not least because it would have encouraged the capital flight at the heart of Indonesia's economic crisis and would have dismayed the IMF and friendly governments from whom Indonesia desperately needed assistance. Nevertheless, fearing that the impetus for change might go too far, the elite placed considerable pressure on Habibie to protect its interests. Either from genuine conviction or as a conscious political strategy, Habibie made no attempt to block the reform wave; instead, he "rode" it and with some surprising adroitness managed for some time to steer it in directions acceptable to both reformers and the establishment.

Thus, Habibie turned out to be a much more reform-oriented president than had been expected. He released political prisoners, ended political censorship of the media, split the police from the army and separated Golkar (at least in formal terms) from the state bureaucracy. He also began moves to give local governments more autonomy and to redress regional economic grievances over their share of export earnings. Most significantly, Habibie fostered a major overhaul of the political system and announced plans for a democratic national election in 1999 under radically different electoral rules. To this end, he allowed the creation of new political parties, a measure that displayed the new political openness in a most emphatic and practical way when dozens of new parties emerged. Through these measures and gestures, Habibie reduced reform pressures and harnessed moderate elements of the reform movement to his presidency, at least temporarily and conditionally. This widened his political support, making him less susceptible to army pressure, but he was careful not to go too far in acting against army interests, forming a successful working relationship with General Wiranto. Wiranto for his part was no reformer, but he recognized the necessity for some reform of Indonesia's political structure, including modification of the army's role.

Habibie also trod delicately (as have all his presidential successors) around the issue of Soeharto, who still wielded considerable influence through informal channels. In response to clamors for prosecution of Soeharto and his family for corruption and related offences, an investigation was launched. But the drawn-out investigation seemed designed only for show. The reluctance to pursue Soeharto stemmed largely from lingering respect for his achievements and loyalty from those who had served under him. This sentiment was especially strong in the army, which made action against him extremely difficult. Self-preservation also contributed to the ineffectual pursuit of Soeharto. Few within the elite had nothing to hide concerning their dealings with Soeharto and his family or had not engaged in behavior that could be considered similarly corrupt. Thus, while the Soeharto family certainly lost the massive business advantages enjoyed during Soeharto's presidency and some even encountered significant business setbacks, the family fortune remained largely intact. Eventually, toward the end of 2000, Soeharto was declared unfit to stand trial due to memory loss following a series of strokes. Only Soeharto's infamous youngest son, Hutomo Mandala Putra (more commonly known as Tommy Soeharto), saw the inside of a cell, charged with ordering the murder of the judge who convicted him for corruption offences in 2000. Ironically, the supreme court eventually overturned the corruption conviction.

While Habibie had modest success with political reform, he was much less successful in effecting economic recovery, although the rupiah stabilized at a less disastrous level during his presidency. The international context was not conducive, given the continuing Asian economic crisis. But the continuation of the factors that had caused Indonesia's economy to be the hardest hit—entrenched corruption, ineffective regulation, and a lack of predictability for investors—also made it the slowest to recover. Lack of progress in the area of economic reform was important in this respect, but far more important was continuing uncertainty about the direction of political events. Under the circumstances, most investors preferred to wait and see. They were not encouraged by renewed violence between rival religious and ethnic groups in early 1999, which Habibie seemed powerless to stop. In January, Muslim-Christian violence suddenly exploded on Ambon, escalating from minor clashes to a complete breakdown in law and order. Spreading throughout Maluku, it lasted for more than two years, during which time thousands were killed or injured and tens of thousands driven from their homes. Many fled Ambon completely, especially members of immigrant communities such as the Buginese. Within weeks, Ambon City was divided into two zones with the Muslim and Christian communities exchanging only bullets and insults across a no-man's-land of burnt-out buildings. By the end of 1999, as much as half of the city's population was living in refugee camps. There were strong suspicions that the clashes were deliberately ignited, or at least fanned and perpetuated, by supporters of the old regime intent on forcing cancellation of the general elections scheduled for June or even creating the circumstances conducive to an army takeover. These suspicions may have some basis, but interreligious and interethnic friction in Ambon and many other parts of Indonesia was real enough. A gradual influx of Muslim Indonesians from elsewhere in the archipelago, mainly from South Sulawesi, had upset the long-standing but delicate balance between Ambon's Muslim and Christian communities. Thus, the conflict may have been brewing for some time and in a context in which strong government and national stability was replaced by weak government and national flux may only have needed one incident to boil over. Events in West Kalimantan provided another example. In March, there was a repeat of the violent clashes of 1997 between indigenous Dayaks and Madurese settlers, which left scores dead and prompted thousands of Madurese to flee.

Such outbreaks of violence between religious and ethnic groups, although confined to small and mostly outlying areas and involving only a tiny proportion of the population, had a major impact on investor sentiment. Not only did they vividly demonstrate the government's inability to maintain order, but also such episodes seemed to indicate that the "doomsday" scenarios of national dis-integration, civil war, and bloody coups were distinct possibilities. Moreover, market sentiment was especially sensitive to outbreaks of ethnic or religious violence in Indonesia at this juncture because a considerable portion of the capital that shifted out of the country belonged to Chinese Indonesians who were so often the victims of such episodes.

Habibie sought to resolve Indonesia's long-running insurgencies, most notably in East Timor. His government entered negotiations with East Timorese independence leaders, the UN, Portugal, and Australia, promoting a policy that offered East Timor considerable autonomy within Indonesia. East Timorese leaders and their inter-national supporters welcomed this offer, which marked a major shift in Indonesia's stance. But their position still differed from that of the Indonesians in one crucial respect. They were pleased to accept autonomy, but only if it were agreed that after an extended period there would be a referendum whereby the East Timorese could choose between continued autonomy within Indonesia or independence. Apparently frustrated by the lack of enthusiasm for what Jakarta regarded as a generous offer, Habibie suddenly decided in January 1999 that the East Timorese would get the choice they desired, but within months not years.

Habibie's bold announcement was calculated to divest Indonesia of the troublesome Timor problem once and for all. He gambled that most East Timorese faced with the stark choice at this stage of their development would vote to remain within Indonesia. But Habibie's risky policy was very unpopular in Indonesia, especially within the army, which feared that the precedent would encourage other sepa-ratist movements, especially if (unthinkably) the referendum result was in favor of independence. Resolved to prevent such an outcome and far more aware than the Indonesian public how unpopular Indonesia's occupation was among the East Timorese, the army employed intimidation on a massive scale in pursuit of its objec-tive. The principal tactic was to set up, train, arm, and pay civilian militias and then direct them to carry out a campaign of beatings, murders, and arson attacks against proindependence supporters. Despite this intimidation, the overwhelming majority (78.5%) of East Timorese voted for independence in a UN-supervised ballot on August 30, 1999.

Immediately after the result was known, the army unleashed the militias in an unrestrained campaign of violence and destruction that drove most East Timorese into the hills and left few buildings in the capital of Dili undamaged. Tens of thousands were loaded onto trucks and deposited in camps in West Timor along with the families of pro-Jakarta militia members. No doubt the army's massive loss of face, incurred by the failure of its campaign to secure a majority in favor of remaining within Indonesia, encouraged this response. But it has also been suggested that there was a strategic objective: to entice the Armed Forces of National Liberation of East Timor (Falantil) into combat so that the horrific events in East Timor could, with some credibility, be labeled a civil war. This would have provided an excuse to declare martial law and to ignore the referendum result. According to this view, the refugee numbers in West Timor were falsely swelled to lend credibility to claims that the ballot was rigged in favor of the independence advocates. Even if this strategy did not succeed, at least the death and destruction would serve as an emphatic warning to others contemplating separation from Indonesia. Given the evident inability or unwillingness of the Indonesian army to stop the violence, intense international pressure was applied to Indonesia to allow UN peacekeeping troops into the territory. Unable to bring the army to heel, Habibie was forced to agree. Upon deployment of the UN force, largely made up of Australian troops, the violence quickly abated and most militia members withdrew to West Timor along with the Indonesian troops. East Timor had obtained its independence, but at great cost. Indonesia also paid a heavy price, losing considerable international goodwill and further alienating foreign investors for whom the unrestrained killings and the generally unrepentant attitude of the Indonesian elite and army signaled a continuing lack of accountability.

Although Habibie's performance had surprised most observers, especially his willingness and capacity to initiate reforms, as early as the end of 1998 it was clear that his troubles were mounting. Patience with the slow pace of reform had worn thin, and concerns that the changes in the offing were largely cosmetic prompted a renewed push by the students. During a special session of MPR in November dealing with reform proposals, demonstrators clashed with security forces and several students were killed. On the other hand, those wedded to the status quo had recovered their equilibrium and were increasingly desperate to derail or limit the reform process as the elections approached. It became increasingly difficult for Habibie to straddle these opposing demands. Then the national humiliation of the East Timor debacle massively under-mined Habibie's already dwindling authority, seriously damaging his prospects of retaining the presidency.

THE 1999 ELECTIONS

Despite Habibie's better-than-expected performance, Indonesia essentially was adrift during his presidency. Although some impor-tant measures were taken, his government had neither the authority nor the desire to push through a comprehensive package of economic, political, and judicial reforms. As a result, the economy continued to stall and political uncertainty continued. Under the circumstances, the 1999 elections were looked toward with perhaps equal parts optimism and trepidation. It was hoped that the first free and fair national elections since 1955 would produce a government with both the legitimacy and capacity to tackle Indonesia's increasingly pressing problems. If not, there were grave fears that Indonesia would descend into chaos and poverty or else revert to dictatorship. Many believed that the army would never allow democracy. Others argued that democracy was culturally inappropriate for Indonesia or that the country was not ready for it because the people were too poorly educated, the logistics were too difficult, or because political, religious, and ethnic divisions were too sharp to allow for peace-ful electoral competition. Thus, if the elections were cancelled or postponed, if the result were affected by coercion or rigging, or if they were accompanied by serious outbreaks of violence, this would represent a serious setback for Indonesian democracy. The "doom-sayers" would have been proved right. Alternatively, if the elections ran fairly, efficiently, and peacefully, then this would be a great boost for the prospects for democracy and reform.

The Team of Seven, an academic working party established by Habibie's government, worked for months to develop a new dem-ocratic electoral and legislative system appropriate for Indonesia. Although some recommendations were not accepted and some compromises were made, most of the key features were imple-mented, and the end product was indeed far-reaching democratic reform. For example, the new political parties were permitted to contest the elections if they could meet certain criteria, such as having branches in at least 9 of the 27 provinces (a measure to pre-vent parties founded on an ethnic basis). Of 147 registered parties, 48 were able to meet the criteria and contest the elections. Another key measure involved reducing the army's reserved seats in DPR from 75 to 38. Similarly, there were to be no presidential appointees to MPR—a stark contrast to the new order, when the executive selected half the MPR membership. Public servants could vote but were no longer able to join political parties or to stand for election, a measure that greatly reduced Golkar's advantage. The creation of a genuinely independent National Election Commission to oversee the elections was another crucial reform.

Although there were some incidents, the fears that widespread violence would break out (or be deliberately provoked) between the various parties' supporters proved unfounded. The behavior at the mass rallies and noisy, colorful processions that choked the streets of Jakarta and other major cities during the campaign period was amazingly good natured. Only when it was Golkar's turn to parade were small-scale clashes common. Voting and counting also went remarkably well on the whole; incidents of vote buying, intimidation, and other irregularities did occur, but not on a scale sufficient to distort the result. The vote count took much longer than expected, however, arousing fears that a major ballot-rigging fix was being perpetrated. In fact, the delay was largely the product of cumbersome checks and balances being implemented painstakingly by the inexperienced local election committees. In short, the conduct of the elections was a democratic success of major proportions, proving the commitment of ordinary Indonesians to the peaceful democratic process. Unfortunately, the results gave far less reason for celebration. As in 1955, the outcome of the free elections emphasized Indonesia's divisions.

In 1955, from the pack of parties, four had emerged to share the bulk of the votes among them (PNI, Masyumi, NU, and PKI). In 1999, a similar pattern took shape: five parties shared almost 87 percent of the vote. Again similar to 1955, behind these "big five" in 1999 there came a handful of small parties with 1 or 2 percent of the vote each who thereby possessed some capacity to influence the composition of governments and their policies. In 1999, however, there were much bigger gaps between each of the "big five." Clearly the most successful party, with 33.7 percent of the vote, was Megawati's new party, the Indonesian Democratic Party of Struggle (PDI-P), a breakaway from the discredited PDI. Like the old PNI, PDI-P was the most secular nationalist of the major parties, drawing support primarily from *abangan* Muslims but also from Christians, Hindus, and Chinese Indonesians. PDI-P also presented itself as strongly proreform, emphasizing democracy and social justice and opposing corruption, although it identified few specific measures that it intended to implement in government.

The once-dominant Golkar came in second with a credible 22.4 percent of the vote. Given its loss of advantage as the party of the state, this was a surprising result. Many expected that in a fair election Golkar would be decimated due to its associations with Soeharto and the new order. Although Golkar had worked hard to distance itself from the Soeharto era, its suddenly claimed reform credentials were received with skepticism, and it continued to be seen as the party of the old status quo. Nevertheless, Golkar remained very well organized, with an effective national network that linked the bulk of the powerful status quo elements in business, government, and the bureaucracy. In other words, Golkar by its very nature constituted an existing network of all those who had benefited from the new order and who (naturally) desired to preserve their positions of wealth and advantage. While this network no longer possessed the unfettered power of the state, it nevertheless still wielded considerable influence and could raise abundant campaign funds. Although the army as an institution largely kept its promise of neutrality, in practice, many serving and retired officers quietly exerted their influence in the political campaign. Golkar was the principal beneficiary of this phenomenon, although in another return to the 1950s pattern, all significant political parties had army supporters.

Wahid's National Awakening Party (PKB) came in third with 12.6 percent of the vote. Although under Wahid's influence PKB was avowedly secular and strongly proreform and prodemocracy, it drew its votes overwhelmingly from the NU membership and was generally seen as NU's party. Reflecting divisions within NU that were as much personal as political, some NU figures formed other parties that claimed the NU mantle, but they were much less successful.

The United Development Party (PPP) came in fourth with 10.7 percent of the vote. This figure was well below its usual proportion of the vote during the new order. Nevertheless, this result was also much better than many expected. PPP had been considered likely to disintegrate since the former parties that composed it were no longer forced to remain. As expected, a number of PPP factions did depart to reestablish old Islam-based parties or to form new parties. But, somewhat surprisingly, it turned out that the new-order decades had molded the bulk of PPP into a genuine political force with its own sense of identity. No doubt some of the same factors that continued to preserve Golkar's relevance were at work with respect to PPP. It too had an established national network at its disposal and thus could continue to provide an effective political vehicle for the many powerful interests it embodied.

The last of the "big five" was the National Mandate Party (PAN) led by Amien Rais. PAN also had political roots in the pre-new order era. Somewhat like Masyumi, it drew most of its votes from Muhammadiyah members, and also like Masyumi, it offered a practical program, drawn up by renowned modernist Muslim intellectuals, comprising a blend of rational economic, social welfare, nationalist, democratic, and (of course) Islamist ideas. But unlike Masyumi, its declared orientation was more secular and much less Islamist. Many opponents held that this posture was a mask and its true Islamist colors would emerge if it came to power. Such suspicions were fed by the more Islamist and less inclusive views that Rais had expressed a decade or so earlier. PAN was the only major party to campaign on issues and to promote a comprehensive program of policy solutions to Indonesia's problems. In this regard, it resembled the old PSI and suffered a similar electoral fate. PAN's unexpectedly low vote (7.1%) indicated that this approach remained unfruitful in Indonesian politics. That it did less well than Masyumi did also suggested that PAN's attempt to appeal to two constituencies had backfired. It was too Islamist to win significant support from those who were not committed Muslims, and it was insufficiently Islamist to win the bulk of the modernist Muslim vote. Those inclined toward a more Islamist agenda voted either for PPP or for one of the smaller, more overtly Islamist parties such as the Moon and Crescent Party (PBB) or the Justice Party (PK).

Much of the new order's social-engineering effort had been justified as putting an end to primordial political divisions. During the new order, it was difficult to discern how much influence primordial identity still exerted in shaping political outlooks because expression of political ideas was censored and political behavior was severely constrained. The 1999 elections revealed that primordial identity, a complex of ethnicity and religious affiliation, remained a major determinant of voter choice. Unlike the 1950s and 1960s, however, it was far less politicized, and the group membership divisions were much less clear. (To what extent this change can be attributed to the policies of the new order is unclear.) Of course, many other factors motivated voter choice, ranging from political issues (in the narrower sense) to coercion. In these elections, for example, PDI-P seems to have gained many "extra" votes because it was identified as the primary mainstream standard bearer of reform.

THE WAHID PRESIDENCY

When after months of speculation and political maneuvering the 700 members of the new MPR met in October 1999 to elect a new president, there were three declared candidates: Habibie, Megawati, and Wahid. Others such as Wiranto and Akbar Tanjung, the chairman of Golkar, were widely believed to be angling for the position should the opportunity arise, for instance, if there were a deadlock. Wahid's candidature was not taken seriously. It was generally expected that the choice would be between Megawati and Habibie, that Wahid would eventually throw his weight behind the former after extracting his political price. Megawati appeared to be in a strong position. She had the largest single bloc of votes and in Habibie was confronted by an opponent whose political stocks had declined sharply in the wake of the East Timor fiasco. But as the leader of the party with by far the largest proportion of the vote, she behaved as if the presidency was hers by right and so put little effort into lobbying and bargaining—a serious mistake as it turned out. The wily Wahid's parliamentary supporters were few in number, but he recognized the political possibilities inherent in the existence of two large but mutually antagonistic parliamentary groupings opposed to Megawati: Golkar and a newly emerged bloc of *santri*-based parties known as the Central Axis. Neither of these groups could win the presidency without the other's support, and neither group could bring themselves to support the other. When Habibie, recognizing he could not win after his presidential report to the MPR was badly received, withdrew his candidacy shortly before the vote, Wahid was the beneficiary. Both groups preferred to vote for him rather than for Megawati. Wahid won by a margin of 40 votes. A shocked and bitter Megawati swallowed her pride and accepted the vice presidency, which sufficed to placate her enraged supporters.

The rotund and avuncular Wahid was generally well liked and renowned for his commitment to social justice and religious and racial tolerance, as well as for his impressive intellect. His eccentricity and unpredictability were often exasperating, but in the Indonesian context, these characteristics were not always perceived as a political weakness. They could also be seen as flexibility and political astuteness. They also lent him a human aura, setting him apart from typical members of the political elite. At the same time, some of his characteristics added to his spiritual (and therefore temporal) authority. Eccentricity and an unprepossessing appearance were traditionally signs of possible mystical prowess, especially for the Javanese. The same could be said for his near blindness. Thus, once people got over the shock of seeing Wahid made president, there was some optimism that perhaps he was a good choice after all. Wahid's credentials as a Muslim figure of consequence while simultaneously a champion of tolerance and dialogue seemed to make him uniquely placed to heal Indonesia's conflicts over religion, ethnicity, and separatism. Also, since he was far more committed to reform than either Habibie or Megawati and was untainted by corruption, Wahid's election offered hope to those unhappy that the reform process had stalled. Further to his advantage, he was not a bogey to the powerful vested interests associated with the new order. They well knew his capacity for pragmatism, an impression he quickly reinforced by signaling that he did not intend to pursue Soeharto and by including a number of Golkar figures in his government. There was some prospect therefore that he could effect meaningful reforms that would nevertheless be acceptable to the elite. Such an achievement would require considerable political skill, which Wahid appeared to possess, as demonstrated through the manner in which he had obtained the presidency.

Unfortunately, Wahid could not capitalize on these apparent advantages. Poor organizational skills, woeful media management, and a lack of discipline and effective teamwork from Wahid and the loose coterie of presidential advisers and spokespersons that swirled around him gave his presidency a chaotic, unfocused, and ineffectual appearance. He proved unable to overcome these weaknesses and incapable of laying out a clear and well-prioritized reform program and pursuing it consistently. Wahid's erratic political behavior and contradictory statements quickly eroded the goodwill originally attached to his presidency. Perhaps this conduct was sometimes intended to keep his enemies off balance (a favorite Wahid tactic), but the general confusion and consternation it created easily offset any benefits. Behavior that might have been merely embarrassing in other circumstances increasingly became a serious political liability when coupled with an absence of progress on the pressing issues of the day. For instance, falling asleep on the podium during a parliamentary sitting and while on national television was very bad politics. It was especially bad politics when the dozing president needed parliament's cooperation and when he was the subject of considerable parliamentary criticism over his performance. Indeed, one of Wahid's principle failures as a politician while president was his inability to make the necessary adjustment to the new reality of a weaker presidency and a stronger parliament. While it might have done him little good, it would surely have been wise for him to refrain from making insulting remarks about the parliament. This indiscipline, essentially a failure to curb his ego, would cost him dearly. However, while Wahid's contributions to the deficiencies of his presidency deserve acknowledgment, the scale of Indonesia's problems, the strength of the opposition to him, and the inherent weakness of his political position are at least equally significant.

Indonesia's powerful bureaucracy, whose departments had run for decades like fiefdoms, was saturated with Golkar supporters intimately linked with the national and local level establishments as well as with the army. It had lucrative interests to protect, its own and those of its "friends," against Wahid's reformist policies, and against Wahid's *kyai* and business supporters who naturally sought to influence and infiltrate the bureaucracy in their own interests. For these "business" reasons as well as because of its political sympathy and connections, the bureaucracy generally did not wish Wahid to succeed. Accordingly, it obstructed his efforts, seriously impeding his ability to govern.

Wahid was also confronted with a problem unknown to Indonesian presidents since the 1950s—that of dealing with a parliament that possessed real power. The combination of reforms to the political structure and the legitimacy supplied by being democratically elected transformed parliament into a much more powerful institution, both constitutionally and in practice. Wahid could rely on only around 10 percent of the votes in parliament and so experienced great difficulty securing parliamentary approval of his program. These problems were not solely a natural consequence of the balance of power within DPR. It was clear that the political leaders of the other parties had no intention of setting aside their own political interests for the sake of the national interest. With their eyes on the next elections, they too had no wish to see Wahid succeed and so obstructed and undermined him consistently. There was also an institutional dimension to parliament's obstructionism. Long treated as a rubber stamp, DPR was naturally inclined to jealously guard its new powers against the previously utterly dominant office of president and to test the parameters of the respective powers at every opportunity.

The biggest problem for Wahid was the army. It had begun the post-Soeharto era internally divided and unsure how much reform of itself and of the Indonesian political system it should allow. It was also rattled by the abrupt exposure of its unpopularity and consequently had difficulty gauging just how far it needed to retreat. By the time Wahid became president, however, the army had regained much of its composure and coherence. The loss of East Timor in particular had reinforced the military's conviction that civilian politicians could not be trusted to maintain Indonesia's territorial integrity. As an affront to the army's pride and sense of mission, it had also galvanized the army's determination to resist policies it deemed injurious to Indonesia and underlined the necessity to maintain army unity and independence to do so effectively. Wahid's position on these sensitive issues was particularly suspect from an army perspective. Few mainstream civilian politicians were more committed to the principle of civilian control over the army, and none were more inclined to engage in dialogue with separatists and to offer concessions.

Wahid soon confirmed army concerns, especially when he supported an East Timor—style referendum for Aceh, a solution for which Acehnese support was made abundantly clear in November 1999 with a massive demonstration in the provincial capital, Banda Aceh. Although quickly forced to backpedal on his referendum statements, Wahid was able to enforce some restraint on the conduct of Indonesian security forces stationed in Aceh. This proved insufficient to improve the prospects for peace but ample to frustrate the army, which regarded the softer approach as merely allowing the Movement for Acehnese Independence (GAM) to strengthen its position. Wahid's policies on Papua aroused similar indignation from the army. Most troubling from the army perspective, however, were his efforts to impose civilian control over the army. To this end, he named a civilian, Juwono Sudarsono, as minister of defense, and in a long drawn-out test of wills, Wahid succeeded in forcing Wiranto to resign as coordinating minister for defense and security. But this victory did little to secure for Wahid the army's cooperation, let alone truly bring it to heel. Later, he tried to make renowned army reformer General Wirahadikusumah army chief of staff but failed due to army resistance, succeeding only in further cementing the army's hostility toward him and pushing the army closer to Megawati.

The consequences of Wahid's losing political battle with the army, and to a lesser extent with the bureaucracy, went far beyond preventing progress on existing problems such as Papua and Aceh. Few observers believe it was coincidental that a rash of additional security problems broke out during Wahid's presidency, with the consequence of diverting his government's attention away from key problems such as the economy and corruption. Within weeks of Wahid's being sworn in, fresh violence erupted in Maluku, including new incidents on the islands of Halmahera, Buru, and Ternate. Then in January 2000, riots occurred on Lombok, during which several churches were attacked. The conflict in Maluku escalated when thousands of Islamist militants from Java, trained and armed by an organization called Laskar Jihad, traveled there to join the fighting. Wahid's instructions to authorities to stop Laskar Jihad forces traveling to Maluku were ignored. In June, the conflict spread to Poso in Central Sulawesi, again with Laskar Jihad involvement, leaving hundreds more dead and thousands more homes destroyed. By the beginning of 2001, there were as many as a million "internally displaced people" throughout Indonesia as a result of these and other conflicts. Then in September, pro-Indonesia East Timorese militia members went on a rampage at Atambua in West Timor, murdering three UN workers, an event that seriously damaged Indonesia's international reputation and threatened to derail UN and other aid programs. In all these instances, the army and other security forces proved either unable or unwilling to intervene to prevent the violence or to bring perpetrators to justice. Indeed, there have been persistent allegations that the army, or elements within it, often stirred up such conflicts and even became involved in the fighting. The perception was widespread that the army and other establishment forces were using these conflicts to undermine Wahid's reformist presidency.

It is difficult to see how Wahid could have overcome these powerful forces. If he had enjoyed massive popular support, he might have been able to mobilize it behind his program and force his opponents to back down. But while he was, initially at least, acceptable as president to a wide range of different groups in Indonesia, for most of them he was only their second choice. Nor did his treatment at the hands of his parliamentary, bureaucratic, and military opponents inspire indignation, except among his most committed supporters—on the contrary. For the most part, the blame for the lack of progress fell upon him. A large part of the problem was that Wahid's only real weapon was the power and prestige of the presidency, both of which had declined considerably by the time he was in office, ironically in large part due to the success of Indonesia's democratic reforms. There is a further irony here in that Wahid's democratic inclinations worked against him because, impatient with pretentious ceremony and a casual dresser by inclination, he did much to demystify the previously rarified office of president.

The ironies continue. Wahid was eventually brought down by misuse of the democratic features of free speech and the parliamentary process that he had championed his whole life. On dubious constitutional grounds, MPR moved to remove Wahid from the presidency, citing equally dubious allegations of corruption. Everyone knew this was merely a pretext, but few Indonesians cared at this point. They simply hoped that his replacement could succeed where Wahid had failed. Ironically also in his last months and weeks, Wahid explored a number of desperate and undemocratic measures to cling to power such as suspending parliament and declaring a state of emergency with army support (which the army refused to give). Perhaps like many other contemporary Indonesian politicians, Wahid had been influenced far more than he realized by Soeharto and the new order's political methods.

Wahid's presidency ended ignominiously. In a last drastic attempt to block the impeachment process, he issued a decree freezing MPR. The supreme court declared the decree unconstitutional and MPR proceeded immediately on July 23, 2001, to vote Wahid out of office and to install Megawati as president. Hamzah Haz of PPP was chosen as Megawati's vice president, providing her administration with the necessary Islamic presence to placate *santri* concerns over her secular nationalist inclinations. That he accepted the position, despite having declared in 1999 that it was against Islamic teaching for a woman to be president, encouraged the view that many who adopted this position did so because at the time it was a useful political weapon rather than a genuine conviction.

THE MEGAWATI PRESIDENCY

Megawati's election to the presidency was generally welcomed, not least by the markets, which immediately lifted the rupiah from

11,300 to 9,900 to the U.S. dollar. Partly this reflected relief that Wahid was gone, combined with the hope that, now that the long, drawn-out struggle to oust him was over, the business of government would resume and attention would be paid to Indonesia's problems rather than to politicking. The cautious optimism was also founded on the belief that Megawati had reached an understanding with the army and so would not encounter the level of obstruction experienced by Wahid. Similarly, Megawati's prospects were considered brighter because her position in the parliament, where she commanded around 35 percent of the votes, was much stronger than Wahid's had been. These were not the only advantages that Megawati enjoyed as she began her presidential term. While losing the presidency to Wahid in 1999 had been galling, perhaps it had actually worked to her advantage. The public's excessively high expectations of 1999 had evaporated by 2001, and as vice president, Megawati had benefited from the opportunity to observe the functions and difficulties associated with the presidency from close quarters. Thus she came into office with a better understanding of the levers of power and, from observing Wahid's mistakes, could avoid some of the pitfalls. Another advantage was the likelihood that she would be allowed to finish her presidential term (until the 2004 elections) undisturbed. Few wished for an imminent repeat of the bruising encounter between presidency and parliament.

Megawati's warm welcome continued with a positive reception to the cabinet she announced on August 9. Weighted toward competent and respected reform-oriented technocrats rather than "political" appointments, it seemed to be a cabinet that would not be held hostage to the special interest groups that had hindered progress during the Habibie and Wahid administrations. Upon coming into office, Megawati also made it clear that she would not tolerate further continuation of the highly symbolic farce involving Tommy Soeharto that had been making a mockery of the police and the justice system for months. Having been convicted of corruption, Tommy Soeharto had gone "on the run," and despite being frequently spotted around town and despite a number of highly publicized searches of likely "hideouts," he continually evaded capture. Few believed it was coincidental that shortly after she assumed the presidency the police had a breakthrough and the notorious fugitive was arrested.

Thus it appeared that Megawati was serious about reform. However, the first suggestion that this benign view was misplaced came with the belated appointment of the new attorney general, a week after the rest of the cabinet. Reform advocates had hoped for the appointment of a "new broom," somebody from outside the notoriously corrupt Attorney General's Office, with the integrity and determination to tackle the corruption problems bedeviling Indonesia's justice system. Instead, Megawati appointed M. A. Rachman, a senior career bureaucrat from within the department. More cynical political observers concluded that Megawati wanted somebody who could be relied upon to pursue only those prosecutions for corruption and human-rights abuses that met with her approval. According to this view, Rachman's appointment would mean that those members of the elite closely associated with PDI-P, Megawati, and her business-man-politician husband, Taufik Kiemas, would be immune from prosecution. It would also mean that other powerful and wealthy individuals could avoid justice unless it suited Megawati's admin-istration to prevent them from doing so.

Events seemed to bear out this view. Human-rights advocates watched aghast as very few convictions were recorded against army personnel accused of human-rights abuses in East Timor and Aceh. The most senior suspects (such as Wiranto) were never charged, and those convicted received light sentences. Observers also noted that, although the number of high-profile corruption cases brought to trial rose during Megawati's presidency, they often involved people who could be considered her enemies, such as Akbar Tanjung. Tanjung was charged in March 2002 with embezzling $4.5 million of public funds (allegedly to finance Golkar's 1999 election cam-paign). Although he was eventually acquitted, the trial probably cost Tanjung his run for the presidency in 2004, assisting his narrow defeat at the hands of Wiranto in a ballot to be Golkar's candidate.

While Megawati's desire to retain this powerful political weapon in her hands was understandable from a realpolitik perspective, the decision had significant negative implications for the reform process and for the problem-solving capacity of her government. The cor-rupt and politicized judiciary was (and is) the linchpin of all corrup-tion in Indonesia. As long as judicial decisions could, as a matter of routine, be bought or "fixed" politically, then Indonesia would con-tinue to suffer from an absence of the rule of law. From this flowed the ineffectual bankruptcy laws, rampant trademark piracy, and inability to enforce contractual obligations (except through bribery and connections), which provided a powerful disincentive to invest-ment. From it too flowed the constant leakage of public funds into the pockets of bureaucrats, politicians, and those in business. Such behavior was not merely immoral; it rendered government projects and state-owned enterprises less effective and uncompetitive and had significant negative impacts on people's lives. In practical terms, for example, it might mean that the funds allocated to connect 10 villages to the national electricity grid only connected 7. Absence of the rule of law also meant that the powerful and well connected were rarely held accountable for power abuse and could with impunity often ignore or obstruct the implementation of laws and the orders of ministers—and even presidents. For genuine reformers, it was for these reasons why reform of the judicial system was paramount and why they were so disillusioned by Megawati's appointment of Rachman. In this context, it is significant that from a judiciary regarded as riddled with corruption, only one judge had been convicted of taking a bribe by the middle of 2003, and he was not even sacked, merely sentenced to two years of probation.

The growing view that Megawati lacked genuine commitment to reform seemed borne out by the experiences of the reform-minded cabinet ministers as they battled to effect change without the political backing needed to overcome resistance. Criticisms were also made of the lack of coordination among the various ministries and the lack of drive and leadership emanating from the top. While vice president, Megawati had remained glumly silent and inactive, keeping her political distance from Wahid lest she be tarnished by his failings. As president, she finally had the opportunity to pursue the noble political objectives she always intimated she had. It soon became apparent, however, that what many had long suspected was indeed the case. Her political silence and quietude had not been "Javanese" reticence hinting at strength and purity of purpose and unsuspected abilities. Instead, Megawati's "stillness" had merely obscured her weaknesses. She was out of her depth politically and intellectually, and she possessed only vague plans and visions for Indonesia. As former minister Sarwono Kusumaadmadja remarked, "It's the New Order without the leadership and without the vision."[1] Thus it is not surprising that her presidency quickly disappointed many supporters, especially many among the millions of ordinary Indonesians who had seen her as their champion. Nevertheless, under her administration, Indonesia saw some improvement. Political stability was achieved, the economy performed better, and interethnic and interreligious strife declined significantly. Ironically, in addition to coming to power at an auspicious juncture, Megawati's successes, as well as their modesty, can be explained largely by her political conservatism.

Megawati saw herself as the authentic standard bearer for her father's nationalist mission, but her interpretation of Sukarnoism was profoundly conservative, paying little more than lip service to the social revolutionary currents that ran through Sukarno's ideas. A natural conservative in terms of her personality, a true child of the establishment in terms of her upbringing and connections, a centralist by inclination, and staunchly nationalistic on questions of Indonesia's territorial integrity, Megawati could readily cooperate with many of the political forces that had so resisted Wahid. In particular, Megawati was able to establish a good working relationship with the army, which, by the time she came to power, had lost its fears of her charting (or being propelled on) a leftward course. Unlike Wahid, she was not inclined to pursue the difficult issue of reforming the army and recasting the army-civilian relationship. In exchange for unobtrusive political support, her administration was content to allow the army to run its "own" affairs. Megawati was (in practice) also in broad sympathy with the army's hard-line attitude toward separatists. As expected, therefore, Megawati did not experience the lack of cooperation that Wahid had from the army in dealing with security problems. While tensions remained high in places like Ambon and Poso, the levels of violence dropped significantly. Local peace efforts and local exhaustion had much to do with the improvement, but the change in the army's stance toward these conflicts made the peace initiatives viable. Simple acts such as arresting key extremists from both sides and curbing armed outsiders such as Laskar Jihad soon restrained the fighting in Ambon. In truth, the latter would not have been difficult if suspicions that Laskar Jihad were a covert creation of the army are correct.

Another contributing factor to Megawati's modest political success, somewhat paradoxically, was her lack of leadership. Her hands-off style may have deprived her ministers of the political backing they needed to drive their reform agendas forward, but it did have the silver lining of allowing them to get on with the job and to make what progress they could. Apparently, Megawati was content with a largely figurehead role as president and possessed sufficient wisdom to accept her limitations and to appoint (for the most part) competent ministers and advisers. Nevertheless, it is difficult to escape the conclusion that Indonesia's slow but steady economic improvement during her presidency had little to do with the modest achievements of the technocrats, though their collective presence in the relevant ministries must have provided some reassurance to the market. More likely to have fostered the moderate improvements in the levels of investment and economic activity was the improved political stability that the tacit Megawati-army partnership delivered.

However, the improved atmosphere of security and political stability was threatened by the emergence of a new and formidable Islamist extremist movement known as Jemaah Islamiah (JI). Although it is a local movement descended from Darul Islam, JI has links with Al Qaeda (the extremist Islamist movement headed by Osama bin Laden), whose internationalist *jihad* perspective it shares. While small, JI has been very difficult to defeat, largely because, unlike Laskar Jihad, the Islamic Defender's Front (FPI), and most other militant Islamist groups that have emerged periodically in Indonesia, JI has proved immune to manipulation or infiltration by army intelligence units. JI's presence was announced with the terrorist bombing of a Bali nightclub frequented by Westerners in October 2002 that killed over 200 people. This was followed by the Marriott Hotel bombing in Jakarta in August 2003 and the Australian Embassy bombing, also in Jakarta, in April 2004. JI had actually begun terrorist operations in Indonesia in 2000 with a bombing in August of the Philippines ambassador's residence and the bombing of numerous churches on Christmas Eve. These earlier incidents however were not understood to be JI operations at the time.

JI has very little support among Indonesian Muslims, and since this is unlikely to change, it poses no serious threat to the Indonesian state. But no government can afford to allow such challenges to its authority to go unanswered without loss of faith in its ability to maintain order. Moreover, because JI's audacious campaign involved high-profile attacks on the Western presence in Indonesia, it threatened an adverse impact on the Indonesian economy. It damaged Indonesia's slowly recovering tourist industry and added further disincentive to Western investment in Indonesia. Clearly, the government needed to respond. But the JI attacks also posed an awkward political challenge because of a widespread initial reluctance of Indonesians (including Vice President Hamzah Haz) to believe that the perpetrators were Indonesian Muslims. Alternative and much more popular accounts blamed either Western intelligence agencies or pro-Soeharto elements in the army. The considerable success of the Indonesian police investigation (with technical help from the Australian Federal Police) and the subsequent prosecutions greatly reduced the currency of these populist conspiracy theories, as did public admissions from several of the arrested bombers. Nevertheless, the Megawati government's response to the JI threat was very cautious, provoking considerable criticism from Western governments. No steps, for instance, were taken to control the network of *pesantren* (Muslim boarding schools) and mosques associated with the JI movement. To do so would be fraught with considerable legal, practical, and above all political difficulties. Such legislation would outrage a wide range of Indonesian Muslim organizations, very few of which have even the most tenuous relationship with JI. Extreme sensitivity to actions by the state that appear to threaten the independence of Muslim organizations is a deeply engrained product of their historical experience from the new order and colonial era.

ECONOMY AND SOCIETY

The Indonesian economy has struggled to recover fully from the Asian economic crisis. Inflation has been kept under control while interest rates and the fiscal deficit have been brought down to levels that have earned praise from the IMF. Yet economic growth and investment have remained too low and foreign debt levels uncomfortably high. Economic growth rallied from a decline of 13 percent in 1998 to run at a slowly rising level of around 3–4 percent between 2001 and 2003, reaching 5 percent in 2004.[2] Such levels, while respectable for developed economies, are inadequate for a developing country like Indonesia, with its large, working-age population. Economic growth of around 7 percent per annum is required to provide enough jobs for Indonesians entering the job market and to make inroads into a combined unemployment and underemployment level estimated at around 40 percent. Similarly, higher levels of economic growth are required to service debt repayments comfortably, without which debt will continue to absorb a high proportion of export earnings. Without a lot more investment, the desired higher levels of economic growth cannot be achieved, let alone sustained. Investment (as a percentage of GDP) has been running at approximately half the precrisis level. Foreign investment remained in negative territory until 2002.

Since the crisis, national infrastructure has been allowed to run down, especially in the area of power generation, as the state has lacked the export earnings to pick up the slack left by private-sector investment. Thus, due to infrastructural bottlenecks, Indonesia risks being unable to take full advantage of the better economic circumstances and higher investment levels that are hoped for. Also of great concern is an economic structure relapse toward heavy reliance on exports of petroleum and mineral products. Indonesia's export-oriented textiles and light manufacturing sector, which boomed in the 1980s and early 1990s, has become less competitive internationally. This is reflected in the shift away from Indonesia by industries such as footwear and clothing to countries such as China and Vietnam where not only are production costs currently cheaper and productivity levels higher but where greater political stability and policy predictability are offered. The concern, if the trend continues, is not only the loss of economic diversity and the accompanying greater vulnerability to world commodity prices, but also the problems associated with higher unemployment since such light manufacturing industries are highly labor intensive.

Indonesia's economic difficulties have been prolonged by the slow progress in effecting the economic reforms deemed necessary to encourage investment and economic growth. The desired reforms include a major overhaul of the finance sector, corporate restructuring, and thorough cleansing of the corrupt legal and economic regulatory system. Implementing such reforms would entail a dramatic change in Indonesia's business-government culture, one that permeates the country's elite and from which most of its members extract major benefits. Despite the seriousness of Indonesia's economic crisis, the elite have displayed little enthusiasm for these drastic changes. Not surprisingly therefore, none of Indonesia's post-Soeharto governments to date have made much progress in this area. Notably, there has been a series of well-publicized cases of powerful and well-connected conglomerates and their owners continuing to successfully evade the consequences of their indebtedness or corrupt behavior. Exerting their influence and taking advantage of corruption, they have escaped charges or evaded bankruptcy and other corporate and financial restructuring measures. Some, far from repaying money owed to the state, have even managed to extract more, receiving rescue funds supposedly reserved for businesses that have cut away their deadwood and reformed their business practices.

The most notorious examples of economic-reform failure have involved the Indonesian Bank Restructuring Agency (IBRA), established to oversee a US$85 billion bank rescue package involving reforms to the system, capital injection, and debt restructuring. A combination of political interference and corruption has at best obstructed and at worst seriously distorted IBRA's endeavors. Such cases vividly illustrate the poor progress of Indonesia's economic-reform efforts and thereby discourage the return of investors and obstruct disbursement of funds from the IMF and other donors. Compounding the problem has been a number of high-profile instances in which foreign companies apparently were badly treated by Indonesian courts, notably where they sought to acquire the assets of bankrupt Indonesian companies. A similar negative impact has been produced by the inability of foreign-owned mining companies to enforce their rights as Indonesian authorities ignore illegal miners operating on foreign concessions.

Indonesian society has experienced change at a bewildering pace since the overthrow of Soeharto. Indeed, significant social changes are still under way, but the extent and speed of the "social revolution" is exaggerated, a product of the fact that many social phenomena frowned on by the stultifying new order are now conducted openly. Herein lies the most obvious and widespread social change, however. The culture, including the political culture, of post-Soeharto Indonesia is much more open than that of the new order. There is now generally much more individual freedom and considerably more space for civil society to operate in as the government's close monitoring of organized human activity has been largely abandoned. Reflecting the relaxation of controls is an outpouring of various forms of artistic and personal expression including literature, film, music, and theater, often exploring controversial themes. Perhaps the clearest sign of the new openness, and also one of its principal drivers, is the newly free media. Formerly, all forms of media were tightly controlled and editors who sought to raise "taboo" subjects or to offer even mild criticism of government policy risked their publishing license whenever they did so. Newspapers and magazines were routinely censored and frequently banned, and on some occasions editors and journalists were jailed for overstepping the mark. The removal of most of these restrictions means that issues previously swept under the carpet are now often aired and discussed in an open and lively fashion, and corruption and government shortcomings that largely escaped public scrutiny before are now frequently exposed. Regrettably, some media irresponsibility has provided authorities with an excuse to begin reining in some of the media freedoms. Nevertheless, the current situation is very different from that which pertained during the new order.

Chinese Indonesians have been notable beneficiaries of the more liberal atmosphere. They are now free, after more than three decades, to celebrate their Chinese identity in public, for instance, by performing traditional lion dances to welcome the Chinese New Year. There are now Chinese-language publications, Chinese television and radio programs, Chinese-language schools, and Chinese characters and products are now openly displayed. Yet considerable prejudice toward Chinese Indonesians remains in some quarters, and most of the laws and regulations that discriminate against them have not been revoked formally.

Among those who have taken advantage of the new freedom of association is the Indonesian trade union movement. Throughout the new order, only one state-controlled trade union, the All Indonesia Worker's Union (SPSI) had legal status. Far from advancing the interests of labor, in practice it prevented workers from organizing themselves effectively in pursuit of improvements in pay and conditions. SPSI could not even be relied upon to enforce the routinely ignored legal minimum pay rates. Now there are numerous trade unions operating freely, some of which had a semiclandestine existence under Soeharto, such as the Union for Indonesian Workers' Prosperity (SBSI). Although only a fraction of the workforce is unionized, a combination of union campaigns and more sympathetic governments has raised wages and improved working conditions, but the gains have been marginal and uneven. The threats of unemployment and collusion between employers and local authorities prevent significant labor gains. Nevertheless, that workers are now free to organize in pursuit of their interests is a major social change. Its significance is better appreciated when viewed as part of a much broader phenomenon whereby ordinary Indonesians are now, for the first time since the early 1960s, voicing their aspirations and forming organizations of their choosing to advance their interests.

Included in the latter phenomenon are women's organizations, although the position of women in Indonesia since the end of the new order has been mixed. Autonomous women's organizations have been able to operate with much greater ease and raise issues of particular importance to women at both the local and the national levels. It also appears that women have generally found more opportunities to engage in the broad spectrum of political life, but they remain rare in leadership positions. Indeed, the number of women in parliament actually fell after the 1999 elections. Of particular concern to many women is the push to implement *sharia* (Islamic law) under the auspices of the decentralization laws in parts of Indonesia. They fear that the form taken by local *sharia* regulations or the manner of their implementation will oppress women, for example, through restricting their movements and opportunities for social and economic engagement.

Devolution of political authority to the regional and provincial levels of government has stimulated a number of important social changes, the full ramifications of which are not yet clear. A revival of local identity and a renaissance of local *adat* has taken place, including, in some instances, a reversion to traditional forms of local governance. For example in West Sumatra, traditional territorial divisions have replaced the administrative villages of the new order. Traditional local authorities have also been reanimated in some places, though it remains to be seen how much real authority they will be able to wield. There is considerable potential for such resurrected social forms to conflict with modernity. To some degree, this phenomenon is largely driven by an emotional need to display symbols of local identity rather than any genuine attempt to turn back the clock. Regional autonomy policy, in some places, is also encouraging grassroots-level democracy (as its designers intended), empowering local people to hold their local officials and governments accountable. In many other places, it has merely provided more scope for local authorities to engage in corruption.

The greater prominence of Islam in Indonesian society, already evident during the new order, has continued into the post-Soeharto era. Public displays of devotion to Islam such as through dress, participation in Islamic rituals, and use of Islamic banks have increased. Removal of the new order's political constraints, however, has not resulted in the transformation in the fortunes of political Islam that some expected. Thus, the results of the free elections of 1999 and 2004 show that the proportion of Indonesian Muslims inclined to give their vote to clearly identifiable *santri*-based parties has if anything declined when compared with the pre–new order period. In the 1955 elections, such parties gained 44 percent of the vote, whereas in 2004 it was only 39 percent. This figure, however, understates Islam's political influence because, as Indonesian Muslims have become generally more *santri*, the "secular" parties such as Golkar and PDI-P have adjusted their stance to also attract *santri* elements. Nevertheless, it is clear that an Islamic state of Indonesia is not imminent. Indeed, in a formal sense it is clearly not a priority for most Indonesian Muslims at this juncture. An illustration was provided in 2002 when the MPR rejected a proposal for the enforced implementation of *sharia* through resurrection of the Jakarta Charter. Only PPP and one or two of the smaller *santri*-based parties supported the proposal.

On the other hand, a radical Islamist minority influenced by extreme forms of Wahhabism (a strict fundamentalist practice of Islam) has become highly visible. This tendency grew significantly, albeit quietly, during the late new order and has made further gains since the fall of Soeharto. Recent events in Indonesia and the world have provided fertile ground for the recruitment activities of militant Islamist groups. Although small in number, they have been able to exercise considerable influence through an ability to capture media attention with their emotive rhetoric and active campaigns against mostly abstract enemies.

Interestingly, in parallel with the upsurge in Islamic religiosity, there has been a similar phenomenon among Indonesian Christians, for whom evangelicalism has a growing appeal. Notwithstanding such trends toward more rigorous expressions of commitment among the Indonesian followers of these monotheistic religions, there is plenty of evidence that traditional animist beliefs retain their mass appeal. Despite the obvious contradictions with the orthodox theology of their respective religions, many Indonesian Muslims and Christians, from all levels of society, continue to adhere also to traditional spiritual beliefs. This suggests that the growth in conspicuous manifestations of devotion to Christianity and Islam is as much about identity politics as it is about spirituality.

By no means are the post-Soeharto social changes universally welcomed. Arguably, Indonesian society remains conservative at heart, and individualistic behavior tends to run against the collectivist grain of traditional culture, although the extent to which this generalization might be true is moderated considerably by ethnicity, age, and urban versus rural location. But disquiet over some social trends since Soeharto's fall is not confined to concerns about declining traditions and excessive individualism. Accompanying the greater openness and freedom has been a breakdown in law and order that has caused many to hanker after the authoritarian controls of the new order. Such problems include a rise in ordinary criminal activity but also activity by vigilante groups that is semicriminal and semipolitical. Sometimes local vigilante activity is merely a reinvigoration of traditional "neighborhood watch" practices, which were incorporated into the new order state. But it often involves excesses, including mob justice handed out to petty thieves, which has occasionally resulted in their being beaten to death. In some rural areas of East Java, this phenomenon even extended to the killing of people accused of sorcery in the late 1990s. Partly such phenomena are a response to frustration with the police, who have been ineffective in preventing the rising tide of crime. The vigilante phenomenon is particularly dangerous for the social fabric when it takes the form of militias formed on the basis of religious membership. Rival Christian and Muslim militias have been responsible for most of the interreligious violence that has swept Indonesia in recent years.

SEPARATIST MOVEMENTS POST-SOEHARTO

Habibie's policies toward Aceh initially seemed to signal that Soeharto's departure might pave the way for peace. Habibie ended the Military Operations Area (DOM) in Aceh and ordered the withdrawal of combat units, signaling his intention to pursue dialogue and reform in order to redress Acehnese grievances. But the most he was prepared to offer was autonomy within the parameters of his proposed national decentralization measures. This was not enough for the hard-line separatists, and in a context in which Acehnese anger over human-rights abuses ran deep, Habibie's overtures were badly received. Distrust of Jakarta's intentions was reinforced in May 1999 when dozens of protestors were gunned down by Indonesian troops in the city of Lhokseumawe. The ensuing upsurge in the conflict saw tens of thousands flee their homes for refugee camps and a wave of school burnings, for which both sides blamed the other. Wahid's election revived hopes for an end to the conflict. During his term, negotiations (with the aid of mediation provided by the Geneva-based Henri Dunant Centre) took place. In theory, there was even a truce, euphemistically termed a "humanitarian pause," to facilitate negotiations. But the peace talks broke down in June 2001. Prospects for Acehnese independence took a further nosedive in the wake of the September 11 terrorist strike on the United States. Although there is no link between GAM and Al Qaeda (indeed politically they are poles apart), much of the already limited international sympathy for GAM's cause evaporated, allowing Jakarta to conduct military operations unfettered.

That Megawati's election was a further blow to Acehnese separatist hopes was confirmed in January 2002 when she declared GAM an enemy of the state. Nevertheless, fighting gave way again to renewed hopes for peace with the signing of a peace agreement in December, under the terms of which a truce and a series of confidence-building steps were supposed to reduce tensions and allow for meaningful negotiations. Amid mutual accusations of cease-fire violations and bad faith, the negotiations collapsed in May 2003. Martial law was declared in Aceh, and the army launched a sustained offensive, which it confidently predicted would crush the rebellion within a few months. Martial law gave way to civil emergency in the middle of 2004 amid army claims that GAM had suffered heavy losses. That fighting continued and troop numbers in the province were not scaled back indicated that, although weakened, GAM was far from finished. Shortly after his election, in 2004, President Susilo Bambang Yudhoyono reiterated Indonesia's special autonomy offer for Aceh, including amnesty for the rebels, but GAM rejected these overtures. It is too early to tell what impact the tsunami disaster of Christmas 2004, which devastated Aceh's coastal areas and killed around 200,000 people, will have on the separatist conflict. The disaster has prompted a shaky truce and renewed peace talks in Helsinki and has provided Jakarta with an opportunity to win Acehnese hearts and minds through a concerted aid and reconstruction program. But Jakarta has proved quite inept in the past with the delivery of aid and development, particularly for Aceh, and the influx of foreign aid workers and journalists also provided GAM with an opportunity to publicize its cause to the world.

The Papuan separatist movement has remained on a much smaller scale than that of Aceh, especially in military terms, since the Free Papua Movement (OPM) has very limited capabilities in this regard. Politically, however, the movement has enjoyed some success recently. Throughout Papua, demonstrations involving raising the Papuan "national" flag, the Morning Star, increased markedly after the fall of Soeharto. Despite repression, including the shooting deaths of dozens of flag-raising demonstrators on the island of Biak in July 1998, this form of defiance of the Indonesian authorities continued as Papuans gained confidence, believing that independence was now attainable. Wahid pursued a policy of dialogue with Papuan nationalists and promoted Jakarta's decentralization policies. In a gesture of conciliation, he changed the name of the province from Irian Jaya to Papua and allowed the Morning Star to be flown, provided it was below the Indonesian flag. Wahid also sponsored a Papuan congress in mid-2000, attended by 2,700 delegates. Much to the army's chagrin, the delegates had the temerity to pass a motion calling for independence. While this decision had no practical consequences, it created a powerful propaganda weapon for the Papuan nationalists and encouraged further displays of nationalist sentiments.

The extreme displeasure with which the army viewed these developments was indicated by the murder of a leading Papuan nationalist leader, Theys Eluay, by Kopassus soldiers in November 2001. The extremely light sentences received by the soldiers involved showed that the army's attitude was shared by much of the Indonesian establishment. (Only lower-ranked soldiers were charged.) Nevertheless, Papuan separatist sentiments have continued to be expressed, albeit guardedly. The less-drastic alternative of special autonomy for the province was made law in 2002, but there is considerable skepticism that it will be implemented in a meaningful way. Indeed, it may have been made effectively redundant almost immediately by a 2003 presidential decree announcing Papua's division into three provinces. Implementation of this measure is bitterly opposed by Papuan nationalists who see it as a ploy to divide the indigenous Papuans. Indeed, ethnic divisions among Papuans are quite strong, and thus the measure enjoys some local support. While the separatist struggle in Papua remains a low-level conflict, it is likely to continue, perhaps even escalate dramatically, in the future if Papuan grievances are not resolved and their aspirations not met within Indonesia.

THE 2004 ELECTIONS AND AFTERMATH

A number of important constitutional reforms were steered through MPR during the Wahid and Megawati presidencies. Of particular significance were further changes to the electoral system, notably provision for direct election of the president and vice president. This meant that in 2004, Indonesian voters would cast ballots to select new representatives for the national parliament and local assemblies in April. Three months later, they would vote again to choose among a number of presidential candidates, each paired with a vice presidential running mate. If no candidate won more than 50 percent of the vote (the likely outcome in Indonesia's fractured polity), there would be a run-off vote between the two leading candidates in September.

Also highly significant was the decision to abolish the army's reserved parliamentary seats. All seats were now open for electoral contest. Ostensibly, the army now no longer has a formal role in the nation's politics. Informally, however, the army continues to exercise considerable influence, especially because the continuation of its territorial structure means that in practice it retains the capacity to control, or at least manipulate, all local affairs from behind the scenes. This capacity in turn strengthens the army's influence at the national level because it means that few national policies can actually be carried out without army cooperation. Officially the "dual function" ideology might have been abandoned, but in practice it remains the army's view of itself and of its mission.

The elections in April 2004 produced a result broadly similar to that of 1999.[3] Again the bulk of the vote was divided among several parties, none of which came anywhere near to achieving a winning margin. PDI-P and Golkar were again the top two parties, with considerable distance between themselves and the rest. This time, however, they finished much closer together and swapped positions. Golkar won 21.6 percent of the vote, down a little from 22.4 percent in 1999, and PDI-P won 18.5 percent, a significant drop from 33.7 percent in 1999. This reversal of their respective electoral fortunes had been expected; indeed, many had predicted that Golkar would win by a bigger margin. Over the intervening years, PDI-P had squandered the opportunity to construct a well-organized national party structure to rival that of Golkar. It remained what has been described as a Megawati fan club rather than a party, and the performance of its representatives in parliament and assemblies had been very poor. Megawati's lackluster performance as president was also blamed for PDI-P's loss of support. On the other hand, Golkar was expected to benefit from a growing nostalgia for the economic prosperity and security it had delivered during the new order, especially as memories of the new order's authoritarian excesses faded and as the succession of post-Soeharto governments failed to deliver on their promises. It seems, however, that these factors were sufficient only to allow Golkar to hold its position as many voters, evidently disenchanted with the major parties, looked to alternatives.

In third place again was PKB. Its relatively stable vote bank of NU-associated Muslims delivered it 10.6 percent of the vote, a fall of 2.0 percent. PPP also preserved its fourth-place finish with 8.2 percent of the vote, a decline of 2.5 percent (which almost exactly matched the percentage of votes obtained by PBR, a PPP splinter). In 1999, PAN had finished in fifth place. Despite its vote declining only a little over 0.7 percent, it was pushed into seventh place. In fifth place with just under 7.5 percent of the vote was the Democratic Party (PD), a new party created by popular presidential aspirant Susilo Bambang Yudhoyono. Just behind PD in sixth place with 7.3 percent of the vote was the Justice and Welfare Party (PKS), formerly PK, which had received less than 1.4 percent of the vote in 1999. Both of the latter two parties were beneficiaries of strong voter sentiment for change and for clean, competent government, which both offered with some credibility. Yudhoyono had a reputation for competence as a senior minister in both the Wahid and Megawati governments, and as a retired general, he automatically possessed some of the army's reputation for getting results. PKS was an Islamist party, which emphasized its opposition to all forms of corruption and through its moral behavior and efficient grassroots operation appeared to practice what it preached. After the "big" 7, the other 17 parties permitted to contest the elections shared the remaining 20 percent of the vote.

Many had expected that the 1999 election result would encourage parties to amalgamate in order to win seats in parliament. And in a conscious effort to reduce the number of small parties that gleaned only tiny percentages of the vote, the number of parties approved by the electoral commission to stand had been halved. Yet the number of "big" parties had increased from five to seven, and the proportion of the vote received by the "small" parties combined had increased from 13 percent to 20 percent. It seems that the fractious Indonesian polity has if anything become even more divided. This outcome impedes the establishment of a stable "governing" coalition majority during the life of the current parliament. It is likely that the passage of legislation through the parliament will continue to be torturously slow and that parliament will continue to be characterized by bickering, posturing, and endless wheeling and dealing. Under such circumstances, it is likely that the public will look for more presidential leadership, potentially making the authority of the presidency greater than might otherwise have been the case. This possibility is also enhanced by the fact that, although the revised constitution has greatly increased parliament's power on paper, it remains unclear where precisely the parameters of power between the executive and parliament will lie in practice. Much will depend upon the personality and political ability of the president over the next few years.

As generally expected, the first round of presidential voting did not produce an outright winner. Yudhoyono with 33.6 percent came first by a significant margin, followed by Megawati with 26.3 percent. Golkar's candidate, Wiranto, finished third, not far behind Megawati with 22.2 percent. Amien Rais performed quite well, receiving just below 15.0 percent. Hamzah Haz finished last with a dismal 3.0 percent. The strong vote for Yudhoyono vindicated proponents of a direct presidential election, proving that voters could have opinions quite different from those of the machine politicians and were prepared to act on them. That Megawati beat Wiranto to a place in the run-off surprised many observers because it reversed the parliamentary election result between PDI-P and Golkar. It suggested that the magic of the Sukarno name still carried some punch and that PDI-P was less popular than its leader. Another part of the explanation lies in the divisions within Golkar. Golkar leader Akbar Tanjung's disappointed supporters did not campaign for Wiranto. Indeed, a considerable portion of Golkar's support defected to Yudhoyono, a tendency much enhanced by his selection of Jusuf Kalla as his vice presidential running mate. Kalla, who had formerly sought Golkar's nomination for the presidency, brought with him a sizable Golkar constituency, especially from his native South Sulawesi.

In the run-off, Yudhoyono won handsomely, although Megawati, with the benefit of incumbency, made it more of a contest than had been expected. Her prospects looked up when Golkar announced it was throwing its support behind her. But most Golkar supporters did not appreciate this political maneuver of Tanjung's, and it seems that the overwhelming majority of Golkar votes went to the Yudhoyono-Kalla ticket. In fact, a few months after the election, Kalla ousted Tanjung from the Golkar leadership. As Kalla and Yudhoyono remained a team, this surprising development effectively shifted Golkar from "opposition" to "government," since its leader now held the vice presidency. The big winner from this political maneuver was Kalla. To the prize of the vice presidency, he added the prize of chairman of Golkar. At the same time, he made himself a very powerful vice president (the most powerful since Hatta) because of the priceless political support he brought to Yudhoyono's presidency (support that Yudhoyono could only retain through maintaining his alliance with Kalla). Of particular importance is the political support in parliament that Kalla's leadership of Golkar brings to the presidential program, in theory at least. The PD and Golkar members of the DPR together comprise a third of the seats, a powerful bloc of votes if it can be wielded as such.

Provided that President Yudhoyono and Vice President Kalla can work together smoothly, there is considerable potential for Indonesia's current government to perform much more credibly than any of its post-Soeharto predecessors. Apart from the advantage of its parliamentary strength, it has the legitimacy of a popularly elected and popular president. Moreover, as a government with impeccable establishment credentials and connections, it can reasonably expect to enjoy far more cooperation from the bureaucracy and the army than did Wahid and Megawati. But turning this potential into reality will provide a serious challenge. Balancing the range of political forces that make up their de facto coalition will in itself require considerable discipline, unity, and political skill from Yudhoyono and Kalla. And there are plenty of political forces keen to see them fail to better their own political prospects. Of course, notwithstanding the new government's better political position, the problems that it must confront remain formidable: economic growth and reform, corruption, insurgency, Islamist extremism, and environmental degradation to name a few. Furthermore, with a conservative government with some authoritarian inclinations, there is the potential for renewed conflict with reformist forces from within the elite as well as from below. It is far from clear that the pressures for change that built up during the new order have run their course.

The dream of a nation stretching across the five thousand kilometers of archipelago from Sabang to Merauke is a very difficult one to realize, not least because this vast space contains so many different peoples with their own rich pasts and legitimate aspirations. Only the abrupt shift in their historical trajectory occasioned by their interaction with the colonial experience brought them together and to the point at which such a novel national territory and identity could be imagined. Achieving the status of an independent nation-state recognized by the world against the stubborn resistance of Indonesia's erstwhile colonial masters was truly an amazing achievement and one in which Indonesians continue, justifiably, to take great pride. But the challenge of building a nation in which all Indonesians recognize themselves and to which they can all feel reconciled is a far greater challenge, and one that yet remains to be met. If it remains unmet, it is possible that, ultimately, the peoples of the archipelago will be reconfigured into a different political unit or units. Yet for all the difficulties that confront Indonesia at this juncture, perhaps there has not been any time since 1928 when the prospects of truly realizing the idea and ideals of Indonesia have been greater.

NOTES

1. Quoted in John McBeth, "Nothing Changes," *Far Eastern Economic Review,* 1 November 2001, p. 18.

2. Deutsche Bank Research. http://www.dbresearch.com.

3. The 1999 election results are in Komisi Pemilihan Umum, *Buku Lampiran IV Pemilihan Umum 1999,* n.d., p. 3. The results of the 2004 elections can be found at Komisi Pemilihan Umum. http://www.kpu.go.id/.

Notable People in the History of Indonesia

Agung, Sultan (1591–1646).   The greatest ruler of the Mataram empire between 1613 and 1646. He succeeded in conquering most of Java and took the Islamic title of sultan in 1641.

Aidit, D.N. (1923–1965).   Became leader of the PKI in 1951. He charted a successful pragmatic political course supportive of Sukarno. He was executed without trial in November 1965.

Coen, Jan Pieterszoon (1557–1629).   Fourth governor general of the Indies. He had a key role in founding the Dutch rule over Indonesia by establishing VOC headquarters in Jakarta in 1618.

Dahlan, Ahmad K.H. (1868–1923).   Born in Central Java, he founded the modernist Muslim movement Muhammadiyah in 1911.

Dewantoro, Ki Hajar (1889–1959).   Born in Central Java, he was a nationalist who was previously known as Suwardi Suraningrat. He established the Taman Siswa educational movement, which combined traditional Javanese arts with European education methodology.

Diponegoro (1785–1855). Born in Central Java, a charismatic prince of the Mataram dynasty and a Muslim mystic, he led an attempt to expel the Dutch from Java and became sultan. Defeated, he was exiled to Makasar. He is regarded as a national hero.

Douwes Dekker, Eduard (1820–1887). Ex-colonial official who, under the pseudonym Multatuli, wrote the novel *Max Havelaar*, credited with prompting liberal and ethical reforms.

Gadjah Mada (?–1364). A semimythical "prime minister" of the Majapahit kingdom, he is reputed to have been instrumental in its expansionist success and is regarded as a national hero.

Habibie, Bacharuddin Jusuf (1936–). Born in South Sulawesi, he was a brilliant engineer. A Soeharto protégé with a reputation for being erratic, he became minister of research and technology in 1978, a founder of ICMI in 1990, vice president, and then president in 1998.

Hamengkubuwono IX (1912–1988). Born in Central Java, he became sultan of Yogyakarta in 1940. Highly revered locally and also nationally for joining the republic in 1945, he was defense minister in 1949 and 1952, deputy prime minister in 1966, and vice president 1972–1978.

Hatta, Mohammad (1902–1980). Born in West Sumatra, he was a leading nationalist figure who coproclaimed independence in 1945. Indonesia's first vice president until 1956 and prime minister 1948–1950, he was a democrat and devout Muslim who was critical of Sukarno and Soeharto.

Imam Bonjol, Tuanku (1772–1864). Padri movement leader who led resistance to the Dutch in central Sumatra during the Padri War. Regarded as a national hero.

Kartini, Raden Ajeng (1879–1904). Daughter of an enlightened Javanese aristocrat, she promoted education for women and opposed polygamy and child marriage before dying in childbirth. She is an important symbol of the aspirations of Indonesian women.

Kartosuwirjo, S.M. (1905–1962). A Muslim mystic and anti-colonial activist with PSII, he founded Darul Islam in West Java, declared an Islamic state of Indonesia in 1949, and opposed the republican government until his death in 1962.

Madjid, Nurcholish (1939–). Born in East Java, he is a controversial Islamic modernist thinker and social commentator who advocates pluralism and democracy. He was an HMI activist in the 1950s and 1960s, a KAMI leader during the overthrow of Sukarno, and prominent in ICMI.

Megawati Sukarnoputri (1947–). Born in Central Java the eldest daughter of Sukarno, she became PDI leader in 1993. Ousted, she founded PDIP in 1998 and became vice president. In 2001 she became president but lost the position in 2004.

Murdani, L. Benny (1932–2004). A Catholic born in Central Java, he was a paratrooper then an intelligence officer. A powerful new-order figure, in the 1970s and 1980s he ran intelligence agencies and was head of the armed forces 1983–1988 and minister of defense until 1993.

Murtopo, Ali (1924–1984). Born in Blora, East Java, he began a military career during the revolution, later specializing in military intelligence. A close confidant of Soeharto, he was instrumental in constructing the new order and helping to consolidate Soeharto's grip on power.

Nasution, Abdul Haris (1918–2001). Born in North Sumatra. Dutch-trained, he played a key military role in the revolution. Head of the army during the 1950s and 1960s, he formulated its ideology, defeated the PRRI rebellion and helped found guided democracy. Narrowly escaping death in the G30S affair, he was MPR speaker in the late 1960s. He was a Petition of Fifty signatory.

Natsir, Mohammad (1908–1993). Born in West Sumatra, he was a major Islamic modernist thinker and Masyumi political leader who famously debated with Sukarno in the 1930s and was prime minister 1950–51. For his role in the PRRI rebellion, he was jailed until 1966, after which he focused on religious education. He was a Petition of Fifty signatory.

Pramoedya Ananta Toer (1925–).   Born in Central Java, he is Indonesia's most renowned writer, principally of novels. He is also a famous, defiant, left-wing social critic whose work was banned. Imprisoned in 1965, he was released in 1979 but forbidden from leaving Jakarta until 1998.

Rais, Amien (1944–).   Born in Central Java, he became a renowned academic and leader of Muhammadiyah with an Islamist reputation. Initially prominent in ICMI, he became a strong critic of Soeharto, after whose overthrow he founded PAN, becoming DPR speaker in 1999 and a presidential candidate in 2004.

Rendra, Willibrordus S. (1935–).   Born in Central Java, he is one of Indonesia's foremost poets and dramatists. His work was often banned for its social and political criticism of the new order.

Sjahrir, Sutan (1909–1966).   Born in West Sumatra, he was a Dutch-educated, major nationalist figure and social democrat who became Indonesia's first prime minister and was instrumental in the negotiations with the Dutch. He founded the PSI and was jailed in 1962 by Sukarno.

Snouck Hurgronje, Christiaan (1857–1936).   A Dutch scholar on Islam, he was an influential adviser to the colonial government, framing its policy on Islam, the civil service, and the war in Aceh.

Soedirman (1915?–1950).   Born in Central Java, he was a Muhammadiyah school teacher. He led a Peta battalion before becoming commander of the army during the revolution. For his feat of leading the guerrilla struggle while dying of tuberculosis, he became a great national hero.

Soeharto (1921–).   Born in Central Java, he rose through army ranks during and after the revolution to Kostrad commander in 1965. Instrumental in crushing the G30S coup, he became army commander and astutely maneuvered himself to the presidency in 1967, which he retained until 1998. His new-order regime was famous for its economic development and corruption.

Sukarno (1901–1970). Born in East Java, he emerged as the primary nationalist leader in the 1920s, largely due to his oratorical talents. He coproclaimed independence in August 1945 and became president until overthrown in 1967. A radical nationalist, he flirted with communism and was renowned internationally for his anti-imperialism.

Sumitro Djojohadikusumo (1917–2001). Born in Central Java, he was a PSI leader and an outstanding economist who held economic ministries in the early 1950s and late 1960s. He joined the PRRI rebellion and lived in exile until 1967. He was the mentor for the "technocrats."

Tan Malaka (1897–1949). Born in West Sumatra, he was a PKI founder, Comintern agent for Southeast Asia, and a "nationalist communist" who founded the Murba party and was prominent during the revolution.

Tanjung, Akbar (1945–). Born in Sibolga, Sumatra, he first rose to prominence during the anti-Sukarno student movement. He rose to lead Golkar after the fall of Soeharto, a position he held until December 2004. He was speaker of DPR between 1999 and 2004.

Tjokroaminoto, H. Umar Said (1882–1934). A charismatic leader of Sarekat Islam and an anticolonialist who served as a role model for Sukarno.

Wahid, Abdurrahman (1940–). An innovative Islamic scholar, he was born in Jombang, East Java, the son and grandson of former NU leaders. A democrat and reformer, he became leader of NU in 1984, founded PKB in 1998, and was president from October 1999 until July 2001.

Wiranto (1947–). Born in Yogyakarta, Java, he was head of the army at the time of Soeharto's removal from power. His handling of this crisis launched his political career. Nominated by Golkar, he was an unsuccessful candidate for president in 2004.

Yamin, Muhammad (1903–1962). Born in Sawah Lunto, West Sumatra, he was a renowned, radical, nationalist poet and historian.

A Youth Oath author and a prominent member of BPUPKI, he was a minister in several 1950s cabinets and a supporter of Sukarno's guided democracy.

Yudhoyono, Susilo Bambang (1949–).   Born in East Java, he was an army general and security minister in the Wahid and Megawati governments. He became president in 2004.

Glossary

abangan: Less observant Muslims who blend Islam with older beliefs
adat: Customary law or traditional law
ASEAN: Association of Southeast Asian Nations
CIA: Central Intelligence Agency
DOM: Military Operations Area
DPD: Regional Representative Council
DPR: People's Representative Council
DPR-II: Provincial Assembly
DPRD-I: Regional Assembly
Falantil: Armed Forces of National Liberation of East Timor
FPI: Islamic Defenders Front
G30S: September 30 Movement
GAM: Movement for Acehnese Independence
Gerwani: Indonesian Women's Movement
GNP: Gross National Product
Golkar: Golongan Karya/Functional Groups
gotong royong: Mutual cooperation
haj: Pilgrimage to Mecca performed by Muslims
IAIN: State Institute for Islamic Studies
IBRA: Indonesian Bank Restructuring Agency
ICMI: All Indonesia Association of Muslim Intellectuals

IMF: International Monetary Fund
inlanders: Natives
ISDV: Indies Social Democratic Association
JI: Jemaah Islamiah
kabupaten: Regency (a territorial division for administrative purposes)
kebatinan: Indigenous spiritual and mystical beliefs
KNIP: Indonesian National Central Committee
Konfrontasi: Confrontation
Kopassus: Special Forces
Kopkamtib: Operational Command for the Restoration of Security and
   Order
Kostrad: Army Strategic Reserve
kyai: Traditional Muslim religious authorities
Malari: January Disaster
MPR: People's Consultative Assembly
MPRS: Provisional People's Consultative Assembly
NU: Nahdlatul Ulama
OPM: Free Papua Movement
PAN: National Mandate Party
Pancasila: Five Principles
Parkindo: Indonesian Protestant Party
PBB: Moon and Crescent Party
PD: Democratic Party
PDI: Indonesian Democratic Party
PDI-P: Indonesian Democratic Party of Struggle
Permesta: Universal Struggle Charter
pesantren: Muslim boarding schools
Peta: Defenders of the Homeland
PI: Indonesian Association
PK: Justice Party
PKB: National Awakening Party
PKI: Indonesian Communist Party
PKK: Family Welfare Movement
PKS: Justice and Welfare Party
PNI: Indonesian Nationalist Party
PPP: United Development Party
priyayi: Traditional aristocratic-administrative elite
PRRI: Revolutionary Government of the Republic of Indonesia
PSI: Socialist Party of Indonesia
PSII: Sarekat Islam Party of Indonesia
pustaka: Magically imbued court regalia
Romusha: Labor battalions
RUSI: Republic of the United States of Indonesia

santri: Observant Muslims
SBSI: Union for Workers' Prosperity
SI: Sarekat Islam
SPSI: All Indonesia Worker's Union
UN: United Nations
VOC: (Dutch) United East Indies Company
wayang: Traditional Javanese dramatic forms

Bibliographic Essay

The authoritative and detailed general history of Indonesia (though it excludes early history) is M.C. Ricklefs, *A History of Modern Indonesia Since c. 1200* (Basingstoke: Palgrave, 2001). An excellent companion work is that of Jean Gelman Taylor, *Indonesia: Peoples and Histories* (New Haven: Yale University Press, 2003), which takes a different approach, blending social history and "history from below" to provide an intimate yet sweeping history. Three extremely useful reference works are Robert Cribb and Audrey Kahin, *Historical Dictionary of Indonesia* (Lanham: Scarecrow Press, 2004); Robert Cribb, *Historical Atlas of Indonesia* (Richmond: Curzon, 2000); and Leo Suryadinata et al., *Indonesia's Population: Ethnicity and Religion in a Changing Political Landscape* (Singapore: ISEAS, 2003).

For early history, there is Peter Bellwood, *Prehistory of the Indo-Malaysian Archipelago* (Honolulu: University of Hawai'i Press, 1997) and the insightful Kenneth R. Hall, *Maritime Trade and State Development in Early Southeast Asia* (Honolulu: University of Hawai'i Press, 1985). Also see Anthony Reid, *Southeast Asia in the Age of Commerce 1450–1680*, vols. 1 and 2 (New Haven: Yale University

Press, 1988 and 1993). Readers interested in the colonial period should start with Giles Milton, *Nathaniel's Nutmeg* (London: Hodder and Stoughton, 1999). This is a lively, popular history that underlines the spice lust that initially drew Europeans to Indonesia. The classic study of the colonial era is J.S. Furnivall, *Netherlands India: A Study of Plural Economy* (Cambridge: Cambridge University Press, 1939). A wonderful antidote to Furnivall's Eurocentric approach to history in this period is M.C. Ricklefs, *War, Culture and Economy in Java, 1677–1726* (Sydney: Allen and Unwin, 1993). More recent outstanding works include R.E. Elson, *Village Java under the Cultivation System, 1830–1870* (Sydney: Allen and Unwin, 1994) and Luc Nagtegaal, *Riding the Dutch Tiger: The Dutch East Indies Company and the Northeast Coast of Java, 1680–1743* (Leiden: KITLV Press, 1996). Also see Heather Sutherland, *The Making of a Bureaucratic Elite* (Kuala Lumpur: Heinemann Educational Books [Asia], 1979) and Robert Cribb, ed., *The Late Colonial State in Indonesia* (Leiden: KITLV Press, 1994).

The nationalist movement has been covered quite extensively. A vivid account of the radical ideas swirling around Indonesia in the early years of the twentieth century is in Takashi Shiraishi, *An Age in Motion: Popular Radicalism in Java, 1912–1926* (Ithaca: Cornell University Press, 1990). Other important studies of this area include John Ingleson, *Road to Exile: The Indonesian Nationalist Movement 1927–1934* (Singapore: Heinemann Educational Books [Asia], 1979). The classic account of the revolution is by George McTurnan Kahin, *Nationalism and Revolution in Indonesia* (Ithaca: Cornell University Press, 1952). Also see Benedict R.O.'G Anderson, *Java in a Time of Revolution: Occupation and Resistance 1944–1946* (Ithaca: Cornell University Press, 1972).

Indonesia's early postindependence period has received outstanding scholarly attention in Herbert Feith, *The Decline of Constitutional Democracy in Indonesia* (Ithaca: Cornell University Press, 1962). The guided democracy period is surprisingly under studied, although its origins are well dealt with in Daniel S. Lev, *The Transition to Guided Democracy: Indonesian Politics 1957–1959* (Ithaca: Cornell Modern Indonesia Project, 1966). No comprehensive work of quality yet exists that deals with the murky events that brought Soeharto to power. The best account is provided in Harold Crouch, *The Army and Politics in Indonesia* (Ithaca: Cornell University Press, 1978), which is also the classic account of the

Indonesian army. Readers should also consult Robert Cribb, ed., *The Indonesian Killings 1965–66: Studies from Java and Bali* (Clayton: Monash University Press, 1990). The new-order period has received much excellent scholarly attention. There is no better starting point than Hamish McDonald, *Suharto's Indonesia* (Blackburn: Fontana Books, 1980). An excellent follow-up is Hal Hill, ed., *Indonesia's New Order: The Dynamics of Socio-Economic Transformation* (Sydney: Allen and Unwin, 1994). For the later new order see Douglas E. Ramage, *Politics in Indonesia: Democracy, Islam and the Ideology of Tolerance* (New York: Routledge, 1995) and Adam Schwartz, *A Nation in Waiting: Indonesia in the 1990s* (Sydney: Allen and Unwin, 1994). The fall of Soeharto prompted a flurry of accounts, most of which suffer from immediacy to the event. The best is Geoff Forrester and R.J. May, eds., *The Fall of Soeharto* (Bathurst: Crawford House Publishing, 1998).

For readers interested in the broad spectrum of Indonesian politics, there is the classic Herbert Feith and Lance Castles, eds., *Indonesian Political Thinking 1945–1965* (Ithaca: Cornell University Press, 1970). Thankfully a follow-up has recently emerged by David Bourchier and Vedi R. Hadiz, eds., *Indonesian Politics and Society: A Reader* (London: RoutledgeCurzon, 2003). The early communist party is comprehensively dealt with in Ruth T. McVey, *The Rise of Indonesian Communism* (Ithaca: Cornell University Press, 1965). Its postwar history can be pursued in Donald Hindley, *The Communist Party of Indonesia 1951–1963* (Berkeley: University of California Press, 1966) and Rex Mortimer, *Indonesian Communism Under Sukarno: Ideology and Politics 1959–1965* (Ithaca: Cornell University Press, 1974). A more recent study of the Indonesian army is Damien Kingsbury, *Power Politics and the Indonesian Military* (London: RoutledgeCurzon, 2003). The growing importance of political tensions between central and local authorities is explored in Edward Aspinall and Greg Fealy, eds., *Local Power and Politics in Indonesia: Decentralisation & Democratisation* (Singapore: ISEAS, 2003). Apart from those dealing with Sukarno, there are few biographies of political figures available in English. For Sukarno, two biographies stand out, the classic J.D. Legge, *Sukarno: A Political Biography* (Sydney: Allen and Unwin, 1972) and Bob Hering, *Soekarno: Founding Father of Indonesia 1901–1945* (Leiden: KITLV Press, 2002), though the latter's period is limited and it is perhaps a little too dense with detail. For Soeharto there is R.E. Elson, *Suharto: A Political Biography*

(Cambridge: Cambridge University Press, 2001). One of the most engaging contemporary Indonesian politicians is studied intimately in Greg Barton, *Abdurrahman Wahid: Muslim Democrat, Indonesian President* (Sydney: University of New South Wales Press, 2002).

Studies concerned with women and gender issues are not plentiful. Readers should start with Jean Gelman Taylor, ed., *Women Creating Indonesia: The First Fifty Years* (Clayton: Monash Asia Institute, 1997). Other fine works include Susan Blackburn, *Women and the State in Modern Indonesia* (Cambridge: Cambridge University Press, 2004); Kathryn Robinson and Sharon Bessell, eds., *Women in Indonesia: Gender Equity and Development* (Singapore: ISEAS, 2002) and Laurie J. Sears, ed., *Fantasising the Feminine in Indonesia* (Durham: Duke University Press, 1996). For the Indonesia economy, three works stand out. Anne Booth, *The Indonesian Economy in the Nineteenth and Twentieth Centuries* (Basingstoke: Macmillan Press, 1998); Hal Hill, *The Indonesian Economy Since 1966* (Cambridge: Cambridge University Press, 1996); and Howard Dick et al., *The Emergence of a National Economy: An Economic History of Indonesia, 1800–2000* (Sydney: Allen and Unwin, 2002).

Indonesia's richness in arts is reflected in the number and quality of works dealing with the subject. For textiles, start with Mattiebelle Gittinger, *Splendid Symbols: Textiles and Tradition in Indonesia* (Singapore: Oxford University Press, 1990). For batik see Inger McCabe Elliott, *Batik: Fabled Cloth of Java* (Harmondsworth: Viking, 1985). Ward Keeler, *Javanese Shadow Plays, Javanese Selves* (Princeton: Princeton University Press, 1987) is a classic study of the *wayang*. A comprehensive study of Indonesian music is provided in the 20 volumes of Philip Yampolsky, *Music of Indonesia* (Washington: Smithsonian Folkways and Indonesian Society for the Performing Arts, 1991–1999). For film, see Krisna Sen, ed., *Histories and Stories: Cinema in New Order Indonesia* (Clayton: Monash University Press, 1988). For literature, see Keith Foulcher and Tony Day, eds., *Clearing a Space: Postcolonial Readings of Modern Indonesian Literature* (Leiden: KITLV, 2002) and Harry Aveling, ed., *Secrets Need Words: Indonesian Poetry, 1966–1998* (Athens: Ohio University Center for International Studies, 2001).

There are many excellent studies of Islam in Indonesia. The best starting point is Ahmad Ibrahim et al., comp., *Readings on Islam in Southeast Asia* (Singapore: ISEAS, 1985), which brings together extracts of key writings on the subject. Other important works include Deliar Noer, *The Modernist Muslim Movement in*

Indonesia 1900–1942 (Jakarta: Oxford University Press, 1972); Greg Barton and Greg Fealy, eds., *Nahdlatul Ulama, Traditional Islam and Modernity in Indonesia* (Clayton: Monash University Press, 1996); Mitsuo Nakamura, *The Crescent Arises over the Banyan Tree* (Yogyakarta: Gadjah Mada University Press, 1983); and Arskal Salim and Azra Azyumardi, eds., *Shari'a and Politics in Modern Indonesia* (Singapore: ISEAS, 2003).

For Darul Islam, see C. Van Dijk, *Rebellion Under the Banner of Islam: The Darul Islam in Indonesia* (The Hague: Matrinus Nijhoff, 1981) and Karl D. Jackson, *Traditional Authority, Islam and Rebellion: A Study of Indonesian Political Behaviour* (Berkeley: University of California Press, 1980). For Aceh, see Anthony Reid, *An Indonesian Frontier: Acehnese and Other Histories of Sumatra* (Singapore: Singapore University Press, 2004). For Papua, see Peter King, *West Papua and Indonesia since Suharto* (Sydney: UNSW Press, 2004).

Index

About the Author

STEVEN DRAKELEY is Professor of Humanities at the University of Western Sydney.